The Life and Times of the Inns, Taverns and Beerhouses of Witney Oxfordshire

"from the 18th Century to the early 21st Century"

Compiled by Douglas Rudlin

Hi, Ernie

I hope you enjoy reading this book

CHEERS,

(AUTHOR)

First published 2018

Copyright © Douglas Rudlin

ISBN: 978-0-244-42953-9

This book is dedicated to all the
Witney pub goers who yearn for the
'Good old days.'

Front cover: *Tavern Scene* by Flemish artist David Teniers c. 1658
National Gallery of Art, Washington, D.C., USA

Contents

Contents

Introduction

When I set out to research the pubs of Witney it was not my intention to give a history of the pubs themselves, nor to give an architectural appraisal of the buildings and certainly not to give a blow-by-blow account of a walk around Witney from pub to pub. Others have already done that. I was more interested in the life that there was in a pub, more to show how much the pub really was the centre of the community. I have spent many hours and days trawling through the newspapers to find the stories that depict life in the pub in days gone by, and many more hours finding out who the people were that ran the pubs, the licensees. Interestingly, some pubs never get a mention in the newspapers, whereas others are referred to frequently. As such this is a collection of articles from the newspapers going way back to the earliest in 1753 and a listing of the licence holders, those who were responsible for running the pubs. My aim was to give as varied a cross section of life in the pubs as possible, from licence changes to murder inquests, births, marriages and deaths. Consequently, the dates that are quoted for the life of a pub are not necessarily the date when it first became a pub or when it ceased being a pub, but more when it was first mentioned in the records that I have been researching and the last. I have deliberately omitted the more modern bars, as they seem to come and go on a frequent basis.

The following format is used to show the pub name: The current name (any former name), address if known, the year of the first and last mention.

I hope the reader finds the life and times of the Inns, Taverns and Beerhouses of Witney as fascinating as I have.

A brief look at Witney in earlier days

'By the 16th century most of the town's inns were probably concentrated, as later, around the market place and High Street. The White Hart, a 'chief inn of the town' visited by Charles I, stood probably on or near the site of the later Corn Exchange on the east side of the market place, and the Crown Inn, mentioned from the early 18th century, a little further south, adjoining Crown Lane. The Lamb (earlier the Bear) stood opposite on the north corner of Corn Street and the market place, the Blue Boar (renamed the Marlborough Arms in the early 19th century) to the north on the site of the modern Blue Boar Hotel, and the Half Moon and the Three Crowns, perhaps alehouses rather than inns, further north beyond Batt House all four of them recorded from the early 18th century. The Salutation Inn, established by the 1660s, seems to have been further north on the east side of High Street, next but one to the later King's Head, while the Staple Hall Inn, established apparently in the mid 17th century and presumably on or near the site of a wool hall, lay at the town's north end near Newland, where it would benefit from traffic between Gloucestershire, Oxford and London.

Some of those inns seem to have been established in existing large houses. The White Hart reportedly occupied part of the Yate family's house, and the Crown part of a house owned by the Wenmans, while the Blue Boar occupied part of a 'late manor house' (presumably mansion house) formerly owned by the clothier Thomas Randall (fl. 1695). Other inns occupied plots created more recently, the Lamb standing on the site of two former houses, and the Star Inn, 'newly erected' on the east side of High Street in 1704, apparently incorporating part of an adjoining property to its north. Like other larger houses most seem to have included a two-storeyed range parallel to the street, often with gabled attics, and with carriageways giving access to courtyard stabling; the Blue Boar and the Lamb were both of that type, while the White Hart may have included a two-storeyed timber-framed range replaced by the Corn Exchange in 1863, which had a large carriage entry on the south. The Staple Hall Inn, on the fringe of the town, occupied a more spacious site, with extensive stabling and closes to the east. In addition, there were numerous smaller inns, public houses, and taverns: in the later 18th century some fifty houses were licensed, many of them at Corn Street, West End, and Woodgreen, with others along Church Green and High Street.'

(Reproduced from A History of the County of Oxford: Volume 14)

'In the hundred of Bampton, is a long, straggling, uncouth, but populous and large, town, with a market on Thursday, and six annual fairs, ... Here is one very capital inn for the accommodation of the nobility, gentry, &c. Here are likewise several other good inns for accommodation of travellers, beside a great number of public houses.'

(Reproduced from 1793 Universal British Directory 1793-1798 Vol 4 N-Y)

'BEER. So in 1549 there is the following entry:-
"At a Cortt holden ye 19 day of April, hytt ys agred byffore ye Cort, ffor ye assysse of Ale, to sell ytt yff hytt be good, and holssomly brewed, to be rated at 20d. ye dossin."

"A order taken att ye same courte ffor ye assise of alle. Item, ytt every brewer sshawle brew good and holsome alle, and so ssell from and after this day by order of the same courte, every dossen of alle beynge brewed, ye som off 2s. 1d. ye dossen, and ye typlar to sell one thurdyndale (three pints) off good alle at 1/2d."

"Item, also ytt is agred by order of the same courte ytt every brewer shall provide for ye comfort off ye pore people, good and holesome drynke, and to allow a gawne and a half ffor a 1d., and every brewer to allow of small drynke ffor ye brewyng off a quarter off mawlt 12 gawnes (gallons)."

It will be perceived, from the above entries, that interference with the liquor trade is of no modern date, and that not only was the price of ale settled by a Court, which sat specially for deciding matters connected with brewing, but that the amount of malt, which should be used, was also determined. In the next year, to the one quoted above, the officials go still further, and recognizing, perhaps, that those who preferred to have their beer at home, should be encouraged, there is the following:-

"1550. A decre made at this Courte that all brewsters in this towne, shall sell a dozen of ale not above iis. viiid., and the ganykar (innkeeper) shall sell a thurdyndale for a penny, as well within the dore, as wt owte the dore."

It is probable that the order made above, was attended with good results, for in the next year there is the following:-

"A decre made by the baylis that all brewsters shall sell a dossene of ale for xxiid., and the ganykar shall selle a quart of good ale owte of the dore, for a halfpenny, and a thurdyndale of good ale within the dore for a penny, and half a thurdyndale within the dore for a halfpenny."

But those connected with the brewing interest appear then to have resented these restrictions of the ruling bodies, and it is easy to see from this resolution, passed in the following year, what particular means they adopted for manifesting their displeasure:-

"That brewsters and tipplers shall sell no better ale or bere within the dore than without, under the payne of forfeiture of ..."

The amount of the fine is not given, perhaps the worthy burgesses were unable to decide on the sum, or they may have been conscious that such an offence would not be easy in those days to discover. In the same year their wrath with regard to the unjust treatment, which those who chose to drink at their own fireside, suffered, brought forth the following definite order:-

"That if any tippler do selle lesse than a quarte of the best ale or bere out of the dore for a halfpenny, shall forfeit five shillings."

Most curious is it to observe, throughout the reign of Mary, how particular he, who made the entries, was that, so far as his own knowledge went, they should be exceedingly correct. ...

... Both these entries come before regulations respecting the brewers; in one of which it is ordered that they "shall sell their ale for iiis. viiid. the dozen, that the tipplers shall sell their ale for iiiis. the dozen, good and stale, and that they shall sell their small drinke for a penny a gawen, good and holesome to man's body."

The dozen contained thirteen gallons.

In the first year of the reign of Good Queen Bess, the authorities appear to have proceeded still further in their efforts to secure a wholesome drink for the people, for we have the following:-

"1558 Ordered that every brewer and tippler, that breweth ale to sale, shall send, and give sufficient warning to the ale taster, at every time of their brewing, to taste their ale under payne of forfeyting iiis. ivd."

In these modern days, any brewer who neglected to send for the excise officer, to test, by certain methods, the gravity of the beer, would be liable to a fine much exceeding the sum, which was exacted from those who in days of old neglected to inform the ale taster that his liquor was ready for his inspection. The excise officer, it may be observed, only takes the place of the ale taster of the 16th century. So far as this is concerned, History does but repeat itself, though it may be perceived that whereas the ale taster came to discover if the ale were "wholesome to man's body," the modern excise-man comes to test the gravity of the liquor, in order to replenish the Imperial Exchequer. Two widely different things. It is not at all certain whether in this particular matter we are wiser than our fathers.

From the commencement of the keeping of the records, the tipplers (innkeepers we should call them now), appear to have been treated with very great strictness. They were required on all occasion to provide two sureties, who had to be responsible for good behaviour; and they were obliged to sell their ale at prices determined by the officials of Court Leet, though the brewers again were also obliged to sell to the former at certain charges, also settled from year to year by the Assize of ale; the latter no doubt being influenced in their decisions by the prices of barley and hops.

An excellent example of the power of Court Leet is afforded in 1566, when it was ordered "that every tippler, within the Borough, which shall after their first warnynge after this p'sent Courte recyve into their houses, or suffer within theire house, or houses, any of the persons whose names are under wyrtten and to this order enexed, to the end to tipple or dryncke therein, or to suffer them to sit tippling or drynking, every such tippler to forfeit for every pot of dryncke so dronken by any of the persons undernamed to the use of the lord of the franchise, iiis. iiiid."

After this follows a list of the persons who were under the displeasure of the Court. There are no means of ascertaining of what offences those mentioned had been guilty; but if they had been guilty of drunkenness or any kindred offence, the punishment was peculiarly fitting. Again, is our modern system of fining a man five shillings and immediately giving him the opportunity of repeating the offence, at all comparable to the more stringent rule of our ancestors?

"1567 It is decree that no tippler shall allow any unlawful games in his howse."

Even then, games with cards, such as backgammon, shovelboard, maw, lodam, noddy, gleek, (see Appendix 6) which except backgammon have now grown obsolete, supplied means to those who were so disposed, to indulge in gambling. Three centuries have gone by since the Witney Conscript Fathers made the decree quoted above, and yet it is found necessary, even now, to make laws dealing with the very same offence.

... There are many other orders with respect to innholders, but those quoted may be regarded as a fair sample.'

(Reproduced from History of Witney by W. J. Monk, first published 1894, pages 106–112)

Bridge Street

Anchor, Bridge St (1753–1786)

It's not clear where this pub was located as there is very little information to be found but it is thought that it may have been situated to the north of the River Windrush and to the west of Bridge Street, possibly where Halfords Autocentre is today. In the Tithe map of the 1840s this area is shown as being densely populated with cottages but by the time the Ordnance Survey map of 1875 was issued this area had been completely demolished and was shown as a field with trees.

From the newspapers:

Oxford Journal – Saturday 29 August 1767
'NOTICE is hereby given, That a Well-accustomed Freehold House and Premisses, situate near the Bridge in Witney, in the County of Oxford, now in the Possession of John Townsend, and known by the Sign of the Anchor, will be sold by Auction, on Thursday the 10th Day of September, 1767, at the Crown Inn, in Witney aforesaid. The Sale will begin precisely at Two o'Clock in the Afternoon. The Premises are all in good Repair, and may be viewed any Day before the Sale, by applying either to the Tenant, or William Woods, of the same place.'

Licensees:

1753–1786	John Townsend
1767	The Anchor was for sale by auction

Black Head, 26 Bridge St (1764–1915)

(Currently a private residence)
(1840 Tithe Awards Map ref 754)

From the newspapers:

Oxford Journal – Saturday 23 June 1764
'To be sold to the Best Bidder, On Monday the Ninth of July next, at the Sign of the Black Head, in Witney, Oxfordshire; THREE Freehold Tenements, adjoining to the Black Head, in Witney aforesaid: ...'

Oxford Journal – Saturday 28 August 1773
'THE Commissioners appointed by a certain Act of Parliament, for inclosing the Open Fields of Stanton-Harcourt, in the County of Oxford, do hereby give Notice, That they intend to meet at the Black's Head, in Witney, in the said County of Oxford, on Monday the 6th Day of September next, when they propose to set out the public Roads intended to pass over the said Fields, and to hear and determine all Disputes and Differences relating thereto, ...'

Oxford Journal – Saturday 06 October 1855
'BAMPTON EAST DIVISION. – Witney, Thursday.
... Thomas Beckinsale, of the Black Head public house, Witney, was charged by

Superintendent Tyrrell with selling beer on Sunday Morning; the case was not fully proved; he was therefore discharged.'

Oxford Chronicle and Reading Gazette – Saturday 10 July 1858
Refer to page 161 for full article for the sale of three Public Houses in Witney.
On 10 March 1859 the Black Head was conveyed from Early & Townsend to J. W. & C. Clinch.

Oxford Times – Saturday 22 May 1869
'CLUB FEASTS. – During the week, the various benefit societies in Witney and the neighbouring villages, have held their anniversaries. In Witney, among others, the King's Head, Bell, Three Horse Shoes, Butcher's Arms, Black Head, Jolly Tucker, and the Griffin (Newland), have had their club feasts. Brize Norton held its feast Tuesday; Standlake, Minster, and Ramsden held theirs on Wednesday; Hailey, on Thursday; and Ducklington on Friday. Many of the village clubs attended divine service at their parish churches. Bands of music have been engaged, and this, combined with the display of flags from the respective head quarters, has given a holiday appearance to the place. The Witney and Burford band, which has given general satisfaction, has been engaged throughout the week.'

Oxford Journal – Saturday 29 September 1883
'PRESENTATION. - At a meeting of subscribers (mostly working men) held at the Black Head Inn on Tuesday se'nnight, Mr. J. M. Clinch in the chair, a presentation of valuable books was made to Mr. Smitheman, station master at Witney, as some acknowledgment of his exertions in carrying out so successfully the recent trip to Bala. Mr. Smitheman, in an appropriate speech, expressed his thanks.'

Oxford Journal – Saturday 27 June 1891
'INQUEST.-F. Westell, Esq. (Coroner), held an inquest on Monday, at the Black's Head, on the body of a newly-born female child, when the following evidence was taken: ... There was nothing remarkable about the body, and the deceased he believed died in a fit of convulsions–A verdict was returned in accordance with the medical testimony.'

Witney Gazette and West Oxfordshire Advertiser – Saturday 11 November 1899
'PETTY SESSIONS, Thursday. HOLDOVER. An application for the holdover of the license of the "Black Head," Witney, from John Davis to Henry Belcher was granted.'

Faringdon Advertiser and Vale of the White Horse Gazette – Saturday 24 May 1902
'PETTY SESSIONS, Thursday. Licensing. Holdovers were granted of the licence of the Black Head, Witney, from A. H. Belcher to S. Harwood, ...'

Oxford Times – Saturday 26 September 1903
'PETTY SESSIONS, Thursday. TRANSFER. – The licence of the ... "Black Head," Witney, from Stephen Harwood to Elijah Miles; ...'

The Stage – Thursday 14 July 1904
'WANTED. Amateur Lady and Gent. Must sing and be willing to give services for a few weeks. Photo if possible. – A. BERTRAM CROUCHER, Black Head Hotel, Witney, Oxon.'

Witney Gazette and West Oxfordshire Advertiser – Saturday 11 September 1909
'TO LET, at Michaelmas, the "BLACK HEAD," Witney (fully licensed). Apply, Clinch and Co., Ltd., Eagle Brewery, Witney.'

Faringdon Advertiser and Vale of the White Horse Gazette – Saturday 30 October 1909
'PETTY SESSIONS, Thursday. A holdover of the license of the "Black Head" Inn, Witney, was granted from Edward John Conway to Joseph Johnson.'

Faringdon Advertiser and Vale of the White Horse Gazette – Saturday 13 November 1909
'PETTY SESSIONS, Thursday. LICENSING. The license of the ... and that of the "Black Head," Witney, From E. G. Connoway to Joseph Johnson. – Theatrical licenses were granted to the Corn Exchange Company, Witney, and also for the Girl's Club House, Witney.'

Faringdon Advertiser and Vale of the White Horse Gazette – Saturday 04 October 1913
'PETTY SESSIONS, Thursday, Sept. 25th TRANSFERS. The license of the ... and that of the "Black Head" Witney, from John Dix to John Davis.'

Faringdon Advertiser and Vale of the White Horse Gazette – Saturday 25 October 1913
'PETTY SESSIONS, Thursday. LICENSING. A holdover of the "Black Head" Inn, Witney was granted from John Davis to William Lunnun.'

Banbury Advertiser – Thursday 25 June 1914
'OXFORDSHIRE COMPENSATION AUTHORITY. SEVERAL HOUSES CLOSED.
The principal meeting of the compensation authority for the county of Oxford was held at the County Hall on Saturday. The list of licensed premises to be dealt with was as follows; – "The Black Head," Bridge Street, Witney, full licence; ...

   Mr. Andrew Walsh said with regard to the Black Head, Bridge Street, Witney, full licence (owners, Clinch and Co., licensee, William Lunnan), and the New Inn, beerhouse, Eynsham (owners, Hall's Oxford Brewery, Ltd., licensee, Robert Buckingham) the magistrates left it to the brewers to nominate two houses for compensation, and these had been chosen. The owners did not offer any opposition to the refusal of the Blandford Arms Inn, full licence, Market Street, Woodstock (owners, Morland and Co., Ltd., licensee, Martha Upstone) and the Prince of Wales Inn, full licence, Horse Fair, Woodstock (owners, Morrell's Trustees, licensee, Emma Kent). The four licences were refused. ...'

Banbury Advertiser – Thursday 07 January 1915
'OXFORDSHIRE QUARTER SESSIONS. REPORT OF THE LICENSING
COMMITTEE.
With regard to the eleven public-houses where the licences were extinguished,
the Committee considered the claims made for compensation, and the reports
of their valuer upon the amounts submitted by the claimants, and gave their
approval to the undermentioned sums as compensation money in respect to
the ten houses set out below. These sums were agreed to by the parties, and the
Committee settled the shares into which the sums were divisible as between the
owners, lessees, and licensees, and the division was also agreed to.

1. The Black Head (full licence), Witney; Claims submitted £814 8s 4d
   Compensation awarded £421 2s ...'

Licensees:

1764	Pub known as the Black Head
1765	William Johnson
1767–1769	Elizabeth Johnson
1770	Buried on 30 Sep 1770
1770–1783	James Johnson
1784–1797	Richard Harbud
1797	Buried on 5 July
1797–1798	Mary Harbud
1799	James Holloway
1801–1817	George Cooper
1830	William Harwood
1840	Public House Garden &c. owned by George Cooper
1839–1858	Thomas Beckinsale (moved to the Roebuck)
	Age 35 victualler, wife Elizabeth age 35 (1841 Census)
	Age 56, born in Witney, Oxon. Wife Elizabeth age 51 (1851 Census)
1858	The Black Head was for sale by auction
1861–1874	William Fyfield
	Age 29, born in Witney, Oxon. Wife Sarah age 32 (1861 Census)
	Age 38, born in Cogges, Oxon. Wife Sarah age 42 (1871 Census)
1876–1895	George George
	Age 44, born in Crawley, Oxon. Wife Elizabeth age 39 (1881 Census)
	Age 58, born in Crawley, Oxon. General Labourer.
	Wife Elizabeth age 49. (1891 Census)
1899	John Davis
1900–1902	Henry Belcher
	Age 35, born in Oxford (1901 Census)
1902–1903	Stephen Harwood
1904–1907	Elijah Miles
1909	Black Head was to let
1908–1909	Edward George Conway
1910–1911	Joseph Johnson
	Age 57, born in Colchester, Essex. Bootmaker.
	Wife Matilda age 39. (1911 Census)

1912–1913	John Dix
1913	John Davis
1914	William Lunnun
1915	Pub closed

Old Court Hotel (Court Inn), 41 Bridge St (1861–present)

(Currently trading, leased by Keshar Sherchan, Free House)

From the newspapers:

Oxford Chronicle and Reading Gazette – Saturday 22 April 1865
'TO BE SOLD BY AUCTION By Seeley & Buckingham, On Wednesday next, April 26th, 1865, at 12 o'clock, at the Court Inn, Bridge Street, Witney, where the property is removed for convenience of sale, - The HOUSEHOLD FURNITURE and various Effects of Mr. Hicks, Grocer, who is leaving.'

Oxford Times – Saturday 29 July 1865
'Inquest. – On Wednesday, at the Court Inn, an inquest was held, before F. Westell, Esq., coroner, on the body of John Viner, aged 73 years, who died at New Yatt, Hailey, the previous day. The deceased lived with his brother. The medical evidence went to show that the deceased died from starvation, and from the other evidence it appeared that he had been very much neglected by his brother during his illness, which was of considerable duration, although he had only received medical treatment for two days previous to his death. The inquest was adjourned until Friday.'

Oxford Chronicle and Reading Gazette – Saturday 05 January 1867
'Inquests. - On the 31st ult, at the Court Inn, Witney, on the body of Joseph Garside, aged 47, a native of Lindley, near Huddersfield. Deceased was a pattern weaver for Mr. Charles Early, and on Sunday last he went with his fellow-lodger and others to Minster, where they had some beer, returning to Witney in the evening. They had a glass of beer together at the Court Inn, and went to their lodgings at Mrs. Harris's, about half-past ten. On getting to their sitting room, which is upstairs, they could not find the matches, and deceased said he could find his way without light, and left the room, his companion remaining behind. Having obtained a light, his fellow-lodger went into the bedroom, but deceased was not there, and thinking that had gone to the privy, undressed and got into bed. Deceased not returning, he went to look after him, and found him lying with his head on the stairs, and his legs straight forward, insensible. He could not rouse him, and thinking that he was overcome with the beer and had fallen, wrapped him up, and went upstairs again, intending shortly to go to him again. Falling asleep, he did not wake until 6 o'clock the next morning, when he immediately went to deceased, who was lying as he had left him, and was snoring loudly, as he was when first discovered. Medical assistance was then called, as all efforts to rouse him failed, and blood came from his mouth when moved, but he died immediately. The jury returned verdict "That deceased died from injuries received by falling down a staircase."'

Oxford Chronicle and Reading Gazette – Saturday 15 June 1867
'Clubs. – On Monday the Benefit Societies held their annual feasts at the Elm Tree, Jolly Tucker, Court Inn, and Butchers' Arms, Witney. – On Tuesday the Benefit

Club held their annual dinner at the Griffin Inn, New Land, Coggs. The Witney Band were engaged playing through the principal streets, after their return from Coggs Church.'

Oxford Journal – Saturday 04 September 1875
'Court Inn, Witney, Oxon. TO BE SOLD BY AUCTION By Mr. WILLIAM SEELY, On the premises of the Court Inn, Bridge-street, Witney, on Monday, Sept. 6, 1875, at Eleven o'clock a.m. – A Two quarter BREWING PLANT, with the Copper Pumps, Furnace, Coolers, and all appliances complete; a capital MALT MILL, some large and small CASKS, HOUSE-HOLD FURNITURE, and various other Effects, as particularized in catalogues, which may be had at the offices of the auctioneer, No. 100, High-street, Witney. The lots will be on view the morning of sale.'

Oxford Times – Saturday 11 March 1876
'BIRTHS. SPIERS. – March 3, at the Court Inn, Bridge-street, Witney, the wife of Mr. Alfred Spiers, of a son.'

Oxford Journal – Saturday 18 March 1876
'SUDDEN DEATH. – On Wednesday last an inquest was held at the Court Inn, Witney, before F. Westell, Esq. Coroner, on the body of Mr. Henry Calcutt, jun., of Middlefield Farm, near Witney, aged 53 years. From the evidence adduced it appeared that deceased had had several attacks of rheumatic fever, and had for some years been subject to a diseased heart. On the night preceding the enquiry deceased and his brother went to Witney, and on their way deceased had a severe fit of coughing, and was sick, he told his brother that it caused him pain at his heart, but he recovered and went on to Witney and returned, and on going to bed was apparently quite well. Nothing more was heard of him until half-past six o'clock the next morning, when his brother tried to awake him, but found him quite dead. Mr. Hyde, surgeon, stated that he had attended the deceased professionally, and was aware that be had a diseased heart; his opinion was that he died from that complaint. Verdict accordingly.'

Oxford Times – Saturday 25 May 1878
'PETTY SESSIONS – May 23rd Henry Kearsey, of Hailey, was charged with refusing to quit the Court Inn, Witney, when drunk on the 11th May; he was also charged with assaulting P.C. Lyford at the same time and place. - Fined including costs 15s for each offence.'

Oxford Journal – Saturday 24 February 1883
'BAMPTON EAST DIVISION PETTY SESSIONS, Witney, February 22. The only business before the Magistrates to-day was the transfer of two licences, viz., The Court Inn, Witney, from R. J. Gibbard to Josiah Heels; ...'

Oxford Journal – Saturday 12 September 1885
'VALUABLE HOUSE PROPERTY. Three substantially stone-built and slated DWELLING HOUSES, with large gardens, Situated on WOOD GREEN, HAILEY, and TWO compact stone-built and slated DWELLING HOUSES,

situated in WEST END & BRIDGE STREET, WITNEY. RICHARD GILLETT is favoured with instructions from the Trustees of the late Mr. Joseph Gardner, to SELL by AUCTION, on Wednesday, September 16th, 1885, at 5.30 for 6.30 o'clock, at the King's Arms Inn Witney, under conditions to be then produced:- ...

Lot 4. – All that Stone-built and Slated DWELLING HOUSE, adjoining the Court Inn, Bridge-street, now and for many years in the occupation of Mrs. Rouse, at a rent of £10 per annum. The occupier of the above is entitled to the use of the w.c. and pump belonging to the said Court Inn. Land Tax 2s.'

Faringdon Advertiser and Vale of the White Horse Gazette – Saturday 01 September 1888
'FOUND DEAD. – Mr John Williams, an old inhabitant of Witney, residing in Bridge-street, was found dead in his bedroom on Monday morning. An inquest was held on Monday by F. Westell, Esq., coroner, at the Court Inn when it appeared from the evidence of Mrs Harwood that deceased, who was 78 years old went to his bed as usual on Sunday night. She heard nothing of him during the night, but when she went to his room about six o'clock the next morning she found him sitting on the floor and leaning against the bed, dressed, but was dead. Mr Edward Hyde, surgeon, said he saw the body about half-past six, and was of the opinion that the cause of death was apoplexy. A verdict was returned in accordance with the medical opinion.'

Witney Gazette and West Oxfordshire Advertiser – Saturday 20 October 1894
'PETTY SESSIONS, TRANSFERS. An application for the transfer of the license of the "Court" Inn, Witney from Josiah Eeles (deceased) to Sarah Ellen Eeles, his widow, was granted.'

Faringdon Advertiser and Vale of the White Horse Gazette – Saturday 30 August 1902
'PETTY SESSIONS, Thursday. – The following licenses were transferred. ... "Court" Inn, Witney, from Sarah Eeles to Joseph Haley; ...'

Witney Gazette and West Oxfordshire Advertiser – Saturday 13 September 1902
'SAD DEATH OF A YOUNG GIRL. On Tuesday evening an inquest was held at the Court Inn by F. J. D. Westell. Esq., deputy Coroner, on the body of Lilian Beatrice Godfrey, who died very suddenly the previous evening. The following evidence was adduced :- John Godfrey, dairyman living at West End, stated that the deceased was his daughter. She was in fairly good health until last Monday. She had not had a serious illness since infancy. She first complained to witness about a quarter to three on Monday morning when he heard someone crying and on going to deceased's room she complained of pain in the bowels. She seemed in great pain, and witness gave her some tea, and she seemed easier, and he left her. He thought she was suffering from constipation. She seemed better, and he went back to bed...

Between 7 and 8 Alice Beale called down to witness's wife to come up as Lily could not speak. Witness ran up first and spoke to deceased, but she only gave a low moan. She then gave two or three more low moans, and died before her mother could get to her. Deceased was 18 years of age last March...

Death was no doubt due to disease and purely natural causes. The disease might have been in progress for months, and no doubt the walls of the stomach gave way early Monday morning when deceased first complained to her father. Had witness been called in early on Monday morning he did not think there would have been any chance of saving her life. He had certainly no reason to think death was due to the operation of poison. A verdict of death from peritonitis was returned.'

Faringdon Advertiser and Vale of the White Horse Gazette – Saturday 29 November 1902

'COLLISION. A somewhat serious collision occurred in Bridge Street on Saturday evening. Mr Millin, baker, of Hailey, was driving into the town, and was turning the corner opposite Staple Hall, when be met the Rev. H. Wilson's horse and trap being driven home to Hailey from Witney Station, and the two collided with such force that the shaft of the clergyman's vehicle penetrated the breast of Mullins' horse a depth of several inches, causing serious injury. The animal was taken to the "Court" Inn stables, where it received attention from a vertinary (*sic*) surgeon. Both shafts of Mr Wilson's conveyance were broken, but the occupants of both vehicles seem to have escaped unhurt.'

Faringdon Advertiser and Vale of the White Horse Gazette – Saturday 02 January 1904

'A WITNEY INNKEEPER IN TROUBLE. Joseph Haley, licenced victualler, of Witney, was summoned for unlawfully permitting drunkenness to take place on his licenced premises, to-wit, the Court Inn, Bridge Street, Witney, on the 19th December. Mr Mace, of Chipping Norton, appeared for the defence. The case was dismissed with a caution.'

Faringdon Advertiser and Vale of the White Horse Gazette – Saturday 13 February 1904

'ANNUAL LICENSING MEETING. Petition for reduction of public houses. This was the annual general licensing meeting for the Bampton East Division, and the following report was presented by Supt. Hawtin: Gentlemen, – There are in the division 71 full licensed houses, beer houses (17 on and 4 off), and 8 wine and sweet licences, total 100. Two licence-holders have been proceeded against during the year for infringement of the Act, but were not convicted, as against one convicted last year. During the past year there have been 31 convictions for drunkenness, being an increase of 7 on last year's total. Of these 10 were resident in the division, and 21 were tramps or strangers passing through the district. I am directed by the Chief Constable to call your attention to the fact that at the "Court" Inn, Witney, the three adjoining houses have back doors opening on to licensed premises, and that in consequence thereof the said premises are rendered difficult for effective police supervision. I have therefore to ask that the renewal of this licence be deferred to the adjourned licensing day. ... Mr. Toy, for the owners of the Court Inn, Messrs. Hitchman, of Chipping Norton, undertook to have the houses at the rear of the inn cut off within three months, and on this condition the license was renewed. ... A petition was presented by Mr C. W. Early, and signed by 1,030 adult persons of the parish of Witney, praying the Bench to act on their promise of last year to reduce the number of licensed houses in Witney. – The Bench having considered the matter, said they felt they could not do anything this year, but they were agreed there were too many licensed houses in Witney, and steps would taken with a view to a reduction being made next year. The licenses were thereupon all renewed.'

Faringdon Advertiser and Vale of the White Horse Gazette – Saturday 16 January 1909
'LICENSING. ... that of the Court Inn, Witney, from Joseph Haley to George Boast; ...'

Faringdon Advertiser and Vale of the White Horse Gazette – Saturday 25 November 1911
'PETTY SESSIONS, Thursday. LICENSING. A holdover of the Witney "Court" Inn license was granted from Mr. G. Boast to Mr. Phillips, of Coats; ...'

Faringdon Advertiser and Vale of the White Horse Gazette – Saturday 05 October 1918
'PETTY SESSIONS, Thursday. TRANSFER. ... and that of the "Court" Inn, from W. Fardon to James William Staines.'

Faringdon Advertiser and Vale of the White Horse Gazette – Saturday 27 November 1920
'OVERHANGING SIGNS AND SHOP BLINDS. An application from Messrs. Hitchman and Co., brewers, for permission to re-place a hanging sign at the "Court" Inn, was granted on condition that it was a fixed sign. A discussion, initiated by the Chairman, followed on signs and window blinds which hung so low as to be dangerous to passers-by. The Surveyor was instructed to inspect and report thereon to the Council.'

Faringdon Advertiser and Vale of the White Horse Gazette – Saturday 07 January 1922
'R.A.O.B. – The first open Lodge, under the auspices of the Windrush Lodge, was held on Wednesday evening at the Court Inn, and was attended by over 100 members and friends. A very pleasant time was spent under the chairmanship of Bro. Stockford.'

Banbury Guardian – Thursday 15 May 1924
'BANBURY DIVISION LABOUR PARTY. GENERAL COUNCIL MEETING AT WITNEY. A meeting of the General Council of the Banbury Division Labour Party was held at the Court Inn, Witney, on Saturday. Sixty delegates were present from all parts of the division. In the absence of Lord Olivier, Mr. V. Jones, Banbury, was elected to the chair. ...'

Licensees:

1861–1874	Joseph Gardner
	Age 49, born in Witney, Oxon. Wife Catherine age 50 (1861 Census)
	Age 59, born in Witney, Oxon. Wife Catherine age 63 (1871 Census)
1876	Alfred Spiers
1877	William Fidler
1881	Joseph Gardner
	Age 69, born in Witney, Oxon. Widower (1881 Census)
1882–1883	John Robert Gibbard
1883–1894	Josiah Eales
	Age 57, born in Eatington, Warks. Wife Sarah age 59 (1891 Census)
1894	Josiah Eales died Jul-Aug-Sep age 61
1894–1902	Sarah Eales (Mrs.)
	Age 69, born in Clifford Chambers, Glos. Widow (1901 Census)
1902–1908	Joseph Haley
1909–1911	George Boast
	Age 40, born in Yarmouth, Norfolk. Wife Mary Ann age 29
	(1911 Census)
1912–1915	Albert Phillips
1918	Ernest Fardon
1919–1921	James William Staines
1922–1958	Frank Edward Tombs
	DOB 26 Jul 1890 Publican. Wife Clara dob 20 Jun 1893 Unpaid
	Domestic Duties (1939 Register)
1959	Tombs Frank of The Court Inn 41 Bridge Street Witney Oxfordshire
	died 8 April 1959 Administration Oxford 2 September to Clara
	Tombs widow. Effects £1465.
1959	Clara Tombs
1960–1966	Geoffrey Richard Cottam
1967–1969	Frank G. Farr
1970–1974	Derek W. Burge
1975	Keith C. Rowley
1976–1977	Derek C. Tooth
1978–1980	Haydn Morgans
2005–2016	Nicholas O'Brien
2017–present	Raj Gurung

Prince Albert, Bridge St (1844–1871)

From the newspapers:

Oxford Chronicle and Reading Gazette – Saturday 16 October 1869
'BRIDGE STREET, WITNEY. EXCELLENT BREWING PLANT, Large and Small COPPER, CASKS, &c., at the late "Prince Albert," TO BE SOLD BY AUCTION By MR LONG, On the premises, Tuesday, October 20, at one o'clock, the property of Mr. John Williams, who has declined the retail beer trade; comprising an excellent 96-Gallon Copper, with grate, lead kirb, and brickwork, 40-Gallon Copper, with lead kirb, lead pump, a 12-Bushel Mash Tub, Underback,

Coolers, and Working Tubs, two excellent 250 Gallon Casks, two 200 Gallons ditto, two 100 Gallons, three 20 and 18 Gallons, and smaller; Pewter Measures, Tap Tubs, Brass Taps, round and oblong Tap Tables, deal seats, signboards, quantity of pipes, beam and scales, corks and bungs, and other utensils.

The Brewery Plant is in excellent condition, and the Casks are sound, remarkably clean, and well kept. Catalogues on the Premises, and of the Auctioneer, Witney.'

Licensees:

1844–1871   John Williams
                      Age 41, born in Witney, Oxon. Baker. Widower (1851 Census)
                      Age 51, born in Witney, Oxon. Baker. Widower (1861 Census)
                      Age 61, born in Witney, Oxon (1871 Census)

Roebuck, 15 Bridge St (1840–1874)

(Currently an empty Retail Premises)
(1840 Tithe Awards Map ref 625)

From the newspapers:

Oxford Journal – Saturday 07 September 1872
'BRIDGE STREET, WITNEY. Freehold Public House, Shop, & Premises, TO BE SOLD BY AUCTION, BY Mr. LONG, At the King's Arms Inn, in Witney, on Friday the 27th of September, 1872, at Five o'clock p.m., under conditions to be then produced, by order of the Executors and Trustees of the late Mrs. Hannah East, in two lots.

Lot 1. - A FREEHOLD BEER HOUSE or PUBLIC HOUSE, called "The Roebuck," in Bridge-street, Witney, containing large tap room, kitchen, scullery, and out-offices; stable, garden, and well of water; three bed rooms, and two attics, in the occupation of Mr. Thos. Beckinsale, a yearly tenant.

Lot 2. - A small FREEHOLD GROCER'S SHOP and PREMISES, containing entrance passage, shop, sitting room, kitchen, and offices; garden and pump; two bed rooms and attic, in the occupation of Mr. James Brooks.

For further information apply to John Early, Esq., Woodgreen; John M. Clinch, Esq., Rock House; Frederick Westell, Esq., solicitor; or the auctioneer, Witney.'

Licensees:

1840   Joseph Clarke
1840   Public House Garden &c. owned by Joseph Tyler
1861–1874   Thomas Beckingsale (moved from the Black Head)
                      Age 66, born in Witney, Oxon. Wife Elizabeth age 60 (1861 Census)

Staple Hall Inn, 30-32 Bridge St (1668–1854)

(Currently a Care Home)
(1840 Tithe Awards Map ref 750)

The stone building that stands there today is mainly 17th century and was almost totally rebuilt as an inn following a fire, by Ursula Marriott (an ancestor of the Marriott blanket making family of Witney) and her husband William Townsend in 1668. It remained in their family until 1795 and although William was killed by a falling tree in 1686, his widow Ursula presided as the Grand Old Dame of the inn for very many years; she died in 1731 at the impressive age of 106. The Staple Hall Inn became popular with local wool merchants and fellmongers on their way to and from the Cotswolds and for many years it was also a staging post for the 'Rival' and 'Retaliator' horse drawn passenger coaches. *(witneyblanketstory.org.uk)*

From the newspapers:

Oxford Journal – Saturday 23 April 1757
'MARCH 21st, 1757. THE Trustees appointed to put in Execution an Act of Parliament made for repairing the Road from the Top of Crickley Hill in Gloucestershire, to Campsfield in the Parish of Kidlington in Oxfordshire; and also the Road from Witney, through Ensham, Cumnor, and Botley, to the City of Oxford, will meet according to their Adjournment on Monday the 25th Day of April, 1757, at Ten of the Clock in the forenoon, at the House of William Townsend call'd *Staple Hall* Inn in *Witney*, in the County of Oxford; ...'

Oxford Journal – Saturday 04 June 1757
'TO BE SOLD, Twenty-Three Couple of Compleat HARRIERS, about two and twenty Inches high. For farther Particulars enquire of Mr. Augustine Batte of Witney in Oxfordshire, or of Mr. Townsend at Staple-Hall Inn in Witney, aforesaid.'

Oxford Journal – Saturday 27 April 1765
'HENRY TOWNSEND, of WITNEY, in the County of Oxford, BEGS Leave to inform his Friends and Customers, that he is removed from the STAPLE HALL Inn in Witney, to the BLACKAMORE's-HEAD Inn in Witney; where all Gentlemen, Ladies, and Others, who shall please to favour him with their Custom, may depend on meeting with the best Accommodations, and most civil Treatment, from Their most obedient humble servant, HENRY TOWNSEND. N. B. Genteel Post-Chaises, with able Horses and careful Drivers.'

Oxford Journal – Saturday 18 February 1775
'February 17th, 1775. ISAAC COBURN, Waiter to Mr. Barke, at the Marlborough Arms, in Woodstock, having taken the STAPLE HALL INN, in Witney, in the County of Oxford, now in the Occupation of Mr. Townsend, (who has declined business) intends entering on the same on the Twenty-fifth Day of March next, by which Time it will be neatly fitted up; he therefore begs Leave to solicit a Continuance of the Commands of the Nobility, Gentry, and other Friends of Mr. Townsend, as well as the Favours of the Public in general, and his own Friends in particular, assuring them, that he will at all Times be provided with the best of all Kinds of Accommodations, which, with a constant Endeavour to please, he hopes will entitle him to their Encouragement; to whom he is Their most obedient Servant, ISAAC COBURN. N. B. Neat Post-Chaises, &c.'

Oxford Journal – Saturday 12 December 1778
'A GREY HOUND CAME into the Yard at Staple Hall, in Witney, on Sunday Evening, December 6, 1778, - A fine Brinded GREYHOUND. – The Owner may have him again, applying to Mr. Coburn, Staple Hall aforesaid, and paying the Expenses.'

Oxford Journal – Saturday 25 August 1787
'To all Alehouse Keepers within the Hundred of Bampton. THE acting Magistrates within the Hundred of Bampton, in the County of Oxford, in Obedience to the Royal Proclamation, and being seriously impressed with Conviction, that the numerous Evils now prevailing and so justly complained of, arise in great Measure from the Licencing of too many Publick Houses; to remedy the same to the utmost of their Power, and to prevent Improper Applications for Licences at their Sessions to be holden at the House of Isaac Coburn, known by the Name of Staple Hall Inn, in Witney, on the Eleventh Day of September next, at the Hour of Ten in the Forenoon, do think proper to chuse this their Notice publickly to be given, that all Persons who shall apply for the Purposes aforesaid, will be expected to severally produce a fresh Certificate, under the Hands of the Minister, Churchwardens, and at least six of the principal Inhabitants, Householders, (if so many there be) of their respective Parishes, attesting the Character and good Behaviour of each Person so applying, and asserting the Expedience and Necessity of such House to be licenced, without which Certificate no Licence will in future be granted: *And it is further required,* That all Publicans at the Time of their being so licenced, do produce good and sufficient Security (to the Satisfaction of the Magistrates then assembled) for the Observance of Rule and good Order; and that no Victualler, or Alehouse Keeper will be accepted as a Surety for another. By Order of the Justices. August 14, 1787'

Oxford Journal – Saturday 27 December 1794
'A CARD and DANCING ASSEMBLY will be held at Mr. COBURN's, STAPLE HALL INN, Witney, On TUESDAY, January 6th, 1795.'

Oxford Journal – Saturday 22 October 1803
'STAPLE HALL INN, WITNEY, OXON. ISAAC COBURN returns his sincere Thanks to the Nobility, Gentry, Gentlemen Travellers, and Public in general, for their Support during his Residence at the above INN, and begs Leave to inform them he has declined Business in Favour of his Son, THOMAS COBURN, for whom he solicits a Continuance of their future Favours and Support.

THOMAS COBURN having entered on the above INN, most respectfully solicits the Favours and Support of the NOBILITY, GENTRY, GENTLEMEN TRAVELLERS, and PUBLIC in general, and begs Leave to assure them he will exert his best Endeavours to render their Accommodation in every Respect comfortable. Neat Post Chaises, able Horses, and careful Drivers.'

Oxford Journal – Saturday 17 December 1803
'STAPLE HALL INN, WITNEY, December 17, 1803. THOMAS COBURN presents his respectful Compliments to his Friends in general, and fearing he should unintentionally have omitted to inform any one of them, either Personally or by Letter, of his HOUSE-WARMING being on WEDNESDAY next, takes this Opportunity of acquainting them, that it is fixed for that Day, when he respectfully solicits the Pleasure of seeing them. Dinner on Table at Two o'Clock.'

Oxford Journal – Saturday 27 April 1805
'On Wednesday last died, aged 60, much lamented and esteemed, Mrs. Susannah Coburn, widow of the late Mr. Isaac Coburn, formerly Master of Staple Hall Inn, Witney.'

Oxford Journal – Saturday 25 January 1806
'IF the Person who left a GREY PONEY at the Staple Hall Inn, in Witney, Oxfordshire, on the 6th of January, does not immediately fetch him away, he will soon be SOLD by AUCTION, to defray the Expences of Keep. *Staple Hall Inn, Jan.* 17, 1806.'

Oxford Journal – Saturday 30 May 1807
'LOST, A Black and White GREYHOUND DOG, answering to the Name of Sting. Whoever has found the same, and will bring it to Mr. Coburn, Staple Hall Inn, Witney, shall be handsomely rewarded for their Trouble.'

Oxford Journal – Saturday 24 June 1809
'LOST,- A Yellow Greyhound BITCH, with a white neck, very fine in the stern, and a white tip at the end of the stern, named FLY.- Whoever has found her and will bring her to Mr. Coburn, Staple Hall Inn, Witney, shall receive ONE GUINEA'

Oxford University and City Herald – Saturday 05 August 1809
'A curious and very unfortunate circumstance occurred at Staple-hall inn, Witney, on Monday last. Mr. Coburn having a horse that he conceived had worked sufficiently long, thought if would be more humane to have him killed, than part with him, and subject him to probable ill usage. In consequence, he gave directions to a man to knock him on the head, and dress his skin. The man went into the stable, and on patting a horse on the hip that was lying down, and finding he did not move, he conceived this was his victim. Unfortunately, however, when the bloody deed was done, it was found that he had killed a valuable post-horse belonging to Mr. James Heath, of Northleach, while the poor superannuated horse had escaped.'

Oxford Journal – Saturday 05 May 1810
'WHEREAS we, the undersigned JOHN GARDNER and WILLIAM BATTS, of Witney, in the county of Oxford, did, on Sunday evening the 18th of March last, assault and ill treat Mary Fyfield, servant to Mr. Coburn, of Staple Hall Inn, in Witney, for which Mr. Coburn has justly caused a prosecution to be commenced against us, but the said Mr. Coburn having, at our solicitation, agreed to stop all proceedings against us in consequence of the contrition we have expressed for the offence, and of paying all expences incurred, and paying One Guinea towards the support of the Sunday School, in Witney aforesaid, we do hereby ask the pardon of the said Mr. Coburn and his said servant, and thank them for the great lenity shewn to us on this occasion. WILLIAM BATTS. The mark of JOHN GARDNER. Witness, W. Osman. Witney, 25th of April, 1810.'

Oxford University and City Herald – Saturday 07 July 1810
'Witney Day Post Coach to London. THE Public are respectfully informed, that a DAY POST COACH, carrying four Insides, will commence running from the Staple Hall Inn, on MONDAY, July 9, at Six o'clock, and arrive at the Angel Inn, Saint Clement's, Strand, London, to Dinner; and at the same hour a Coach will commence to run from the Angel Inn, St. Clements, and arrive at Witney to

Dinner. Performed by COSTAR and Co. The Proprietors cannot be accountable for any parcel or packages whatever, above the value of Five Pounds, unless entered as such, and paid for accordingly.'

Oxford University and City Herald – Saturday 02 November 1811
'Valuable Freehold and Copyhold ESTATES, WITNEY, COGGS, and HAILEY, OXON.
TO BE SOLD BY AUCTION, by Messrs. Churchill & Turner, At Staple Hall Inn, in Witney, in the County of Oxford, on FRIDAY, the 18th day of DECEMBER, 1811, at Twelve o'clock at Noon, under such conditions as shall be then and there produced, by order of the Assignees of Thomas Coburn, a Bankrupt, SEVERAL Valuable FREEHOLD and COPYHOLD ESTATES, at Witney, Coggs, and Hailey, in the county of Oxford, in the following lots:-
FREEHOLD. LOT I. – All that long-established well-accustomed and very respectable Inn, The STAPLE-HALL INN, at Witney aforesaid, in the high road from Gloucester and Cheltenham to Oxford and Woodstock, excellent stabling for forty horses, with good wool and hay lofts, spacious yard, coach houses, and other requisite buildings, kitchen and pleasure gardens, together with a close of rich pasture land adjoining the Inn, containing about Four Acres. ...'

Oxford University and City Herald – Saturday 14 December 1811
'TO BE SOLD BY AUCTION. By CHURCHILL & TURNER. On THURSDAY NEXT, DECEMBER the 19th, 1811, (by order of the Assignees Thomas Coburn, a Bankrupt,) ALL the valuable Stock of POST and COACH HORSES, Chaises and Harness, on the premises, at Staple Hall Inn, in Witney, in the County of Oxford; consisting of 40 capital post and coach horses in high condition, 6 excellent Post Chaises, 10 pair of short and 4 pair of long chaise harness, and 4 sets of coach harness. The Sale to begin at 12 o'clock precisely.'

Cheltenham Chronicle – Thursday 02 January 1812
'STAPLE HALL INN, WITNEY, OXON. TO BE SOLD BY AUCTION, By CHURCHHILL and TURNER, On the Premises, Wednesday the Eighth day of January, 1812, at Twelve o'clock at Noon, under such Conditions as shall be then and there produced, (by Order of the Assignees of Thomas Coburn, a Bankrupt, Mr. Henry Leake, the purchaser of the Estate at the last Sale having refused paying the deposit and to comply with the Conditions.)
ALL that long-established and very respectable INN, THE STAPLE HALL INN, at Witney aforesaid, on the High Road from Gloucester and Cheltenham to Oxford and Woodstock, excellent Stabling for 40 Horses, with good Wool and Hay Lofts, spacious yard, Coach Houses, and other requisite Buildings, Kitchen and Pleasure Gardens; together with a Close of rich Pasture Land adjoining the Inn, containing about Four Acres, and part of a rich Meadow, as the same is now staked out. Also, a Pew in the Church.
The Land-tax is redeemed, and the Estate Freehold. Printed particulars may be had at the Office of Messrs. North and Harrison, solicitors, and of the Auctioneers, in Woodstock, Oxfordshire ; Mr. Lovell, solicitor, Towcester, Northamptonshire; at the place of Sale; the Inns in the Neighbourhood; and at the Office of Mr. Turner, solicitor, Edward-street, Cavendish-square, London.'

Oxford Journal – Saturday 14 March 1812
'Staple Hall Inn, Witney, Oxon. The Nobility, Gentry, and Public, are respectfully informed, that the above Inn is continued open for their reception, where

every attention will be paid to their comfort and accommodation, and all favors thankfully acknowledged. – Neat post chaises, good horses, and careful drivers.'

Oxford University and City Herald – Saturday 03 October 1812
'THE Creditors who have proved their Debts under a Commission of Bankrupt, bearing date the 4th day of October last, awarded and issued forth against THOMAS COBURN, of Witney, in the County of Oxford, Woolstapler, Dealer and Chapman, are desired to meet the Assignees of the Estate and Effects of the said Bankrupt, on the 9th day October, 1812, at Eleven of the clock in the Forenoon, at the Marlborough Arms Inn, in New Woodstock, in the said County Oxford, to assent to or dissent from the said Assignees commencing and prosecuting a suit at law or in equity, against Henry Leake, late of Kidlington, in the said County of Oxford, Gentleman, the Purchaser of Staple-Hall Inn, with its Appurtenances, part the said Bankrupt's Estate, for refusing to pay the Deposit, and to comply with the Conditions of Sale; and other Special Affairs. By order of the Assignees, H. J. NORTH, J. V. HARRISON, their Solicitors. *Woodstock, 4th Sept.* 1812.'

Oxford Journal – Saturday 12 December 1812
'STAPLE HALL INN, WITNEY. JOSEPH MASTERS, having taken and entered on the above well-known and long-established INN, begs leave to solicit the favours of the Nobility, Gentry, and others, and to assure them that every attention will be paid to their comfort and accommodation. Neat Post-chaises, good horses, and careful drivers. Gentlemen Travellers are respectfully informed, that they will meet with the utmost civility and attention at the above Inn. The wholesale wine and spirit trade carried on as usual.'

Oxford University and City Herald – Saturday 10 December 1814
'STAPLE-HALL INN, WITNEY, DECEMBER 8, 1814; JOSEPH MASTERS BEGS leave to return his sincere and grateful thanks to the Noblemen, Gentlemen, and the Public, who have been pleased to honour him with their patronage and support since his commencement as Landlord at the above Inn, and does assure them that exertion on his part shall be wanting to merit a continuance of those favors which have been so liberally bestowed on him.

    J. Masters also flatters himself that his Horses, &c. Wines and Spirits, with well-aired Beds, have been, and will be found equal to any in the kingdom. – He also solicits his Friends and the Public, who wish to favour him with their commands, to be particular in ordering the drivers to STAPLE-HALL INN, as chaises are sent to another House, in opposition to him and his connexions.'

Oxford University and City Herald – Saturday 25 March 1815
'On Monday se'nnight died, of a decline, Mr. Robert Shepherd, son of Mrs. Masters, of Staple-Hall Inn, Witney, in this county. He bore his illness with resignation, and was greatly esteemed by those who enjoyed the pleasure of his acquaintance.'

Oxford Journal – Saturday 05 February 1820
'On Thursday last King George the Fourth was proclaimed at Witney, with every degree of loyalty and regularity, under the directions of the Bailiffs of the Town. The proclamation was first read at Staple Hall Inn, when the procession proceeded to the Blanket Hall, Market Place, and Church Green, at each of which places it was also read.'

Oxford Journal – Saturday 16 August 1823
'His Royal Highness the Duke of Gloucester and suite changed horses at the Star Inn, in this city, on Wednesday last, on their road to Cheltenham. The noble party dined at the Staple Hall Inn, Witney, and reached Cheltenham the same evening.'

Oxford Journal – Saturday 16 July 1825
'On Tuesday last his Royal Highness the Duke of Gloucester and suite dined at Staple Hall Inn, Witney, on his way to Cheltenham, where he arrived the same evening, taking up his residence in St. James's-square.'

Oxford Journal – Saturday 01 July 1826
'THE friends of G. F. STRATTON, Esq. will dine together at the Staple Hall Inn, Witney, on Wednesday next, July 5, at Four o'clock. Mr. Stratton has consented to be present. – Tickets may be had at the bar of the Staple Hall Inn.'

Oxford Journal – Saturday 15 July 1826
'On Tuesday last his Royal Highness the Duke of Gloucester and suite passed through this city, on their route to Cheltenham, and changed horses at the Star Inn. His Royal Highness dined at the Staple Hall Inn, Witney.'

Oxford Journal – Saturday 18 July 1829
'The Duke of Glocester, attended by Colonel Higgins, Major Forster, and Captain Stevens, passed through this city on Wednesday last, on their way to Cheltenham. His Royal Highness changed horses at the Star Inn, and proceeded to the Staple Hall Inn, Witney, where the party dined, and reached Cheltenham the same evening.'

Oxford Journal – Saturday 21 August 1830
'On Tuesday last his Royal Highness the Duke of Glocester and suite, on their return from Cheltenham, dined and slept at the Staple Hall Inn, Witney, and the following morning, on taking his departure, his Royal Highness was pleased to express his perfect satisfaction at the attention and most excellent accommodation he had experienced at the above Inn.'

Oxford Journal – Saturday 04 August 1832
'On Wednesday last the Duke and Duchess of St. Alban's lunched at the Staple Hall Inn, Witney, on their way to Cheltenham.'

Oxford Journal – Saturday 29 July 1837
'On Tuesday last the E Troop of the Queen's Own, O. Y. C. sat down to a sumptuous dinner provided by Messrs. Masters and Son, of the Staple Hall Inn, Witney. The banquet was given, in the most liberal manner, by the Hon. Major George Charles Agar, to his late troop. The party spent the afternoon in high glee, and separated at an early hour, much gratified with the entertainment.'

Oxford Journal – Saturday 21 December 1839
'On the 16th inst. was married Mr. C. Rouse to Miss Gardiner, only daughter of Mr. J. Gardiner, of the Staple Hall Inn Tap.'

Oxford Journal – Saturday 01 October 1842
'Staple Hall Family Hotel and Posting House, Witney, Oxon. JOSEPH MASTERS, Jun. BEGS Permission most respectfully to inform the Nobility, Clergy, Gentry,

Commercial Gentlemen, and the Public generally, that, in consequence of the advertisement for Sale of the Household Furniture and Effects of Mr. George Smith, under an assignment for the benefit of Creditors, ample and comfortable accommodation is provided at the WHITE HART INN, WITNEY, until the requisite arrangements are made for re-establishment at the Staple Hall; the Hotel and Inn Department *only* of which has been for some time conducted by Mr. Smith, his late Clerk.

Mr. Masters begs to state he has *alone* continued as heretofore the Posting Business, Stabling, and Yards of the Staple Hall; where, and also at the White Hart Inn, will be found excellent Post Horses and Chaises, Flys, Gigs, and other Carriages; and he respectfully solicits a continuance of that patronage which he and his father have had the honor to be favoured with at the Staple Hall for more than thirty years.

All orders addressed to Mr. Masters, at the Staple Hall, or White Hart Inn, Witney, will meet with instant attention, and be gratefully received. Witney, Sept. 19, 1842.'

Oxford Chronicle and Reading Gazette – Saturday 14 March 1857
'WITNEY, OXFORDSHIRE. important and VALUABLE FREEHOLD AND LEASEHOLD HOUSE and INN PROPERTY, CLOSES of PASTURE and GARDEN LAND, At WITNEY, Oxon. TO BE SOLD BY AUCTION By Mr. LONG, At the Staple Hall Hotel, Witney, on Thursday, the 2nd day of April. 1857, at 5 o'clock in the afternoon (by direction of the Devisees in Trust for Sale, under the will of Daniel Westell, Esq. late of Witney, Solicitor, deceased, and under conditions of sale to be then produced), as follows:-

In one lot – and if not told then, in three lots, as stated below

All that FREEHOLD ESTATE and capital MANSION, celebrated as THE STAPLE HALL HOTEL, in Bridge-street, in Witney, with very extensive buildings attached and belonging, comprising entrance hall and portico, several parlours and commercial rooms, 2 smaller parlours, bar, and kitchen, on the first floor; a large ball or assembly room, now used as the County Court room, and 15 bedrooms, water closet, extensive arched cellaring, back kitchen, and other numerous convenient out offices, and also several stables, of different dimensions, and coach-houses, granary, wool warehouses and lofts, pleasure and kitchen gardens, and 2 closes of rich meadow and pasture land, containing together 5 acres, all adjoining to the Hotel, in Bridge street, Witney, and now occupied by Mr. Wm. Salmon.

Outgoings on this lot – Land tax, 5s. 4d.; Quit Rent, 2s. 8d.

N.B. – If this Property is not disposed of in one lot, as above described, it will be immediately offered in the following 3 lots, viz. :-

Lot 1. – A substantial and desirable stone-built and genteel RESIDENCE, fronting south, and standing on a raised terrace, next to the pleasure and flower gardens of the Hotel, attached, and with kitchen garden and close of rich meadow land adjoining, situate in Bridge-street, Witney (part of the present Hotel), and commanding an eligible frontage of 180 feet to the street.

This lot, with moderate outlay, is readily convertible into a valuable residence, suitable for the family of a gentleman of good position, or professional man, and would comprise 4 good rooms, entrance hall and offices, on the ground floor, excellent arched and extensive cellaring, breakfast, and occasional room, good kitchen room, and 6 bedrooms, and attics of various sizes. The land is 1A. 3R. 9P., all conveniently situated for occupation with the house.

Lot 2. – A neat and very comfortable sashed RESIDENCE (other part of the Hotel adjoining Lot 1), with portico and entrance hall, parlour, breakfast, dining, and occasional room, a good kitchen, arched cellaring, with 6 large bedrooms and attics, and a garden and courtyard attached, and lying convenient.

Lot 3. – The STAPLE HALL INN, to be retained, the remaining part of the Hotel, with the gateway entrance to the yard, the tap and stabling reduced, it would be proposed, and adapted to the comparatively smaller requirements of its present with its former trade and business. The excise licences would attach and belong to this Lot as "The Staple Hall," for which it could be conveniently altered and arranged, and at moderate expence, with excellent stabling, granary, and coachhouses, around a large yard, pigeon house, and another back yard, and coach horse stables, together with a large kitchen garden, and a close of 4 acres of superior upland pasture land, called Hill Closes, adjoining.

This Lot offers for investment or occupation a most eligible inn property, deserving the attention of brewers and innkeepers, as a place of still extensive trade and business.

The outgoings on these Lots, if separately sold as stated above, will be apportioned.

Lot 4. – The BRIDGE HOUSE, a respectable RESIDENCE, dwelling house and offices, being freehold, with well-arranged parlours, dining and drawing rooms, 7 bedrooms and attics, entrance hall and passage, kitchen, cellaring, laundries, and out offices, &c. The business offices, detached from but adjoining the house, extensive lawns, front flower garden, and ornamental kitchen gardens, stabling and coachhouse, yards, courts, and premises, with close of superior pasture and meadow land adjoining, and a neat pleasure ground, well planted with choice ornamental timber and shrubs in full growth, and preserved trout stream, containing in the whole 2A. 2R. 0P., and bounded on the northern side and in front of the house by the river Windrush, affording excellent trout and other fishing, besides the trout stream in the close, which is preserved, the whole situate near the Bridge, in Witney late the residence of Daniel Westell, Esq., and now of Mr. Jas. Westell, solicitor.

Outgoings – Land Tax, £1 5s. 5d; Quit Rent, 2s. 6d.

Lot 5. – A FREEHOLD CLOSE of very excellent market garden land, inclosed by stone walls, and well planted in Puck Lane, in Witney, near adjacent lot 4, called Castle's Close, containing 1A. 2R. 25P., now in the occupation of P. Buckingham, with hovel, &c.

Outgoings, land tax, 8s. 6d.

Lot 6. – A LEASEHOLD respectable and roomy DWELLING HOUSE, and Residence, in Corn Street, in Witney, with stable and gighouse, court yard, garden, and offices attached, now in the occupation of J. W. Clinch, jun., Esq.; and a CLOSE of capital Arable or Garden Land, containing 2R. and 33P. in the Crofts,

Witney, lying near adjoining thereto, and held under the same lease and title; and two substantial stone-built and slated COTTAGES thereon, now rented by Wm. Perkins, and his under tenants.

Outgoings, land tax, 8s. 6d.

Lot 6 is held by lease from the Churchwardens and Trustees of the parish of St. Giles, in the city of Oxford, for a term of 21 years, from 5th Oct., 1848, at a reserved rent of £20 per annum, granted to Messrs. James Westell and Hy. Bateman.

Descriptive particulars, with conditions of sale and lithographed plan of lots 1, 2, 3, and 5, shewing their relative adjacent situations, and of lot 6, and an enlarged plan of the buildings and proposed division into lots of lot 1, and information may obtained on application to Messrs. James and Frederick Westell, solicitors, or the Auctioneer, Witney, or Mr. Henry Bateman, Asthally, near Witney, and to view the several properties apply to the respective tenants.

Banbury Guardian – Thursday 02 June 1859
'TO BE LET, IN WITNEY, THE INN and PREMISES, known as the STAPLE HALL which been thoroughly restored and re-arranged, and is a part of the old-established and well-known Inn. It comprises a Smoking Room, 21 feet by 16 feet, Bar and Parlour, Cellar, Kitchen, Larder, Brewhouse, &c.; a Water Closet, approached from the House; Sitting and Bed Room, or two Bed Rooms, on first landing; three Bed Rooms on the first floor. There is also a six-stall Stable and other accommodation for 20 Market Horses, with extensive Lofts over; a Carriage House and Club Room above; a good walled Garden, and a Close of Three Acres of excellent Pasture Land, if required. –For further Particulars apply to Mr. James Long, Auctioneer, Witney.'

Licensees:

1753-1759	William Townsend
1760	Buried on 13 June 1760
1760-1774	Henry Townsend
1775-1803	Isaac Coburn
1804	Isaac Coburn snr was buried 13 December
1805	Susannah Coburn died 24th April, age 60
1804-1811	Thomas Coburn
1811	Thomas Coburn was bankrupt, 2-11-1811
	Staple Hall Inn for sale by auction
1813-1840	Joseph Masters
1840	Staple Hall Inn &c. owned by Daniel Westell
1841-1844	George Smith
	Age 24, wife Emma age 25 (1841 Census)
1850-1857	William Salmon
	Age 50, born in Witney, Oxon. Wife Anna age 50 (1851 Census)
1857	Staple Hall Inn for sale by auction
1859	Staple Hall to be let

White Hart Inn, 10 Bridge St (1753–1857)

(Currently unoccupied)
(1840 Tithe Awards Map ref 766)

From the newspapers:

Oxford Journal – Saturday 29 January 1763
'WITNEY, Jan. 28, 1763. Dropped or mislaid somewhere near the White-Hart Inn, in Witney, Oxfordshire, on Monday the 22nd of November last, a Sum of Money amounting to Nine Pounds. Whoever will bring the same to Mr. Smith, at the White Hart, in Witney aforesaid, shall receive a Guinea Reward.'

Oxford Journal – Saturday 29 August 1772
'TO be SOLD to the BEST BIDDER, on Saturday the 12th of September, 1772, between the Hours of Three and Seven in the Afternoon, unless disposed of before by private Contract, of which Notice will be given, at the House of George Smith, the White Hart Inn, in Witney, Oxfordshire. – All those MESSUAGES or TENEMENTS, Back Buildings, Gardens, &c. and an inclosed Ground of about two Acres, adjoining to the same, now in the Occupation of Elizabeth Sellman, and William Maddocks, and their Under-Tenants, situate on the West Side of the High-Street, in Witney aforesaid, -near the Bridge. – For Particulars enquire of Benjamin Bradshaw or John Fardon, in Witney, who will shew the Premises. N. B. Also sundry Implements belonging to the Carrying Business at the same Place.'

Oxford Journal – Saturday 27 April 1776
'THE Trustees appointed to put in Execution Two several Acts of Parliament, made for repairing the Road from the Top of Crickley-Hill, in the County of Gloucester, to Campsfield, in the Parish of Kidlington, in the County of Oxford; and also the Road from Campsfield to the Turnpike Road at or near Enslow-Bridge, in the said County of Oxford, will meet on Friday the tenth Day of May, 1776, at Eleven o'clock in the Forenoon, at the House of George Smith, called the White-Hart Inn, in Witney, in the County of Oxford; ...'

Oxford Journal – Saturday 31 January 1789
'ALL Persons indebted to William Howlett, late of the White Hart Inn, Witney, Oxfordshire, Carrier, deceased, are forthwith desired to pay their respective Debts to John Biggers, of Witney aforesaid, Schoolmaster: And all Persons having any Demands on the said William Howlett, are desired to send their accounts to the said John Biggers.'

Oxford Journal – Saturday 03 August 1805
'CAPITAL INN TO LETT. TO be LETT, and entered upon immediately, - All that old-accustomed and well-established INN, called the White Hart, conveniently situate in a central Part of the Town of Witney, in Oxfordshire; comprising a spacious House with every Convenience for an Inn, a large Brew-House, Stabling for forty Horses with Lofts, roomy Wool-Lofts, two large Gardens, an Orchard well planted with Fruit Trees, Chaise-House, Pig Sties, and every other Requisite for carrying on the public Business, or the Trade of Wool Dealer, or any other Business in an extensive Line.

For a View of the House and Premises apply to the Tenant, and for Terms to Mr. William Long, of Witney aforesaid.'

Oxford Journal – Saturday 26 April 1806
'TO COVER this SEASON, 1806, at the White Hart Inn, Witney, Oxon, at ONE
GUINEA each Mare, and 2s. 6d. the Groom, That beautiful Chesnut Horse
YOUNG DOGE, now the Property of Mr. Atkins, of Witney.'

Oxford University and City Herald – Saturday 23 May 1807
'WHITE HART INN, WITNEY, OXON, TO BE LET, and entered on
immediately, All that Old-accustomed and Well-established INN, called the
WHITE HART, situate at Witney, in the County of Oxford comprising good
parlours, kitchen, bed rooms, brew house, cellars, and every other convenience
for an inn, stabling for 30 horses, extensive lofts for the storing of wool or grain,
two large gardens, and an excellent orchard well stocked with fruit trees, now in
fine bloom.'

Oxford University and City Herald – Saturday 19 September 1807
'WHITE HART INN, WITNEY. JOHN FREEMAN, Late of the King's Head
Inn, Oxford, BEGS leave to inform his friends and the public, that he has entered
on the above Inn, which has lately undergone thorough repair, and which he
has fitted up in a neat and elegant style. N.B. An Excellent Stock of WINES,
LIQUORS, &c. Good BEDS and Extensive STABLING.'

Oxford University and City Herald – Saturday 10 December 1814
'Last week died, greatly regretted by his family, and a numerous circle of friends,
Mr. Smith, formerly master of the White Hart Inn, at Witney, in this county.'

Oxford University and City Herald – Saturday 14 November 1818
'... This is to give Notice, whoever will give such information to Mr. Salmon,
White Hart Inn, Witney, to Mr. John Collingwood, Abingdon, Berks, as shall lead
to the discovery of the above property, shall receive a Reward of Five Guineas.
And, if stolen, any person giving information of the offender or offenders, that
they may be brought to justice, shall, on conviction, receive the above Reward,
on application to the said Mr. Salmon, or Mr. J. Collingwood. Abingdon, Nov. 11,
1818.'

Oxford University and City Herald – Saturday 17 May 1823
'BELL INN, BAMPTON. Royal Defiance Post Coach, TO LONDON. THE
Public are respectfully informed, for the better accommodation of BAMPTON and
its Neighbourhood, the above Post Coach leaves the Bell Inn, Bampton, every
Morning at 6 o'clock; White Hart Inn, Witney, at 7; and arrives in London at ½
past 3. Performed by C. Holmes and Co.'

Oxford Journal – Saturday 17 March 1832
'WHITE HART INN, POSTING AND COMMERCIAL HOUSE, WITNEY,
OXON.
J. COMPTON, (late of the Royal Hotel, Chapel House,) having entered upon
the above establishment, begs respectfully to solicit the continuance of those
favours enjoyed by his predecessor: and hopes by assiduous attention to the
accommodation of those Noblemen, Gentry, Commercial Travellers, and others

who may honour him with their preference, to merit that support which it will be
his most diligent and persevering endeavours to deserve.

J. C. embraces this opportunity of returning thanks for the kind patronage
he experienced at Chapel House; and flatters himself that by the same attentive
regard to the comfort of families or individuals, in every part of the establishment,
which procured him that preference, will again entitle him to a share of their
support.

Neat Post Chaises, steady horses, and careful drivers. Well-aired beds.'

Oxford Chronicle and Reading Gazette – Saturday 04 February 1837
'WHITE HART COMMERCIAL INN and POSTING HOUSE, Witney,
Oxon. J. WOMACK, having recently taken the above Inn of Mr. J. COMPTON,
begs leave to call the attention of Families, Commercial Gentlemen, and the
Public generally to the great improvements he has made in every department in
the Establishment, which flatters himself, combined with strict attention to the
comforts of his guests, and moderate charges, will ensure to him a share of their
patronage. N. B. Superior OLD WINES and SPIRITS of the very best quality.
– Well-aired Beds. Good stall Stabling, loose boxes and lock-up Coach-houses.'

Oxford Chronicle and Reading Gazette – Saturday 01 July 1837
'LOST, from Witney, A Yellow and White POINTER DOG. He is old, and rather
grey in the face. – Whoever will bring the same to the White Hart Inn, Witney,
shall be rewarded for his trouble. Any one detaining him after this notice will be
prosecuted.'

Oxford Chronicle and Reading Gazette – Saturday 14 July 1838
'W. MEGINNIS, Veterinary Surgeon, At the White Hart Inn, WITNEY, BEGS
respectfully to inform the Nobility, Gentry, and Inhabitants of Witney and its
Vicinity, that (in consequence of the unfortunate termination of Mr. Staley's
business) he has commenced practising on his own account, and hopes, by
assiduity and attention to their commands, and to all cases placed under his care,
to merit a share of their support. W. M. begs also to inform his friends that he
is the only person in Witney having authority from the Board of Examiners to
practise as Veterinary Surgeon. Horse and Cattle Medicines, made of the best
Drugs, and on the most reasonable terms. Witney, July 3, 1838.'

Banbury Guardian – Thursday 26 December 1850
'Coroner's Inquest. – An inquisition was taken on Saturday last, before F. Westell,
Esq., of Witney, deputy-coroner, at the White Hart Inn, touching on the death
of a child, aged about 3 months, who died very suddenly the previous night. The
verdict recorded was "Water on the brain," and attributed no neglect to the
parents, James and Ann Faulkner.'

Oxford Journal – Saturday 26 January 1856
'ATTEMPTED ROBBERY. - On Monday last a robbery was attempted at the residence
of Mr. Smith, Bridge-street, better known as "The White Hart." The thief in
this case is a man named Flexony, and brother-in-law to Mr. Smith, who for at

considerable time lived at the White Hart tap, when it was used as a public house. Since the house has been closed for the sale of beer, liquors, &c., and the tap uninhabited, Mr. Smith has, from time to time, missed many things from his house and premises, and, amongst others, there was a gradual disappearance of food from the larder. Night after night was spent in vain to catch the delinquent, but it appeared that the watch was not prolonged till after twelve or one o'clock. Still several articles were continually being missed, and accordingly our superintendent devoted several whole nights to detect the rogue. About four o'clock on Monday morning a noise was heard in the back premises, the bolt of the door, we believe, was gradually pushed back by means of a knife, and the thief walked in, the superintendent at the same time being concealed in one of the rooms on that part of the premises which the thief had entered; he began searching about from one room to the other, but, we believe, finding no booty, he went into the room where the superintendent was, but did not perceive him; he, however, made a second search in the same room, and came within hands' grasp of the superintendent, who instantly turned his "bull's-eye," and seized him; a struggle commenced, and the prisoner, being a strong robust man, released himself, and got off; a chase then took place, and the prisoner made away for Wood Green Hill, but from his corpulency he was "winded" on reaching the summit of the hill; he was then re-captured, and would have made a further resistance, but the superintendent immediately drew his cutlass, and dared him to move; this so terrified him that he was quietly led away and lodged in "durance vile." He was taken the same day before the Rev. W. S. Bricknell, at Ensham, and committed to take his trial at this ensuing Assizes. Bail was accepted for his appearance.'

Oxford Chronicle and Reading Gazette – Saturday 27 June 1857
'Extensive Freehold Business Premises & Land, In BRIDGE STREET, Witney; And TWO COPYHOLD COTTAGES, with Large Garden, At HAILEY, TO BE SOLD BY AUCTION By Mr. LONG, At the King's Arms Inn, in Witney, on Tuesday next, June 30th, at 3 o'clock, by order of the executors of the will of the late Mr. Hollis, under such conditions as will then be produced;

Lot 1. – The extensive FREEHOLD BUSINESS PREMISES, with commanding frontage of 65 foot, in Bridge Street, Witney, comprising the whole of the property, formerly the White Hart Inn, but now occupied by Mr. Smith, manufacturer, and Mr. Margetts. It is a modern sashed building, with entrance hall, office, 3 sitting rooms, and two large parlours, six good bedrooms with attics over. Also excellent kitchens, cellars, and other offices, and the extensive warehouses and stabling, extending 120 feet in length; besides coach houses, bleaching house, piggeries, workshops, and other warehouses. A large yard, with carriage entrance from Bridge Street, and one acre, one rood, and 20 poles of valuable garden land, with abundant fruit and other trees thereon. The present is a low rental of £33.

The outgoings are – A land tax of 19s. 7d., and quit rent of 3s. 0d. ...'

Licensees:

1753–1784	George Smith
1785–1787	William Howlett
1788	William Howlett died at the end of the year
1788–1790	John Dix
1791–1795	William French
1796–1805	Thomas Smith
1803	White Hart to be sold by auction
1805	White Hart to be let
1806	Joseph Hopkins
1807	White Hart to be let
1807	Joseph Freeman
1808–1809	William Lambert
1814	Thomas Smith died in December
1810–1830	Henry Salmon
1832–1936	John Compton
1837–1844	James Womak
1840	Public House Outbuildings &c. owned by John Hollis
1852–1854	William Smith Closed
1857	The White Hart to be sold by auction
1875	William Smith died in July age 72

White Lion, 37 Bridge St (1772–1804)

(Currently Retail Premises & Private Clinic)
(1840 Tithe Awards Map ref 630)

From the newspapers:

Oxford Chronicle and Reading Gazette – Saturday 22 February 1851
'PETTY SESSIONS, Thursday. Mary Robinson was charged with assaulting Mrs. Cook, of the White Lion public-house, Witney. The assault was proved. The adjudged to pay 1s. fine and costs, – Paid accordingly.'

Oxford Chronicle and Reading Gazette – Saturday 23 October 1852
'ROBBERY AT THE OXFORD WORKHOUSE. Wm. Preece, alias Wm. Priest, 23, and George Field, 21, were charged with having, on the 16th of July, at the parish of St. Giles's, Oxford, stolen two pairs of boots and other articles, the property of the Guardians of the Poor within the city of Oxford. – Mr. Mallam prosecuted; the prisoners defended themselves.

Charles Collier said: I am one of the constables at Witney; I apprehended both prisoners at the White Lion, Witney ; they had a large bundle containing shoes and clothes. On witness putting certain questions to prisoners, Priest said, "Where is your warrant?" Witness immediately took them into custody with the assistance of the superintendent. Priest said he was a tailor, and Field said he was a shoemaker.

... In less than a minute the jury found both prisoners guilty. A previous conviction for felony was proved against Priest, and he was sentenced to be transported for seven years. Field 12 months' imprisonment.'

Oxford Chronicle and Reading Gazette – Saturday 03 October 1857
'PETTY SESSIONS, Thursday. – John McKensey, tramp, was committed for one mouth's hard labour for feloniously stealing a coat, the property of John Woodcock, of the White Lion beer house, Witney. ...'

Licensees:

1772–1795	Edward Higgins
1795	Buried on 3 June
1795–1796	Elizabeth Higgins
1797–1799	Charles Harwood
1800–1801	Edward Wright
1802	Thomas Fauchon
1804	William Bennett
1840	House Outbuildings Garden &c. owned by Eldrid Hugh
1857	John Woodcock

Church Green

Fleece Hotel (Marlborough Head), 11 Church Green (1774–present)

(Currently trading, owned by Greene King Retailing, leased by Peach Pubs)
(1840 Tithe Awards Map ref 983)

In about 1811, John Clinch, a prominent Witney banker and landowner, and his son James Clinch purchased the Marlborough Head PH at Church Green, Witney. James founded the first Clinch Brewery at the Marlborough Head between 1811 and 1814. His brother John Williams Clinch 1 was also involved in the enterprise.

From the newspapers:

Oxford Journal – Saturday 20 April 1776
'TO be LETT, and entered on at Michaelmas next. – A large good HOUSE, with a very good Close, Garden, Malt-house, &c., situate on the Church-Green, in Witney, Oxfordshire. – Enquire of Mr. Leverette, in Witney.'

Oxford Chronicle and Reading Gazette – Saturday 18 September 1841
'An Inquest was taken before Jas. Westell, Esq. Coroner. On Tuesday last, at the Marlborough Head, Witney, on view of the body of William Bennett, aged 70, who suddenly expired the previous morning. A verdict "Died by the visitation of God," was returned.'

Oxford Journal – Saturday 21 February 1852
'John Judge, of the Marlborough Head, Witney, was charged by Superintendent Mitchell with selling beer on Sunday morning the 5th inst.; the case was proved, but the Magistrates taking the circumstances into consideration, he having been in the trade only about three months, mitigated the penalty to 10s. and 10s. costs; paid.'

Oxford Times – Saturday 01 June 1867
'ALE-HOUSE OFFENCE. – Mr. James Gillett, of the Fleece Hotel, in this town, was charged by the police with keeping open his house for the sale of beer after 11 o'clock Sunday night last. Fined, with costs, £1.'

Oxford Times – Saturday 28 December 1867
'Gillett. – Dec. 20, on Church Green, Witney, of bronchitis, Mr. James Gillett, landlord of the Fleece Hotel, aged 42.'

Oxford Chronicle and Reading Gazette – Saturday 05 December 1868
'FEOFFEE DINNER. The Feoffees of the Freeland Charity Estate held their annual feast at the Fleece Hotel, on Friday, November 28th, when upwards of 40 sat down. The Rev. F. M. Cunningham (the Rector) presided, faced by Mr. Henry Townsend, the acting feoffee. A very excellent dinner was provided by the hostess Mrs. Gillett, and after the usual toasts of the evening were disposed of, the song

and glass went merrily round, and a very pleasant evening was spent, and kept up till an early hour.'

Oxford Chronicle and Reading Gazette – Saturday 14 August 1869
'MARRIAGES. - ... Mrs. Selina Phillips Gillett, of the Fleece Hotel, Witney (widow of the late Mr. James Gillett), to Mr. Frederick John Townsend, of Fullbrook.'

Oxford Times – Saturday 16 July 1870
'FLEECE HOTEL, WITNEY. Three minutes walk from the Railway Station. Visitors attending the Oxford show will find COMFORTABLE APARTMENTS and moderate charges at the above Hotel. F. Townsend, Proprietor.'

Oxford Chronicle and Reading Gazette – Saturday 13 August 1870
'August 1, the wife of Mr. F. Townsend, Fleece Hotel, Church Green, Witney, of a daughter.'

Oxford Journal – Saturday 13 April 1872
'ATHLETIC SPORTS – The prizes competed for on Easter Monday were distributed on Friday the 5th inst. at the Fleece Hotel. The recipients present suitably acknowledged the gifts, and a pleasant evening was spent.'

Oxford Times – Saturday 08 April 1876
'A PAPER CHASE came off here on Monday last. It was got by the football club, and the meet took place at the Fleece Hotel. Messrs. H. Smith and T. Howse started as hares and proceeded down at the back of the east side of High-street, coming through Mr. French's yard, crossing the street into the premises of Mr. Young, and then across country to Leafield. The hounds followed in a quarter-of-an-hour but the hares were too nimble for them, the latter returning to cover in a little over an hour, while the hounds were a considerable distance behind!'

Oxford Times – Saturday 10 March 1877
'AMERICAN BEEF. – A dinner took place at the Fleece Hotel, last week, to which about twenty sat down. American beef being the principal item in the bill of fare. There was also an American turkey provided, and all present appeared to enjoy the novelty.'

Oxford Journal – Saturday 26 May 1877
'FOR SALE, a Full-sized BILLIARD TABLE, including Balls, Cues, and everything requisite for the game; together with Gas Chandelier (18 lights) and Shades (complete), and entire Furniture of Billiard Room. - Apply Fleece Hotel, Witney.'

Oxford Times – Saturday 16 August 1879
'DESTRUCTIVE AND ALARMING THUNDER STORM. During a severe storm, which passed over our town on Wednesday morning, the residence of W. Clinch, Esq., was struck by lightning, which entered the chimney and threw the stack with a tremendous crash on to the roof of the adjoining house, occupied by Mr. East, leaving the roof a ruin. A considerable amount of damage was also done to the interior. It appears that the electric fluid passed from the chimney into the wall,

making one of the bedrooms a complete wreck; it then descended to the kitchen, ran along the gas pipe and bell-wires and left the house by the open kitchen door. The servants who were in the kitchen were thrown down upon the floor with great violence, but happily, beyond being frightened, no one was hurt. The shock was felt by many in the immediate neighbourhood. Mr. Townsend, of the "Fleece Hotel," for a time lost the use of one side, and another gentleman with him was also affected, but both have, we understand, now recovered.'

Oxford Journal – Saturday 27 January 1883
'... George Smith, landlord of the Fleece Hotel, Witney, said that he recollected sending the saddle produced to P.C. Price about a fortnight ago. He received the saddle about two years ago from a boy whom he believed to be Mr. Blundell's son. Mrs. Blundell owed him a guinea, and he did not therefore give him any money for it. ...'

Oxford Journal – Saturday 10 November 1883
'FLEECE HOTEL, First-class Family and Commercial. Newly Furnished and under New Management, CHURCH GREEN, WITNEY. WM. BODDINGTON, Proprietor.'

Witney Gazette and West Oxfordshire Advertiser - Saturday 26 September 1891
'CRICKET SUPPER. – The members and friends of the Witney Cricket Club had supper together at the Fleece Hotel, on Saturday evening. A first rate spread was placed on the tables by Mrs. Lancefield, whose catering as usual was much appreciated. Mr. W. Smith occupied the chair, and Mr. J. Ravenor the vice-chair...'

Witney Gazette and West Oxfordshire Advertiser – Saturday 20 April 1895
'GENTLEMEN should at once insure their MARES and FOALS – Agent F. MORICE, Fleece Hotel, Witney. Agent for Employers Liability and Personal Accidents.'

Oxford Times – Saturday 25 January 1896
'THE FLEECE HOTEL, Witney. Pleasantly situated and within five minutes' walk of the Railway Station. SPECIAL ACCOMMODATION for Commercial Gentlemen, Tourists and Picnic Parties at Reasonable Charges. For the convenience of farmers a Market Ordinary is provided every Thursday at One o'clock. Price Two Shillings. Football Teams catered for at special rates. Wine and Spirits of the best quality. Excellent Posting Accommodation. MISS READING, Manageress.'

Witney Gazette and West Oxfordshire Advertiser – Saturday 01 September 1900
'WANTED. – A GENERAL SERVANT. Apply, Fleece Hotel, Witney.'

Witney Gazette and West Oxfordshire Advertiser – Saturday 05 April 1902
'WANTED – A thoroughly experienced COOK-GENERAL for London; two in family; wages £20. Apply to Mrs. Green, Fleece Hotel, Witney.'

Witney Gazette and West Oxfordshire Advertiser – Saturday 13 December 1902
'WANTED. – A young girl as NURSE-MAID, must be clean. – Apply, Mrs. Green, Fleece Hotel, Witney.'

Witney Gazette and West Oxfordshire Advertiser – Saturday 09 May 1903
'FLEECE HOTEL WITNEY – WANTED. A steady useful MAN for Hotel. – Apply as above.'

Faringdon Advertiser and Vale of the White Horse Gazette – Saturday 23 January 1904
'CHOIR TEA. The junior members the two church choirs were entertained at tea and games at the Fleece Hotel Assembly Room Saturday evening.'

Faringdon Advertiser and Vale of the White Horse Gazette – Saturday 02 April 1904
'PETTY SESSIONS, Thursday, March 24th. LICENSING. ... Mrs. Green, of the Fleece Hotel, Witney, was given an extension of one hour for the Volunteer dinner and smoking concert on April 8th. ...'

Witney Gazette and West Oxfordshire Advertiser – Saturday 31 December 1904
'WANTED, at once, a strong girl as GENERAL SERVANT, for a London Suburb. Apply, Mrs. Lloyd, Fleece Hotel, Witney.'

Oxford Times – Saturday 28 January 1905
'PETTY SESSIONS, Thursday. Licensing. – A holdover of the licence of the Fleece Hotel, Witney was granted to John Owen, of Kingston-on-Thames, a brother-in-law of the late Mrs. W. Green.'

Witney Gazette and West Oxfordshire Advertiser – Saturday 08 April 1905
'WITNEY. THE FLEECE HOTEL (under entirely new management), Facing Church Green, and close to station. Wines, Beers, Spirits, Cigars, etc., of the best quality. Excellent accommodation for Commercials, Tourists, Cyclists, and Private Families. Hot and Cold Baths alway (*sic*) Ready. Market Ordinary every Thursday. Hot Luncheon daily at 1.15 p.m. Breakfasts, Dinners, Tea, Suppers. Afternoon Teas for Ladies. Terms exceptionally moderate. Cricket Clubs, Parties, etc., catered for at reasonable rates. Large Room for Dances, Dinners, Smoking Concerts, Auctions, etc., or as a sample show room. Good Stabling and Forage. Lock-up for Cycles. R. J. EASTERBROOK, PROPRIETOR.'

Faringdon Advertiser and Vale of the White Horse Gazette – Saturday 10 February 1906
'PETTY SESSIONS, Thursday. Extension. An extension from 11 p.m., on the 16th inst, to 5 a.m., on the 17th was granted Mr. Easterbrook, of the Fleece Hotel, Witney, on the occasion of a subscription ball.'

Faringdon Advertiser and Vale of the White Horse Gazette – Saturday 01 December 1906
'THE EDGAR RIFLE CLUB. – A match between members of the above and a team of

Volunteers took place at the Fleece Hotel Assembly Room on Thursday evening last week, resulting in a win for the latter by 39 points, the scores being 190 and 151. Subsequently the teams sat down to an excellent supper, provided by Mr and Mrs Easterbrook, at the Fleece Hotel.'

Faringdon Advertiser and Vale of the White Horse Gazette – Saturday 09 February 1907
'INVITATION BALL. – The farmers' annual invitation ball was held at the Fleece Hotel Assembly room on Friday evening, and was very successful. The room was tastefully decorated with flags and evergreens. The company numbered 75, and dancing, which began at 8.30, continued till between 3 and 4 a.m., to the strains of the Witney String Band. Messrs J. Wilsdon and S. Hawkes were M.C.'s, and the catering was most satisfactorily carried out by and Mrs Easterbrook.'

Witney Gazette and West Oxfordshire Advertiser – Saturday 07 September 1907
'2ND VOLUNTEER BATTALION OXFORDSHIRE LIGHT INFANTRY. "F" Company orders for the week ending 14th September, 1907. Wednesday. – Recruits drill at the Fleece Hotel, at 8 p.m.; plain clothes. Saturday. – Class firing at 2 p.m. It is requested that those who have not completed their class firing will do so as early as possible. By order. E. N. BENNETT, Captain, Commanding "F" Company.'

Faringdon Advertiser and Vale of the White Horse Gazette – Saturday 16 November 1907
'VOLUNTEER DINNER. – The annual dinner and distribution in connection with the Witney Company 2nd V.B.O.L.I., was held at the Fleece Hotel Assembly Room on Tuesday. Captain E. N. Bennett, M.P., presided, and the company numbered about 90. A capital dinner was provided by Mr and Mrs Easterbrook. After dinner the usual toasts were honoured...'

Faringdon Advertiser and Vale of the White Horse Gazette – Saturday 21 December 1907
'WITNEY CHRISTMAS FAT STOCK SHOW DINNER. – The annual dinner in connection with the Fat Stock Show, was held at the Fleece Hotel Assembly Room on Thursday se'nnight. Mr Herbert Smith (Senior Bailiff) presided. The company numbered about 90. An excellent dinner was provided by Mr and Mrs Easterbrook...'

Witney Gazette and West Oxfordshire Advertiser - Saturday 19 December 1908
'VOLUNTEER DINNER. The annual dinner of the "F" Witney Company, 4th Battalion Oxfordshire and Bucks Light Infantry, was held at the "Fleece" Hotel on Monday evening last. There was a good attendance, for whom Host Moore catered excellently...'

Faringdon Advertiser and Vale of the White Horse Gazette – Saturday 16 January 1909
'LICENSING. ...that of the Fleece Hotel, Witney, from R. J. Easterbrook to Fredk. Moore; ...'

Faringdon Advertiser and Vale of the White Horse Gazette – Saturday 26 February 1910
'PETTY SESSIONS, Thursday. ... - Occasional licenses were granted to Mr F. Moore, of the Fleece Hotel, Witney, for a Conservative Smoking Concert at the Corn Exchange on Saturday, the 26th inst. ...'

Witney Gazette and West Oxfordshire Advertiser – Saturday 16 July 1910
'FOOTBALL. WITNEY TOWN FOOTBALL CLUB. the annual GENERAL MEETING of the above, will be held at the Fleece Hotel on MONDAY, JULY 25th, 1910 at 8-30 p.m. All interested in Football are invited to attend. T. J. FINNIS, Hon. Sec.'

Faringdon Advertiser and Vale of the White Horse Gazette – Saturday 24 June 1911
'TERRITORIALS' SMOKER. – A smoking concert was given to the "F" Witney Company of the 4th Oxon and Bucks Light Infantry at the Fleece Hotel on Saturday (the eve of the Battle of Waterloo), by the Bailiffs of Witney and other gentlemen. Mr R. F. Cuthbert presided, and there was a numerous company. The room was tastefully decorated by Ex-colour Sergeant Moore, Sergeant Goatley, and others. A capital programme was provided, and a pleasant time was spent.'

Faringdon Advertiser and Vale of the White Horse Gazette – Saturday 22 July 1911
'PETTY SESSIONS, Thursday. Licensing. A holdover of the license of the Fleece Hotel, Witney, was granted from Frederick Moore to Samuel Herbert Cruly, of Shipton-on-Stour.'

Faringdon Advertiser and Vale of the White Horse Gazette – Saturday 29 July 1911
'FOOTBALL ASSOCIATION. – The annual general meeting of the Witney and District Football Association was held at the Fleece Hotel Assembly Room, on Friday evening. Mr H. Sharpe presided. Mr W. Smith was re-elected president for the ensuing year, and Mr H. Dingle was chosen secretary. The radius was extended to eleven miles, so as to include Oxford, and it was agreed that no runners-up medals should be offered unless more than four teams entered for the competition.'

Faringdon Advertiser and Vale of the White Horse Gazette – Saturday 26 August 1911
'PETTY SESSIONS, Thursday, August 17th. Licensing. The license of the Fleece Hotel, Witney, was transferred from F. Moore to W. H. Cruly.'

Faringdon Advertiser and Vale of the White Horse Gazette – Saturday 25 November 1911
'FIRE BRIGADE DINNER. – The members of the Witney Volunteer Fire Brigade, with a few specially invited guests, dined together at the Fleece Hotel Assembly Boom on Wednesday evening in last week, by invitation of the officers of the Brigade. Chief officer, Herbert Smith, presided, and was supported by second officer, E. C.

Early, third officer, W. Long, Messrs. W. Smith and F. Habgood (bailiffs), E. Tarrant (chairman), and R. F. Cuthbert (clerk, Urban District Council), Dr. Harvey (hon. surgeon to the Brigade), etc., the company numbering altogether about 40...'

Faringdon Advertiser and Vale of the White Horse Gazette – Saturday 23 March 1912
'WITNEY BOWLING CLUB. – The first annual meeting of the above club was held at the Fleece Hotel Assembly Room on Thursday in last week. Mr E. Tarrant presided, and there was a good attendance. A satisfactory report showing a membership of 52 was presented by Mr Fletcher (hon. sec.), and the financial statement submitted Mr E. J. Barnes (hon. treasurer), revealed a balance in hand of £3 4s 6d. These statements were adopted, and the election of officers followed, Mr W. Smith being unanimously chosen president for the ensuing year.'

Faringdon Advertiser and Vale of the White Horse Gazette – Saturday 07 March 1914
'PETTY SESSIONS, Tuesday. ... An occasional license was granted to Herbert Cruley, of the Fleece Hotel, Witney, from 9 a.m. to 6 p.m. on Tuesday, the 17th March, for the Old Berks Hunt Point-to-Point Races at Compton Beauchamp.'

Faringdon Advertiser and Vale of the White Horse Gazette – Saturday 06 November 1915
'OBITUARY. – Three deaths occurred within the space of a few hours at Witney in the early part of the week. On Sunday afternoon Mrs Moore, formerly of the Fleece Hotel, passed away in the 51st year of her age. She had not been well for a long time. At the funeral which took place at Witney Cemetery Wednesday afternoon, the Sergeants' Mess, 34th Com., M.T., A.S.C., sent a lovely wreath of arum lilies and chrysanthemums, and four N.C.O.'s acted as bearers. ...'

Faringdon Advertiser and Vale of the White Horse Gazette – Saturday 16 February 1918
'PETTY SESSIONS, Thursday. Brewster Sessions. Supt. Smith presented his annual report on the conduct of licensed houses in the division during the past year. One inkeeper was proceeded against for supplying a girl under 14 years of age with beer in an unsealed vessel. Five persons were convicted for drunkenness, a decrease of two on last year. Last year a number of houses were temporarily transferred to the wives of inkeepers who were serving in H. M. Forces, and the houses had been satisfactorily conducted. There were 67 fully licensed houses, 30 beer houses, and 5 wine and spirit licenses. He made no objection to any of the renewals, which were accordingly agreed to. Three houses were temporarily closed during the war, but certificates were granted in respect to two, the Fleece Hotel, Witney, and the White Hart, Eynsham, though both houses would remain closed for the period of the war.'

Banbury Guardian – Thursday 05 July 1923
'WANTED, a good GENERAL. Good wages and outings, State full particulars and references. – Apply, W. T. Felton, Fleece Hotel, Witney.'

Birmingham Daily Gazette – Thursday 20 May 1943
'PORTER, Kitchen, Required, own room, any age, £2. – Fleece Hotel, Witney, Oxford.'

Birmingham Daily Gazette – Tuesday 21 September 1943
'CHAMBERMAID Wtd., good home and gratuitites, own bedroom. State wages required. – Fleece Hotel, Witney, Oxon.'

Birmingham Daily Post – Tuesday 19 September 1961
'BEQUESTS TO CHARITIES. Four charities receive big bequests in the will published yesterday of Mr. Henry Arthur Blake, of The Fleece Hotel, Witney. Oxfordshire. Mr. Blake left £157,810 (£155,913 net) duty of £80,940 has been paid. After a number of personal bequests, Mr. Blake left the residue equally between the R.S.P.C.A., the Guide Dogs for the Blind Association, the R.N.L.I. and the British Limbless Ex-servicemen's Association.'

Licensees:

1774–1783	John Piesley
1784–1820	Henry Bolton
1821–1830	Thomas Edwards
1839–1844	William Bond
	Age 48, wife Rebecca age 55 (1841 Census)
1840	Public House, Garden &c. owned by James Clinch
1847	William Brown
1852–1854	John Judge
1861	William Gunter
	Age 41, born in Shillingford, Berks. Wife Jane age 34 (1861 Census)
1863–1867	George North
	Age 49, born in Leeds, Yorks. Wine Merchant & Chelsea Pensioner. Wife Emily age 32 (1871 Census)
1867	James Gillett
1867	James Gillett died aged 42
1868–1869	Mrs. Selina Gillett
1869	Selina Gillett married Frederick Townsend
1870–1881	Frederick Townsend
	Age 28, born in Fulbrook, Oxon. Wife Selina age 30 (1871 Census)
	Age 38, born in Fulbrook, Oxon. Wife Selina age 40 (1881 Census)
1883	George Smith
1884–1888	William Bonnington
1891	Mary Lanchfield
	Age 36, born in West End, London. Widow (1891 Census)
1895–1898	Frank Morice
1899	Mrs. F. Morice
1901–1904	Minnie Green (Mrs.)
	Age 29, born in Cheltenham, Glos. Widow (1901 Census)
1905	John Owen
1905–1908	Robert John Easterbrook
1909–1911	Frederick Moore

1911–1915	Samuel Herbert Cruley
	Fleece Hotel was closed for the duration of the war.
1925	Owned by Clinch & Co
1920–1931	William Thomas Felton
1932	Arthur Phillips
1933	William Henry Varney
1934	William Varney died in June age 57
1934	Cerise Varney
1935	Stanley Herbert Osborne
1936	Cedric Margetts
1937–1940	William George Esling
	DOB 10 June 1905 Hotel Proprietor. Married (1939 Register)
1941–1942	Mabel Emilie Esling
1943–1947	Bernard John Garrington
1948–1949	Peter Fowler Walker
1950–1952	William Reginald Gladstone
1953–1964	William Frederick Small
1965	Maurice O. Stoneham
1966–1980	Frederick A. V. Jenkins
2003	Lease taken by Peach Pubs
2005–2007	John Johnstone
2008–2010	Amie Moore
2010–2011	Adam Saunders
2011–2013	Peter Nicholas
2013	Nicholas Skinner
2014–2015	Catherine Jones
2016	Duncan Froomes
2017	Frazer Sutherland
2018	Mike Tenant

Corn Street

Bell Inn, 57 Corn St (1774–1915)

(Currently a private residence)
(1840 Tithe Awards Map ref 97)

From the newspapers:

Northampton Mercury – Saturday 08 August 1812
'DIED. On Wednesday se'nnight ... Same day, aged 32, after a lingering illness Mr. John Dix, of the Bell inn, Witney, Oxfordshire.'

Oxford Chronicle and Reading Gazette – Saturday 09 December 1837
'WITNEY, Dec. 6. We regret to state that as Mr. Shuffrey, ... was coming out of the Bell Inn, his foot slipped, ... fall his leg was broken in two places. We are ... he is doing as well as could be expected.'

Oxford Chronicle and Reading Gazette – Saturday 01 June 1839
'On Tuesday last, Charles, the eldest son of Mr. James Sellman, of the Bell Inn, in this town, was sent by his father to the Park Farm, in this neighbourhood, with a horse and cart, to fetch some straw; on his return, having, against the express orders of his father, provided himself with some reins, he imprudently got on the top of the load to ride, and on descending a Hill, a short distance from his home, the horse becoming restive, the straw slipped, and the boy, in his endeavours to stop the horse, was precipitated to the ground with such violence as to cause his death in a few hours. The poor boy was about 14 years of age. An Inquest was held on the body on Thursday, by Mr. James Westell, Coroner, and a verdict of "Accidental Death" returned.'

Oxford Chronicle and Reading Gazette – Saturday 13 July 1844
'On the 3rd inst. a match at cricket was played at Standlake (11 single games) between James Martin and Samuel Kitchen, of Witney, and John and Benjamin Perry, of Standlake, for 5*l.* a side and a dinner, which was won by the latter. Score: Martin 81, Kitchen 85 – total 116; John Perry 96, Benjamin Perry 99 – total 195. The return match will be played at the Bell Inn, Witney, on the 19th inst.'

Oxford Chronicle and Reading Gazette – Saturday 11 March 1848
"Died. March 8, at Witney, Mr. James Silman, aged 46, landlord of the Bell Inn, Corn-street.'

Oxford Journal – Saturday 10 May 1851
'BELL INN, CORN STREET, WITNEY. WILLIAM HAYNES FRY begs respectfully to inform his friends and the public that he has taken to and entered upon the above old-established house; and trusts, by unremitting attention and punctuality, to merit a continuance of that support so long shewn to his predecessor. N. B. A Market Ordinary every Thursday. - Wines and Spirits of the finest quality. – Home brewed Ales. GOOD STABLING. - HORSES TO LET ON HIRE.'

Oxford Journal – Saturday 20 November 1852
'NOTICE is hereby given, that, by Indenture dated this 18th day of November, 1852, WILLIAM HAYNES FRY, of the Bell Inn, in Witney, in the county of Oxford, publican, has assigned all his Estate and Effects unto Leonard Warrington, of Witney aforesaid, grocer, and Thomas Whitlock, of the same place, Sheriff's officer, upon Trust, for the general and equal benefit of all his Creditors. All Creditors executing the said Indenture, within three calendar months from the date thereof, will be paid such dividend as the Estate will produce; and Creditors refusing or neglecting to execute the same, within such time, will he excluded from all benefit thereunder.-Dated 18th November, 1852. ROSE and BULLEN, Bampton, Oxon, Solicitors to the said Trustees. N.B. The Stock, Furniture, and Brewing Plant of the Bell Inn, Witney, to be disposed of, with immediate possession of the Premises. - Apply as above.'

Oxford Journal – Saturday 31 January 1857
'The Bell Inn, Corn Street, Witney. HOUSEHOLD FURNITURE, BREWING PLANT, excellent BEER CASKS, BREWING COPPER, Utensils, Fixtures, and Effects. TO BE SOLD BY AUCTION, By Mr. LONG, On the premises, at the Bell public house, in Corn-street, Witney, on Friday the 6th of February, at Twelve o'clock, in consequence of the proprietor leaving. The valuable HOUSEHOLD FURNITURE, excellent BREWING PLANT, comprising a large brewing copper and apparatus, mash tub, coolers, underback, and utensils; a 700-gallon beer cask, one of 500 gallons, eight casks of 120 gallons each, three casks of 50 gallons, and smaller ditto ; several gallons of excellent ale, a pocket of prime hops ; also all the grates and other fixtures in and about the premises; catalogues of which may be had at the place of sale, or of the auctioneer, Witney.'

Oxford Journal – Saturday 21 February 1863
'BAMPTON EAST DIVISION, - Witney, Feb. 12. Alfred Nunney, landlord of the Bell Inn public-house, Corn-street, Witney, was fined 4*l.* and 1*l.* 14s. 6d. costs, for keeping his house open for the sale of beer at an illegal hour on Sunday the 8th instant.'

Oxford Journal – Saturday 12 September 1863
'BELL INN, CORN STREET, WITNEY. BREWING PLANT, 100-gallon COPPER, BEER CASKS, BEER ENGINE, CUPS, JUGS, BOTTLES & GLASSES, and part of the HOUSEHOLD FURNITURE, TO BE SOLD BY AUCTION, By Mr. LONG, On the premises at the Bell Inn, Corn-street, Witney, the latter part of this month, the property of Mr. A. Nunney, who is leaving.'

Oxford Journal – Saturday 26 November 1864
'TO BE SOLD BY AUCTION, By Messrs. SEELY & BUCKINGHAM, (By direction of the Trustees of the Will of the late Mr. Dix), at the Red Lion Inn, Witney, on Tuesday the 29th of November, at Two for Three o'clock in the afternoon precisely, in eight lots, and under conditions to be then produced. Valuable FREEHOLD PROPERTIES, situate in Corn-street and the Market-place, Witney, in the county of Oxford ; comprising a very convenient Stone-built

- and Slated RESIDENCE, with necessary out offices; a Six-quarter MALT HOUSE, with fittings complete; the BELL INN, with stabling, brew-house, large club room, and appurtenances; ...'

Oxford Journal – Saturday 22 March 1879
'Messrs. JONAS PAXTON, SON, & CASTLE ARE instructed to SUBMIT the undermentioned PROPERTIES to PUBLIC COMPETITION, sometime in April next:- ... The BELL INN, at Witney, in the occupation of Mr. George Goodall; and a HOUSE, GARDEN, and PREMISES (formerly the Blandford Arms), in the village of Coombe. Particulars are being prepared, and may be had three weeks previous to the sale of Messrs. Morrell and Son, solicitors, Oxford, or of the auctioneers, Bicester.'

Oxford Times – Saturday 29 March 1879
'PETTY SESSIONS – March 27 George Hall was charged by George Goodall, of the Bell Inn, Witney, with being drunk and refusing to quit licensed premises; also with assaulting him. – Defendant proved that complainant was himself drunk at the time. The case was consequently dismissed with costs, £1 8s. 6d., which the complainant paid.'

Oxford Times – Saturday 21 June 1879
'TO LET, - With immediate possession, The BELL INN, Witney. – For particulars apply, Eagle Steam Brewery, Oxford.'

Oxford Times – Saturday 14 June 1890
'PETTY SESSIONS – June, 5th William Benjamin, a tramp, was sentenced to 10 days' hard labour for stealing money from the Bell Inn, Witney, on the 29th ult.'

Faringdon Advertiser and Vale of the White Horse Gazette – Saturday 25 October 1902
'PETTY SESSIONS, Thursday. A VIOLENT WOMAN. Mary Sullivan, tramp, was charged with being drunk and disorderly and committing wilful damage to the windows of the "Bell" Inn Witney, on the 13th, to the extent of 2s.; and further with committing wilful damage to the windows of the police cell, to the extent of 10s. – The prisoner, who pleaded guilty to being drunk and damaging the cell, was fined £1 or a month's hard labour for each offence.'

Faringdon Advertiser and Vale of the White Horse Gazette – Saturday 11 December 1909
'COUNTY COURT, Tuesday. CLAIMS ON DEFAULT SUMMONSES. ... Mary D. Grace Sanders, Corn Street, Witney, v. Henry William Smith, Bell Inn, Corn Street, Witney, printer. The amount due was £2 10s.'

Licensees:

1774–1808	Thomas Dix
1809–1812	John Dix
1812	John Dix died in August age 32
1814	John Price
1840	Public House Outbuildings &c. owned by Thomas Dix

1830–1847	James Tilman
	Age 38, wife Mary age 38 (1841 Census)
1848	James Tilman died in March aged 46
1851–1852	William Haynes Fry
1853–1854	William Underhill
1857	The Bell Inn was for sale by auction in January
1861–1863	Alfred Nunney
	Age 64, born in Brize Norton, Oxon. Plasterer. Wife Mary age 65 (1861 Census)
1864	Bell Inn was for sale by auction in November
1864–1868	Charles Hitchman
1869–1871	William Bolton
	Age 48, born in Witney, Oxon. Carpenter. Wife Ann age 58 (1871 Census)
1874–1877	William Barnes
1879	George Goodall
1879	Bell Inn was for sale by auction in March
1879	Bell Inn was to let in June
1883–1909	Joseph Phipps
	Age 50, born in Witney, Oxon. Wife Sarah age 50 (1891 Census)
	Age 60, born in Hailey, Oxon. Wife Sarah age 60 (1901 Census)
1910–1915	John Prior
	Age 35, born in Witney, Oxon. Wife Gertrude Ellen age 32. Groom (1911 Census)

Black Swan (aka Swan), Corn St (1775–1844)

From the newspapers:

Oxford Journal – Saturday 05 July 1755
'Thursday Morning about Eight o'Clock a Fire broke out at Widow Collier's at the Swan in Witney in this County, which might have been of dreadful Consequence had it happened in the Night; but the Town being quickly alarmed, it was happily extinguished before it had done any very considerable Damage.'

Oxford Journal – Saturday 29 June 1833
'Freeholds, Witney, Oxfordshire. TO BE SOLD BY AUCTION, By Mr. LONG, At the Black Swan, in Corn-street, Witney, on Monday next the 1st of July, 1833, at Five o'clock in the afternoon; -Seven newly and substantially-built COTTAGES, situate on the North side of and behind Corn-street, in Witney aforesaid, in the occupation of Widow Burford, Henry Townsend, Hannah Haddon, John Miles, Henry Gadfield, John Hern, and - Allen. ...'

Oxford Chronicle and Reading Gazette – Saturday 13 January 1838
'Inquests by James Esq. Coroner. – On Friday the 5th instant, at the Black Swan, Witney, on the body of John Organ, who died suddenly from internal bleeding. Verdict, "died by the visitation of God."'

Oxford Chronicle and Reading Gazette – Saturday 24 September 1842
'BLACK SWAN public house in Corn-street, Witney. HOUSEHOLD FURNITURE, Fat and Store Pigs, Quantity of Potatoes, &c. TO BE SOLD BY

AUCTION, By Mr. Long, On the premises of Mr. Nelson (who is leaving), at the Black Swan, in Corn-street, Witney, on Tuesday next, the 27th of September, at Eleven o'clock. ...'

Oxford Journal – Saturday 15 October 1842
'FREEHOLD PREMISES, THE SWAN PUBLIC HOUSE, in WITNEY. TO BE SOLD BY AUCTION, By Mr. LONG, At the Crown Inn, in Witney, on Friday the 28th day of October, 1842, at Two o'clock in the afternoon,-All that substantial Stone-built and Slated INN and PUBLIC HOUSE, called the *Swan Inn*, with a frontage of 54 feet, having a sash front, and entrance gateway, with a large room over; excellent kitchen, with projecting bow window, bar, parlour, and sitting room ; spacious entrance ; extensive basement cellaring, detached kitchen and offices; seven airy bed rooms and attic floor; also brewhouse, dairy, smith's shop, large barn, slated shed, stabling for 12 horses, yard and large productive garden, well planted with fruit trees and walled in. The whole recently let at 42*l.* 10s. per annum. Land tax 2s. 6d. and chief rent 10d.

This Freehold Property offers considerable advantage to persons wishing to carry on the business, as the occupier, by brewing his own beer, secures a certain and considerable custom from the great manufacturing population, and eligible situation in the town. May be viewed by applying to the auctioneer, Witney; and particulars obtained of Messrs. Morland and Godfrey, solicitors, Abingdon, and Charles Leake, Esq. solicitor, Witney.

Part of the purchase money may remain on mortgage, if required.'

Licensees:

1775–1784	William Farbrother
1839	William Hutt
1841–1844	William Nelson
	Age 25, wife Phœbe age 20 (1841 Census)
1842	The Swan was for sale by auction in October

Butcher's Arms, 104 Corn St (1839–2011)

(Currently The Mortgage Co.)
(1840 Tithe Awards Map ref 326)

From the newspapers:

Oxford Chronicle and Reading Gazette – Saturday 15 June 1867
'Clubs. – On Monday the Benefit Societies held their annual feasts at the Elm Tree, Jolly Tucker, Court Inn, and Butchers' Arms, Witney. – On Tuesday the Benefit Club held their annual dinner at the Griffin Inn, New Land, Coggs. The Witney Band were engaged playing through the principal streets, after their return from Coggs Church.'

Banbury Advertiser – Thursday 29 August 1878
'FATAL ACCIDENT. – An inquest was held by F. Westell, Esq., coroner, at the "Butchers Arms" inn, on Wednesday, the 21st inst, on the body of Samuel Haines. It appears that the poor man for a short time had been employed by Mr Wainwright, Corn

Street, and while going on a journey on Monday last slipped from the top of his load to the ground, causing concussion of the brain. On Tuesday it being thought advisable to send him to the Infirmary, he was placed on a bed in a conveyance, but they had only proceeded a short distance from the town when the poor fellow died. A verdict of "Accidental Death" was returned.'

Faringdon Advertiser and Vale of the White Horse Gazette – Saturday 02 March 1889
'PETTY SESSIONS, Thursday. Sarah Jordan, a travelling woman, was brought up in custody, charged with breaking six panes of glass at the "Butcher's Arms" Inn, Corn Street, on the 24th ult. Thomas Haines, the landlord, proved the case, and the prisoner was fined 10s, and allowed a fortnight to pay.'

Oxford Journal – Saturday 22 February 1890
'JOHN HABGOOD and SON Have received instructions from the Trustees of the late Mr. Thos. Haines, to SELL by AUCTION, at the Butcher's Arms, Corn-street, Witney, on Friday, February 28th, 1890, at Five for Six o'clock in the evening, in one lot, subject to conditions to be then produced, ...'

Witney Gazette and West Oxfordshire Advertiser – Saturday 29 December 1900
'TO LET. – The "BUTCHER'S ARMS," Corn Street, Witney. Possession January 14th, 1901. Apply, Tower Brewery Stores, Witney.'

Faringdon Advertiser and Vale of the White Horse Gazette – Saturday 14 February 1903
'TRANSFERS. ... the "Butcher's Arms," Corn Street, Witney, from John Harris, to Ralph Busby.'

Witney Gazette and West Oxfordshire Advertiser – Saturday 14 November 1903
'DEATHS. COOK – November 8th, at the "Collingwood Arms," Plough Road, Battersea, S.W., after a long and painful illness, Charlotte Sarah Cook, late Mrs. Haines, of the "Butcher's Arms," Corn Street, Witney, Oxon, in her 58th year. Interred in family grave, Woolwich Cemetery.'

Witney Gazette and West Oxfordshire Advertiser - Saturday 07 October 1905
'PETTY SESSIONS, Thursday. HOLDOVERS. Applications for the holdover of the licenses of the ... and the "Butcher's Arms," Witney, from Ralph Busby to Adolphus Talbot were granted.'

Witney Gazette and West Oxfordshire Advertiser – Saturday 16 November 1907
'PETTY SESSIONS, Thursday. TRANSFERS. The following licenses were transferred:- ... the "Butcher's Arms," Witney, from A. Talbot to Horace Neal Baker; ...'

Faringdon Advertiser and Vale of the White Horse Gazette – Saturday 24 October 1908
'HOLDOVERS. Holdovers of the licenses of the "Butchers Arms" Witney from A. E. Stanford to Charles M. Fox; ...'

Faringdon Advertiser and Vale of the White Horse Gazette – Saturday 09 July 1910
'LICENSING. ... and that of the "Butchers Arms," Witney, from F. Orpwood to F. W. Smith.'

Faringdon Advertiser and Vale of the White Horse Gazette – Saturday 22 October 1910
'PETTY SESSIONS, Thursday. REFUSING TO QUIT. Charles Walker, of Witney, was summoned for refusing to quit the licensed premises of F. W. Smith, at "The Butcher's Arms," on the 9th inst. Defendant, who was said to have absconded, was fined 15s.'

Licensees:

1839–1840	Robert Spittle
1840	Public House Yard &c. owned by Thomas Dix
1841	Robert Spittle moved to the Red Lion
1861–1889	Thomas Haines
	Age 47, born in Witney, Oxon. Publican & Foreman at a Blanket Maufacturer. Wife Ann age 49 (1861 Census)
	Age 57, born in Witney, Oxon. Wife Ann age 59 (1871 Census)
	Age 67, born in Witney, Oxon. Wife Ann age 69 (1881 Census)
1889	The Will of Thomas Haines late of Corn-street Witney in the County of Oxford Licensed Victualler who died 7 August 1889 at Witney was proved at Oxford by William Cook of Wood Green Witney Retired Licensed Victualler and George Collier of Corn-street Witney Grocer the Executors. Personal Estate £129 0s 3d
1890–1891	Charlotte Haines (Mrs.)
	Age 45, born in Woolwich, Kent. Widow (1891 Census)
1895–1902	William Henry Cooper
1900	The Butcher's Arms was to let in December
1903	Charlotte Haines died in November aged 58
1903–1905	Ralph Busby
1906–1907	Adolphus Talbot
1908	Horace Neal Baker
1925	Owned by Hall & Co
1910–1941	Frederick William Smith
	Age 28, born in Swindon, Wilts. Wife Annie age 28 (1911 Census)
	DOB 13 Nov 1882 Inn Keeper. Wife Annie dob 11 Jun 1881 Unpaid Domestic Duties (1939 Register)
1942–1966	Ernest Henry Lock
1967–1972	Gladys E. Lock
1973	Pearl J. Humber
1976–1980	Harvey P. Wicks
2002	Pub bought by Enterprise Inns 12 Nov
2002–2007	Graham Henderson
2008–2013	Andrew Coggins
2014–2015	Sharma Prakash
2015	Pub closed 06 May

Chequers, 47 Corn St (1753–present)

(Currently trading)
(1840 Tithe Awards Map ref 86)

From the newspapers:

Oxford University and City Herald – Saturday 25 June 1814
'TO BE SOLD BY AUCTION, By Mr. JOHN LUCKETT, At the Crown Inn, Witney, at Four o'clock in the Afternoon, on THURSDAY, the 14th of JULY, under such conditions as shall be then and there produced, ... At the same time and place will be sold, the CHEQUER PUBLIC-HOUSE, situate in Corn street, Witney. ... Immediate possession may be had.'

Oxford University and City Herald – Saturday 18 March 1815
'TO BE LET and entered on at Lady-day, THE CHEQUERS PUBLIC HOUSE; also the COACH and HORSES PUBLIC HOUSE; both situate in Corn-street, Witney. For further particulars, and to treat, apply to Mr. J. N. Lawrance, common brewer, Witney, Oxon.'

Oxford University and City Herald – Saturday 01 May 1819
'TO BE LET, And may be entered upon immediately, THE CHEQUERS PUBLIC-HOUSE, situate in Corn-street, WITNEY, Oxon. Apply to Mr. J. N. LAWRANCE, of Witney.'

Oxford Journal – Saturday 05 March 1859
'DIED. – March 3, Mrs. Dailey, widow of the late Mr. G. Dailey, of the Chequers Inn, Corn-street, aged 66 years.'

Oxford Times – Saturday 09 July 1864
'CLUB FEAST. - The first Tuesday in July has now come to be regarded a general holiday, being the day on which the various Friendly Societies, or clubs, with, we believe, only one exception, hold their annual feasts. The morning opened clear and fine and soon the bright sun scattered the few clouds that were drifting over the sky, and imparted a cheerfulness to the scene. In the town every one seemed astir. The day before, a number of stalls, photographic studio, shows, merry-go-rounds, and shooting galleries had taken up their place to contribute to the amusement of the juveniles, and early in the morning others arrived, making the Market Place quite a busy scene. ... The club at the Chequers Inn had engaged the Coombe Band, who performed in a most creditable manner at the Inn and in various parts of the town; ...'

Oxford Times – Saturday 21 August 1869
'MELANCHOLY DEATH OF THE LANDLORD, OF THE "CHEQUERS." – An inquest was held on Monday last, before F. Westell. Esq., Coroner, at the "Chequers" Inn Corn-street, Witney, respecting the death of John Simpson, landlord of the Chequers Inn, who died on Sunday morning last, aged 63 years. – Nellippa Casson, sworn, said: The deceased is my father. I have been at home for two or three weeks. I have heard him complain of his head being heavy, several times. He went to bed

on Saturday, about three o'clock, and got up at half-past five to tea, and seemed very lively. He did not complain of any illness. After he had had his tea, he went out, but I do not know where he went. I did not see him when he came in. In the night I heard a noise, and went down, my mother was with him; he was in the arm chair. I and my mother went upstairs to bed again. He had been drinking, but I do not think he had drank more than ordinary. He seemed very well when I left him; he was smoking his pipe. Soon after I was in bed, I heard another noise down stairs; I went down; my brother James was with him. My father was sitting in the chair and looked as though he was faint. He died about two minutes after I got there. He died in the chair. No one was down with him but my brother and me. He never spoke once. I did not notice his breathing. James Simpson, called, said: The deceased is my father. I have heard him complain about his neck and head. I did not see him come in yesterday morning. I heard a noise in the night, and came down stairs, and found father on the floor, on his left side. I lifted him up, and put him in the chair. He was not sensible, for he did not know me. I did not notice anything particular in his breathing. I did not see his end, for I went for the doctor, and he was dead before I got back. – Dr. Batt, sworn, said: I did not attend deceased on Sunday morning, my assistant attended, but he was dead before he reached there. I have made an investigation of the body; there is a mark on the left cheek, which was caused by the fall. I cannot positively say the cause of deceased's death, but I believe it was a fit of apoplexy.-This being the whole of the evidence, the jury returned verdict that deceased died in a fit of apoplexy.'

Oxford Times – Saturday 15 February 1873
'BIRTH, WEAVER – February 8, at Corn-street, Witney, the wife of Mr. Weaver, of the Chequers Inn, of a son.'

Oxford Journal – Saturday 10 April 1875
'TO BE SOLD BY AUCTION, By Messrs. JONAS PAXTON & G. CASTLE, In seven lots, at the Fleece Hotel, Witney, on Tuesday, May 11, 1875, at Three for Four o'clock, by order of the Trustee of the late Mr. Wm. Shuffrey.

Lot 1. – "THE BRITANNIA BREWERY," in the Market Square, Witney, including two good dwelling houses, the brewhouse, excellent 8-quarter malt-house, working room, hop room and store rooms, with stable, granary, grinding house, piggery, wagon hovel, 2 walled gardens and paddock, now occupied by Mr. T. Shuffrey.

Lot 2. - A FREEHOLD PUBLIC HOUSE, in Corn-street, Witney, known as "The Eagle," occupied by Mr. Moses Midwinter.

Lot 3. - A FREEHOLD PUBLIC HOUSE, "The Chequers," also situate in Corn-street, Witney, occupied by Mr. Thos. Weaver.

... The several lots may be inspected by permission of the occupiers, and descriptive particulars may be obtained of Frederick Westell, Esq., solicitor, Witney; G. H. Saunders, Esq., solicitor, Chipping-Norton; and of the auctioneers, Bicester, Oxon.'

Oxford Times – Saturday 31 March 1877
'TO BE LET, WITH IMMEDIATE POSSESSION, - The "CHEQUERS INN,"
situated in corn-street, Witney. – For particulars, Apply Messrs. Hunt, Edmunds
and Co., brewers, Banbury.'

Faringdon Advertiser and Vale of the White Horse Gazette – Saturday 14
February 1903
'PETTY SESSIONS, Thursday. TRANSFERS. The following licences were
transferred:- ... "The Chequers" Inn, Corn Street, Witney, from John East to
Henry East, his son; ...'

Licensees:

1753–1763	John Clapton
1764	Buried on 8 Sept.
1764–1780	Mary Clapton
1780	Buried on 8 December
1781–1793	Thomas Bolton
1794	Buried on 21 March
1794–1808	Elizabeth Bolton
1809–1811	James Green
1812	William Page
1814	Chequers was for sale by auction in June
1815	Chequers was to let in March
1819	Chequers was to let in May
1830–1847	George Dailey
	Age 45, wife Mary age 45 (1841 Census)
1840	Public House Yard &c. owned by William Shuffrey
1848	George Dailey was buried on 8 November aged 60
1848–1854	Mary Dailey
	Age 58, born in Witney, Oxon. Widow (1851 Census)
1859	Mary Dailey died in March aged 66
1861–1869	John Simpson
	Age 55, born in Witney, Oxon. Wife Mary age 52. Mason (1861 Census)
1869	John Simpson died in August aged 63
1869–1871	Mary Simpson
	Age 61, born in Witney, Oxon. Widow (1871 Census)
1873–1874	Thomas Weaver
1875	Chequers was to be sold by auction in April
1877	Chequers was to let in March
1883–1887	John Bartlett
1891–1902	John East
1903–1907	Henry East
1908–1932	Mary Baker (Mrs.)
	(moves from the Malt Shovel)
	Age 54, born in Walworth, London. Widow (1911 Census)
1933	Mary Baker died in March age 81
1933–1951	Charles Frederick Jenkins
	DOB 4 Feb 1882 Licensed Victualler. Wife Marie dob 13 Mar 1887
	Unpaid Domestic Duties (1939 Register)

1952–1962   Arthur Champion
1963–1969   Edith May Champion
1970–1980   Arthur F. Reeves
2005–2013   Jennifer Kelly
2013   Pub bought by Enterprise Inns 07 Jun
2014–present Martin Ogden

Eagle Tavern (Coach & Horses), 22 Corn St (1783–present)

(Currently trading, owned by Hook Norton Brewery)
(1840 Tithe Awards Map ref 391)

From the newspapers:

Oxford University and City Herald – Saturday 22 February 1812
'TO BE LET, and entered on immediately, ... Also, All that PUBLIC HOUSE, called the Coach and Horses, situate in Corn-street, in Witney, Oxon. For particulars, and to treat, apply to Mr. J. N. Lawrance, common brewer, Witney.'

Oxford University and City Herald – Saturday 18 March 1815
'TO BE LET and entered on at Lady-day, THE CHEQUERS PUBLIC HOUSE; also the COACH and HORSES PUBLIC HOUSE; both situate in Corn-street, Witney. For further particulars, and to treat, apply to Mr. J. N. Lawrance, common brewer, Witney, Oxon.'

Oxford Journal – Saturday 20 May 1820
'TO be LET, and may be entered upon immediately, - The COACH and HORSES PUBLIC HOUSE, situate in Corn-street, Witney, Oxon. For particulars apply to Mr. J. N. Lawrance, Witney.'

Oxford University and City Herald – Saturday 14 June 1823
'TO BE LET, the COACH and HORSES PUBLIC HOUSE, situate in Corn Street, Witney. For particulars apply to Mr. J. N. Lawrance, Witney.'

Oxford Journal – Saturday 19 June 1824
'TO be LET, with immediate possession, - That old established PUBLIC HOUSE, the COACH and HORSES, situated near the Market Place, in Witney, Oxon. – For particulars apply to Mr. James Curtis, Corn-street, Witney.'

Oxford Journal – Saturday 12 March 1842
'DIED, March 7, in Corn-street, Witney, aged 48 years, Mr. G. Clarke, landlord of the Coach and Horses public house.'

Oxford Chronicle and Reading Gazette – Saturday 06 November 1847
'At our Petty Sessions on Thursday transfers of licenses were granted from Mr. Richard Stevens, of the Coach and Horses, Witney, to Mr. Henry Woodington,'

Oxford Chronicle and Reading Gazette – Saturday 12 January 1850
'DIED. – On the 7th inst., Jane, daughter of Mr. Woodington, of the Coach and Horses public house.'

Banbury Guardian – Thursday 19 June 1851
'BAMPTON. Petty Sessions, Town Hall. - ... Charles Bernard was charged with stealing from W. Bridgman, at the Coach and Horses, Witney, a pair of shoes and other articles, his property. He made no defence, and was committed for trial.'

Oxford Chronicle and Reading Gazette – Saturday 14 June 1856
'Coach and Horses Public-house, CORN STREET, WITNEY, TO BE LET, - Apply to J. Early, Maltster, Witney.'

Oxford Journal – Saturday 02 January 1858
'Died. – Dec. 26, at Witney, Susanna, widow of the late Mr. Giles Clark, formerly of the Coach and Horses, Corn-street, aged 65 years.'

Oxford Times – Saturday 16 July 1864
'PETTY SESSIONS, July 14, DRUNK AND DISORDERLY. – John Hearn, of Witney was charged with being drunk and refusing to leave the Eagle Tavern, Witney, when requested to do so by the landlord. Fine 2s. 6d., costs 12s. Being unable to pay, and having no goods, was committed for 7 days.'

Witney Gazette and West Oxfordshire Advertiser – Saturday 25 January 1890
'EAGLE TAVERN, WITNEY. TO LET, the above full licensed PUBLIC HOUSE, with Good stabling. Apply, F. W. Edwards, Agent for Hunt Edmunds & Co., the Hill, Witney.'

Oxford Journal – Saturday 29 November 1890
'PETTY SESSIONS, Nov. 20. Thomas W. Townsend, 18, and Lewis W. Richards, 15, of Witney, were charged with having stolen, on Nov. 14, a bottle of gin, 40 cigars, and four ounces of tobacco, the property of John Stayt, landlord of the Eagle Tavern, Witney. Townsend was fined 3*l.* or a month's imprisonment, and Richards 2*l.* or a month: allowed a week.'

Witney Gazette and West Oxfordshire Advertiser - Saturday 20 December 1890
'ASSAULTING AN OLD MAN. John Evans, a tailor, lodging at the "Eagle" Tavern, was charged with assaulting George Stayt, aged 71, landlord of the "Eagle" Tavern, on December 4th.
Defendant pleaded guilty...
The Bench fined defendant 30s. including costs. Defendant asked for time, but this was refused, and he was removed in custody.'

Witney Gazette and West Oxfordshire Advertiser - Saturday 30 December 1893
'AN ASSAULT IN CORN STREET. WAS HE DRUNK? George Rusher, a travelling hawker, was summoned for assaulting George Stayt, the landlord of the "Eagle" Tavern, on 21st December. He was also charged with being drunk while in charge of a horse and cart on the same date.
Defendant pleaded guilty to both charges ...

Defendant said he had been a total abstainer for some time, but broke the pledge on that day, and the beer overcame him. He was sorry for what had occurred, and had he been in his right senses it would not have happened. Fined £1.'

Witney Gazette and West Oxfordshire Advertiser – Saturday 12 May 1894
'TO LET. – The "EAGLE" TAVERN, Corn Street. Full Licensed. – Apply, Hunt, Edmunds, and Co., the Hill, Witney.'

Oxford Journal – Saturday 23 June 1894
'PETTY SESSIONS, June 14. A holdover of the licence of the Eagle Tavern, Witney, to Joseph Seely, of Hailey, was granted; ...'

Faringdon Advertiser and Vale of the White Horse Gazette – Saturday 03 December 1904
'ALLEGED LARCENY. Annie Winfield, alias Vouler, of 14, Corn Street, Witney, on bail, was charged with feloniously stealing a bottle of brandy, one of rum, one of whisky, and two of gin, value 16s. the property of Joseph Seeley, at the Eagle Tavern, Witney, on the 26th ult. She pleaded guilty, and was fined £1, and allowed 14 days to pay.'

Witney Gazette and West Oxfordshire Advertiser – Saturday 10 February 1906
'PETTY SESSIONS, Thursday. LICENSING BUSINESS. TWO PUBLIC HOUSES PROPOSED TO BE CLOSED.

This being the annual licensing meeting, Supt. Hawtin reported that there were 71 full licensed houses, 21 beer houses, and 8 wine and sweet licenses, giving an average of 1 licensed house to every 126 persons in the division. The whole of the houses had been well conducted. During the year there had been 14 convictions for drunkenness against 12 persons, showing a decrease of 12 compared with last year. Of this number 6 were residents and 6 were strangers passing through the district. The population of the division was 12,553.

Supt. Hawtin stated that he had no complaint to make against any licensed houses, but there were one or two things which he wished to point out to the Bench. There was a door in the passage at the "Eagle Tavern," Witney, leading to the back of the premises. It was possible to get into the house from the back without being interfered with in the front. It was desirable that the front door should be left open, so that the police could have access to the premises at any time.

Messrs. Hunt, Edmonds' representative promised that this should be done.

Supt. Hawtin said he also wished to call the attention of the Bench to the fact that in the "Cross Keys" yard there was a cottage which at present was unoccupied. The tenant of the "Cross Keys," controlled the yard gates, and when these were closed the only way to get into the licensed premises was by the front door. In order to get over that difficulty the small door in the gates should be left open.

Mr. Storey for Messrs. Clinch & Co. stated that he had written to the tenant instructing him to leave the door open.

Supt. Hawtin said a cottage adjoining the "Three Pigeons," was let by the landlady of this public house, and at the back the two houses were not divided. He believed alterations were now being made for the purpose of dividing these premises and when that was done the police would be satisfied.

The Chairman said with regard to the licenses, the Magistrates had been very carefully through the houses, and subject to the alterations suggested by the police, nearly all would be renewed. With regard to the "Jolly Tuckers" and the "Malt Shovel," they would have to be referred to the Licensing Committee and they would have to adjourn them for a fortnight. The Magistrates did not think it was necessary to grant those licenses.

Mr. Hinton, on behalf of Messrs. Clinch and Co., applied for a retail license to sell spirits off the premises.

Supt. Hawtin explained that the application did not give any greater facilities for the selling of spirits, but was made in order to comply with the excise regulations.

The application was granted.'

Faringdon Advertiser and Vale of the White Horse Gazette – Saturday 16 January 1909
'LICENSING. ... A holdover of the Eagle Tavern, Witney, was granted from Joseph Seeley, deceased, to T. W. Felton; ...'

Faringdon Advertiser and Vale of the White Horse Gazette – Saturday 06 February 1909
'PETTY SESSIONS, Thursday. The following licenses were transferred:- "Eagle Tavern," Witney, from the late Joseph Seely to John Horne; ...'

Faringdon Advertiser and Vale of the White Horse Gazette – Saturday 08 October 1921
'LICENSING ACT. Mr Andrew Walsh, instructed by the Oxford and District Licensed Victuallers Association, appeared in support of certain license holders in the district, who had presented a petition to the Bench, with regard to the fixing of the hours of opening licenced premises in the district. He made no application for the additional half-hour after ten, but asked that the hours on weekdays might be from 10 till 2 p.m. and 6 till 10, and on Sundays from 12 noon till 2, and from 7 p.m. to 10. The petition had been signed by 27 license holders in Witney, 12 at Bampton, 11 at Eynsham, 3 at Stanton Harcourt, 4 at Brighthampton and Standlake, 2 at Ducklington, 2 at Aston and one at Curbridge. – There being no opposition, the Bench fixed the hours of opening in accordance with the petitions. The new hours came into operation on Monday, October 3rd.

Mr Walsh made further application under Section 55 of the 1910 Act on behalf of certain license holders in the vicinity of Witney Market, to keep their licensed premises open for the sale of intoxicating liquors between the hours of 2 and 5 p.m. on Market days (Thursdays).

54 The Inns, Taverns and Beerhouses of Witney

Evidence was given in support of the application by Mr S. H. Cruley, Marlborough Hotel; George F. George, the Vaults, Market Square: William Cubbidge, Bull Inn; F. O. Fisher, Cross Keys; Mrs Hudson, Angel Inn; W. C. Moss, Royal Oak ; and Mr J. H. Horne, Eagle Tavern.

Mr Franklin (Oxford) opposed the application on behalf of the Witney Social Service Committee, which was representative of all the Churches in the town, submitting that it would be unfair to grant the application of only a number of the licence holders to the exclusion of the others; that the concentration of men in fewer public houses would lead to increased drinking; but it was admitted there was no great influx of visitors on small market days; and there was no necessity for hours of opening asked for, and that with regard to big market days the suggested hours of from 2 till 5 were too long.

Mr Walsh, in reply, said he had no objection to the extension being granted to the whole of the license holders in the town.

The Chairman asked if any other licence holder in the town desired to make application, whereupon F. E. Tombs, of the Court Inn, Bridge Street, said it would be a very great disadvantage to him if his house was closed on market days.

The Bench deliberated in private, and on their return the Chairman said they had decided to allow an extension from 2 till 4 on big market days to the nine licence holders who had signed the petition. They were not able to give the same advantage to other licence holders.'

Licensees:

1783–1787	Edwards Hawkes
1788–1795	Samuel Wright
1796–1802	Edward Druce
1804–1811	William Sheppard
1812	Coach & Horses was to be let in February
1812–1814	John Garnton
1815	Coach & Horses was to be let in March
1820	Coach & Horses was to be let in May
1823	Coach & Horses was to be let in June
1824	Coach & Horses was to be let in June
1830	John Busby
1840	Public House Yard &c. owned by William Shuffrey
1839–1841	Giles Clarke
	Age 44, wife Susan age 47 (1841 Census)
1842	Giles Clarke died in March aged 48
1842–1844	James Mason
1847	Richard Stevens
1848–1854	Henry Woodington
	Age 48, born in Hailey, Oxon. Wife Martha age 35 (1851 Census)
1856	Coach & Horses was to be let in June
1858	Susan Clarke, widow of the late Giles Clarke died in December aged 65
1862	Pub renamed Eagle Tavern
1861–1878	Moses Midwinter
	Age 45, born in Ducklington, Oxon. Boot & Shoe Maker employing 2 men & apprentice. Wife Jane age 40 (1861 Census)

	Age 55, born in Ducklington, Oxon. Book Maker. Wife Jane age 50. (1871 Census)
1875	The Eagle is for sale by auction in April
1878	Moses Midwinter died age 63. Buried 5 October in Ducklington.
1878–1883	Moses Walter William Midwinter
	Age 28, born 10 December 1852 in Alesowen, Staffs. Wife Thirza age 31 (1881 Census)
1887	George Williams
1890	The Eagle Tavern was to let in January
1890–1894	George Stayte
	Age 74, born in Charlbury, Oxon. Wife Ellen age 34 (1891 Census)
1894	George Stayte died Jan-Feb-Mar age 76
1894	The Eagle Tavern was to let in May
1894–1907	Joseph Seeley
	Age 52, born in Witney, Oxon. Widower (1901 Census)
1909	Joseph Seeley died in January aged 59
1925	Owned by Hunt Edmunds & Co
1908–1930	John Henry Horne
1931–1941	John Luckett
1941	Luckett John of 22 Corn-street Witney Oxfordshire died 5 September 1941 Administration Oxford 7 November to Matilda Luckett widow. Effects £209 15s 7d.
1942–1944	Matilda Luckett
1945–1948	Laura Torrance
1949–1956	Britton Clark
1957–2001	Gordon Rollins
2001	Hook Norton Brewery bought the pub.
2004–present	Ian Payne – moved from the Red Lion

Holly Bush, 35 Corn St (1781–present)

(Currently trading, owned by Greene King Retailing)
(1840 Tithe Awards Map ref 75)

From the newspapers:

Oxford Journal – Saturday 07 December 1805
'TO be LETT,-All that old-established and well-accustomed PUBLIC HOUSE, in full Trade, called the HOLLY BUSH, with the Malt House, convenient Stables, and Out-Buildings, and Garden, thereto belonging, situate in Corn Street, in Witney, Oxon, now in the Occupation of Mr. WIGGINS. Immediate Possession may he had. The Stock and Utensils to be taken to at an appraised Price.- Enquire of Mr. Wiggins, on the Premises, or of Mr. Macey, Solicitor, Witney.'

Oxford Journal – Saturday 05 July 1828
'A PUBLIC HOUSE to LET. THE HOLLY BUSH PUBLIC HOUSE, in Corn-street, Witney, to be LET, and may be entered on immediately. For further particulars apply to the present occupier, Mr. John Tandy.'

Oxford Chronicle and Reading Gazette – Saturday 13 June 1840
'The annual hunt on Whit Monday, in the Forest of Whichwood, afforded excellent
sport to a large company of equestrian as well as pedestrian. Lord Churchill kindly
sent his hounds, and as early as six o'clock they broke cover, and soon found a
deer, which was killed after a good run; two others were also killed in the course
of the day. We regret that any contention should have arisen as to the right of
parties claiming to have the deer killed, for the township of Witney, dressed in
their house. Lord Churchill, with his usual good feeling, ordered a buck to be
killed for one of the parties, which had the effect of restoring peace. On Thursday
evening a large party sat down to supper at Mr. Willett's, the Holly Bush, where
one of the bucks was dressed, together with other good cheer, and under the able
presidency of Mr. Charles Jones, the company spent a very pleasant evening.'

Oxford Chronicle and Reading Gazette – Saturday 23 December 1843
'Died, Dec. 21, at Leafield, aged 86 years, Mrs. Sophia, mother of Mr. R. Willett,
of the Holly Bush, Witney.'

Oxford Chronicle and Reading Gazette – Saturday 02 December 1848
'[duty free] Insolvent Debtor to be heard before the Judge of the County Court of
Oxfordshire, at the County Hall, Oxford, on Thursday, the 14th day of December,
1848, at 2 o'clock in the afternoon precisely. JOHN WILLETT, late of the Holly
Bush, public house, Corn-street, Witney, in the county of Oxford, licensed
victualler and brewer, and occasionally letting horses for hire. John Looker,
Attorney for the Insolvent, Queen Street, Oxford.'

Oxford Journal – Saturday 21 April 1849
'Died, at the Witney Union-house, Richard Willett, for many years landlord of the
Holly Bush, in this town, aged 71.'

Oxford Chronicle and Reading Gazette – Saturday 29 May 1858
'The seventh anniversary of the Friendly Society, established at the Holly Bush
Inn, in this town, was held on Monday last, when the members were entertained
with a plentiful supply of "the good things," provided by the worthy landlord.
Several members enrolled their names and the day was spent with the utmost
conviviality.'

Witney Gazette and West Oxfordshire Advertiser – Saturday 02 May 1885
'Was he drunk? George Higgs, of Witney, licensed victualler, was charged with
assaulting Stephen Painter, on the 26th March, at Witney. Defendant pleaded not
guilty, and all witnesses were ordered out of Court. Mr. Wall appeared for the
defendant. Stephen Painter deposed--On the 25th February I went to the "Holly
Bush" Inn, and called for a pint of ale, and asked defendant to drink. I then missed
4d.; defendant then jumped up and said be would have me locked up. I then went
to the back, and on again going to the house defendant knocked me down, and
broke the small bone of my leg. I have had it attended to by the doctor, and he
says it may never be well again...

John Higgs deposed - I am a son of defendant. On the 25th February, as I came
home, I saw Painter on the path; father was there. Painter struck at my father

twice, the second time he fell. My father did not strike him nor kick him, neither did he trip him up.

Case dismissed.'

Witney Gazette and West Oxfordshire Advertiser – Saturday 08 January 1887

'LEAVING HORSES IN THE STREET. George Robinson, of Minster Lovell, Haulier, was charged with obstructing the highway, by leaving his horses and carts thereon, at Witney the 31st ult.

P. C. Simmons deposed – On the 31st he saw defendant's two horses and two carts standing opposite the "Holly Bush" Inn, for 20 minutes. He saw three conveyances turned out of the road in consequence of one of the horses having strayed near the middle. Fined 6d. and costs 11s 6d.'

Witney Gazette and West Oxfordshire Advertiser – Saturday 21 November 1903

'PETTY SESSIONS, Thursday. transfers. The transfer of the license of the "Holly Bush," Witney, from F. W. Watts to Ann Brooks was granted; ...'

Witney Gazette and West Oxfordshire Advertiser – Saturday 12 January 1907

'PETTY SESSIONS, Thursday. transfers. Transfers of the licenses of the "Holly Bush," Witney, from Ann Brooks to Alfred William Walker; ...'

Oxford Mail – Saturday 12 May 1984

'Goodbye to Fanny, 103. The funeral of Witney's oldest woman, 103-year old Mrs. Fanny Walker, was held at the Chapel in Witney cemetery yesterday. Mrs. Walker, an ex-publican who kept up the tradition of drinking a Guinness a day, was born in 1880. She lived with her daughter Miss Dorothy Walker, of 33 Ashcombe Place, Witney, where she died. With her late husband Alfred she kept the Hollybush pub in Corn Street, Witney. Five of her children are still alive and she also has nine grandchildren and eighteen great-grand children. A friend, Mr. Ron Hathaway, of 35 Hailey Road, Witney, said yesterday: "She was a great old lady and will be sadly missed. Many people in Witney knew her and I can recall the lively pub she used to keep." Mrs. Walker was born at Field Assarts, near Leafield, and after her husband's death at the age of 48 kept on the Hollybush pub while looking after her seven children.'

Licensees:

1781–1784	Thomas Brooks
1785–1807	John Wiggins
1805	Holly Bush was to let in December
1808	William Smith
1809–1810	William Hale
1816–1817	John Wiggins
1828	Holly Bush was to let in July
1828	John Tandy
1830–1844	Richard Willett
	Age 55 (1841 Census)

1840	Public House outbuildings &c. owned by John Williams Clinch
1847–1848	John Willett
1849	Richard Willett died aged 71
1851–1854	John Busby
	Age 32, born in Leafield, Oxon. Wife Hannah age 31 (1851 Census)
1861–1867	Mary Smith
	Age 56, born in Martin (?), Northants. Widow (1861 Census)
1869–1877	Joseph Phipps
	Age 30, born in Hailey, Oxon. Wife Sarah age 30 (1871 Census)
1881–1891	George Higgs
	Age 44, born in Bampton, Oxon. Sergeant Pensioner. Wife Anne age 38. (1881 Census)
	Age 58, born in Bampton, Oxon. Wife Ann age 45 (1891 Census)
1895	William Davis Attwood
1899–1903	William Frederick Watts
	Age 29, born in Witney, Oxon. Wife Ellen age 31 (1901 Census)
1904–1906	Ann Brooks
1925	Owned by Clinch & Co
1907–1931	Alfred William Walker
	Age 29, born in Witney, Oxon. Wife Fanny age 30 (1911 Census)
1931	Alfred Walker died age 48
1932–1939	Fanny Walker (Mrs.)
1940–1941	Jesse Warner
1942–1958	Sam Purbrick
1959–1962	Ronald Alexander Richings
1963–1964	Martha Mabel Richings
1965–1967	George J. Rich
1968–1972	Cecil J. Leask
1973–1976	Alec J. Cuthbert
1977	Allen T. Orme
1978–1979	Richard J. Wray
1980	Anthony R. Jamieson
2005–2014	Anne Champion
2015–present	Alexander Vaughan

Malt Shovel, 17 Corn St (1840–1907)

(Currently a Dental Clinic & Barbers Shop)
(1840 Tithe Awards Map ref 62)

From the newspapers:

Oxford Journal – Saturday 24 October 1840
'FREEHOLD PUBLIC HOUSE, BUCHER'S SHOP, MALT-HOUSE, DWELLING HOUSE, & PREMISES, in WITNEY; also 6½ ACRES of ARABLE LAND, in CURBRIDGE, TO BE SOLD BY AUCTION, By Mr. Long At the Marlborough Arms Inn in Witney, on Thursday the 5th day of November, at Four o'clock, subject to such conditions as will be then produced (by order of the Trustees under the will of the late Mr. John Stevens, deceased), in two lots.

Lot 1. – The MALT SHOVEL PUBLIC HOUSE, BUTCHER'S SHOP, &c. now in full trade; comprising spacious well-built Premises, with a frontage to the street of 66 feet, having a kitchen, cellaring, 4 bed rooms, and offices; yard, pigstye, stable, a butcher's shop, slaughter-house, and desirable malt-house at the back, with other out-buildings thereto belonging; also adjoining, a DWELLING HOUSE, with a shop, three bed rooms, bake-house, yard, and out-buildings, and a back entrance to the premises, the whole situate in Corn-street, Witney, and now in the occupation of Richard Stevens and Edward Tims. ...'

Oxford Chronicle and Reading Gazette – Saturday 06 November 1847
'Died. Oct. 31, at Witney, aged 55, Mr. Wm. Griffin, of the Malt Shovel public house, maltster, formerly of Shipton Oliffe, Gloucestershire.'

Banbury Guardian – Thursday 11 August 1853
'Deaths. August 2, Mr. Richard Stevens, butcher, late of the Malt Shovel, Corn Street, Witney, aged 46 years.'

Oxford Journal – Saturday 04 September 1858
'BAMPTON EAST DIVISION. – Witney Thursday. John Stevens, of the Malt Shovel public house, Corn-street, charged with keeping his house open for the sale of beer at an illegal hour, was fined 20s,. and costs.'

Oxford Chronicle and Reading Gazette – Saturday 17 August 1861
'WITNEY, Oxon, & SHIPTON OLIFFE, Gloucestershire, TO BE SOLD BY AUCTION By Mr. Hussey, At the Marlborough Arms Inn, Witney, on Friday, August 30th, at One for Three o'clock.
    Lot 1. – FREEHOLD PUBLIC HOUSE and small BREWERY, with the House adjoining, situate in Corn Street, Witney, and known as the "Malt Shovel," in the occupation of Mr. Stevens and Mr. Turner as yearly tenants, at £24 per annum. ...'

Faringdon Advertiser and Vale of the White Horse Gazette – Saturday 15 October 1870
'REWARD. – LOST, on Saturday, October 1st, supposed between Witney and Clanfield, a BOX and its contents. – Whoever has found the same, and will take it either to the Malt Shovel Inn, Witney, or to the New Inn, Bampton, will be rewarded. Anyone detaining the same after this notice, will be prosecuted.'

Witney Gazette and West Oxfordshire Advertiser – Saturday 16 July 1904
'PETTY SESSIONS, Thursday. TRANSFERS. The transfer of the "Malt Shovel," Witney, from Thomas Adams to Tom Baker, ...'

Oxford Times – Saturday 02 June 1906
'The case of the "Malt Shovel" beerhouse was next taken.
    Mr. Ames said the main questions were the ownership, the brewer's monopoly, and the size of the house and the accommodation generally.
    Superintendent Hawtin gave a list of the licensed houses in the locality of the "Malt Shovel" and the owners. The "Malt Shovel" was a small house, there was no accommodation for lodgers, and there was stabling for one horse. The "Eagle," opposite, had three rooms for lodgers and stabling for six horses: the

"Hollybush" was a larger house than the "Malt Shovel," but did not take in lodgers, and there was stabling for six horses; the "Chequers" had also stabling for six horses and four bedrooms for lodgers; the "Bull" consisted of large premises, with stabling for six horses, and in his opinion less trade was done there than the "Malt Shovel"; the stabling at the "Angel" was for four horses. If the "Malt Shovel" was closed, people could get the same kind of beer at the "Angel," the "Hollybush," and the "Bull." Comparing the "Malt Shovel" with the other houses in the matter of accommodation he should think it was the worst of the lot, but it did a fair trade.

By Mr. Walsh: The last tenant was in the house for 28 years, and the "Malt Shovel" was the only beerhouse in the area.

Mr. Bryan said the "Malt Shovel" and the "Three Horse Shoes" were the two selected to be visited by the committee, and they found the "Three Horse Shoes" had better accommodation for the public than the other, though the stabling was practically the same. There was a most objectionable back-entrance to the "Malt Shovel." He did not think this would be a final reduction of licensed houses in Witney.

The tenant, Mr. Baker, was called by Mr. Walsh, and stated that he had been in the house two years. He paid £9 a year rent, but was rated at £15. He had put his money into the house, and obtained a living. His trade was two barrels of ale, nine galloons of bitter, nine gallons of stout, and 18 gallons of best, weekly, beside minerals and cyder. He had been asked twice for lodgings.

Mr. Walsh said his arguments in this case were the same as in the last, that he would make an appeal on behalf of the tenant. It seemed very hard that after retiring from service and putting his savings into the house he should be turned out, and he was not in a good state of health. If there was any objection to the bark-entrance the owners would close it up permanently.

The Chairman said it was more a matter for the licensing authority than for the County Licensing Committee.

The Committee retired for deliberation, and on returning, the Chairman said they had agreed to confirm the decision of the licensing justices, but they thought it would be right to suggest to the Witney Bench, as they had intimated that they were going to continue the reduction of licensed houses, that they should consider the possibility of beerhouses being preferred by some persons to fully-licensed houses.

Mr. Ames applied for the justice's costs, and the Chairman said they would be granted.'

Witney Gazette and West Oxfordshire Advertiser – Saturday 17 November 1906
'PETTY SESSIONS, Thursday. TRANSFERS. The transfer of the "Malt Shovel," Corn Street, from the late Mr. T. Baker to his widow; ...'

Oxford Times – Saturday 05 January 1907
'... The Licensing Committee presented a report on the year's work, which showed that nine licences had been referred to them by the licensing justices, five

from Banbury, two from Bampton, two from Henley. The renewal of six had been refused, and the following sums allowed as compensation in respect of four of them; "The Malt Shovel." Witney, £761; ...'

Witney Gazette and West Oxfordshire Advertiser – Saturday 11 May 1907
'TO BE SOLD OR LET. No. 17, Corn Street, Witney, formerly known as the "MALT SHOVEL." Apply, M, Gazette Office.'

Licensees:

1840	John Stevens
	Public House Garden &c. owned by John Stevens
1840	Malt Shovel was for sale by auction in October
1841–1844	Richard Stevens
	Age 30, Butcher. Wife Rebecca age 31 (1841 Census)
1847	William Griffin
1847	William Griffin died in October aged 55
1853	Richard Stevens died in August aged 46
1861	Malt Shovel was for sale by auction in August
1851–1871	John Stevens
	Age 29, born in Witney, Oxon (1851 Census)
	Age 48, born in Witney, Oxon. Wife Jane age 59 (1871 Census)
1876–1877	John East
1891–1904	Thomas Adams
	Age 44, born in Ducklington, Oxon. Wife Jane age 39 (1891 Census)
	Age 54, born in Ducklington, Oxon. Wife Jane age 48 (1901 Census)
1904–1906	Tom Baker
1907	Mary Baker (Mrs.) (moved to the Chequers)
	Pub closed

Nag's Head, 100 Corn St (1840–1980)

(Currently an Antique Shop)
(1840 Tithe Awards Map ref 328)

From the newspapers:

Oxford Journal – Saturday 14 June 1879
'TO BE SOLD BY AUCTION, By Mr. James Long, On the premises, the Nag's Head, Corn-street, Witney, on Tuesday, June the 17th, at One o'clock (by order of the Executrix of the Will of the late Mr. Richard Redgate, coal merchant, &c.)'

Oxford Journal – Saturday 17 July 1886
'Freehold and Copyhold PROPERTY, to be sold by auction, By John Habgood and Son, At the Marlborough Hotel, Witney, on Wednesday, July 21st, 1886, at Five for Six o'clock in the evening, in five lots, consisting of
    A FREEHOLD BEER HOUSE, known as the "Nag's Head," situate in the Corn Street, Witney, in the occupation of Mr. Jesse Brown, and let to Messrs. Clinch and Co., with Lot 5, at £26 per annum. ...'

Faringdon Advertiser and Vale of the White Horse Gazette – Saturday 05 January 1901
'PETTY SESSIONS, Thursday. - ... The following holdovers were granted:- ... the "Nag's Head," Witney, from Jesse Brown, deceased, to his widow. ...'

Banbury Advertiser – Wednesday 04 November 1942
'PRISONERS OF WAR WEEK. "Playing the game" at Oxon Licensed Houses. ... Bar Billiards and shove ha'penny at Nag's Head, Witney. ...'

Licensees:

1840	House Outbuildings Garden &c. owned by James Long
1840–1878	Richard Redgate
	Age 30. Wife Charlotte age 35 (1841 Census)
	Age 45, born in Witney, Oxon. Carrier. Wife Charlotte age 46 (1851 Census)
	Age 55, born in Witney, Oxon. Railway carrier & Coal dealer. Wife Charlotte age 57 (1861 Census)
	Age 65, born in Witney, Oxon. Coal Merchant. Wife Charlotte age 67 (1871 Census)
1879	Richard Redgate died Jan-Feb-Mar aged 73
1879	Nag's Head was for sale by auction in June
1879–1881	James Redgate
	Age 46, born in Witney, Oxon. Coal merchant. Wife Martha age 47. (1881 Census)
1886	Nag's Head was for sale by auction in July
1886–1900	Jesse Brown
	Age 65, born in Witney, Oxon. Wife Ann age 60 (1891 Census)
1900	Jesse Brown died end of year aged 76
1925	Owned by Clinch & Co
1901–1931	Eliza 'Lizzie' Brown (Mrs.)
	Age 33, born in Crawley, Oxon. Widow (1901 Census)
	Age 43, born in Hailey, Oxon. Widow (1911 Census)
1932–1933	William Maling
1934–1939	Jesse Warner
	DOB 18 Feb 1901 Licensed Victualler. Wife Ethel dob 23 Jul 1899 Unpaid Domestic Duties (1939 Register)
1940	Cyril Edward John Lord
1941–1944	Albert Edwin Hayward
1945	Letty Louise Hayward
1946–1951	Arthur Albert Henry Hayward
1952–1957	Frederick Edward Conway
1958–1966	Cyril Pratley
1967–1969	Dyson Rogers
1970–1975	Nicholas F. State
1977–1978	James Cookson
1979–1980	John H. Coleman

New Inn (Waggon & Horses), 111 Corn St (1840–present)

(Currently trading, owned by Punch Taverns Ltd)
(1840 Tithe Awards Map ref 156)

From the newspapers:

Oxford Chronicle and Reading Gazette – Saturday 30 April 1842
'CORONER'S INQUEST. – On Tuesday last an inquest was held by James Westell, Esq.
at the Waggon and Horses, on view of the body of Mary Ann Partlett, aged 6
years, who came by her death by going into a field and seating herself close to
a heap of burning squitch, which ignited her clothes, and before any one could
render her assistance was so dreadfully burnt that she expired in about five hours.
– Verdict, Accidental Death.'

Oxford Times – Saturday 13 September 1862
'Waggon & Horses Public House, Corn Street, Witney. Capital BREWING
COPPER   and   PLANT,   excellent   CASKS,   BREWING   UTENSILS,
FURNITURE, and Effects. TO BE SOLD BY AUCTION, BY. MR. LONG, On
the premises at the Waggon and Horses, Corn-street, Witney, on Friday the 26th
of September, at Twelve o'clock, the property of Mr. Pumfrey, in consequence
of having disposed of the premises; comprising a capital 240-gallon copper, with
large brass discharge tap, and stack, complete: large mash tub and underback, five
brewing tubs, two large coolers, copper wort pump and lead pump, as fixed; sweet
and well-made oak beer casks, consisting of one 1200, one 1000, one 800, one 350,
two 300 and 200, four 112, and seven about 60 gallons each, and sundry utensils.
The Furniture will comprise four-post, tent, and other bedsteads, several flock
beds and bedding, chairs, bed room and other furniture and effects.'

Oxford Chronicle and Reading Gazette – Saturday 17 December 1864
'Waggon and Horses Inn, Witney, Oxon. THE above Old-Established INN, now
in full trade, TO BE LET, with immediate possession. A portion of the Premises
having been recently let off to an eminent engineer, brings the rent, licences, and
taxes very low. Apply to Mr. Tustin, St. Clement's, Oxford.'

Oxford Times – Saturday 06 May 1865
'PETTY SESSIONS, May 4. ALEHOUSE LICENCES. – This being a special session for
the transfer of victuallers' licences, the following transfers were made:- Elm Tree,
Witney, Mark Knight to Henry Townsend; Waggon and Horses, Witney, Frederick
Lyford to William Thornton; The Angel, Henry Paine to Charles Hitchman.'

Oxford Chronicle and Reading Gazette – Saturday 12 October 1867
'DIED. - ... Oct. 3. In Corn Street, Witney, at the Waggon and Horses, Mr. William
Thornton, aged 59.'

Oxford Times – Saturday 14 March 1868
'JUSTICE ROOM, - March 12. ALEHOUSES. – The following alehouse licenses
were transferred:- Waggon and Horses, Witney, from Mary Carpenter to Michael
Carpenter. ...'

Oxford Journal – Saturday 20 March 1869
'BAMPTON EAST DIVISION. – Witney, March 4. The following transfers were made: ... The application for the Waggon and Horses, Witney, was refused.'

Oxfordshire Telegraph – Wednesday 10 March 1875
'DEATHS. February 13, aged 41, Mr. James Porter, Waggon and Horses Inn, Witney.'

Oxford Times – Saturday 29 January 1876
'"A Gipsy's Life for Me." – On Monday last Sergt. Baker, a young man, at the Waggon and Horses Inn, in this town, was brought up on a charge of having absconded from his duties as a police-constable in the Gloucestershire Constabulary. It appears he had been stationed at Northleach, and having become acquainted with some gipsies determined to abandon official life for one of a more romantic kind. His uniform, handcuffs, &c., were found in the van. The prisoner was handed over to the justices at Northleach to be dealt with by them.'

Wilts and Gloucestershire Standard – Saturday 26 October 1878
'County Court, Wednesday. – (Before W. H. Cooke, Esq., judge.) – Lee v. Hudson. – The plaintiff, for whom Mr. Assheton Cross, barrister, appeared, is landlord of the New Inn, Witney, but was formerly a farmer near Fairford, and he sued the defendant, a corn dealer at Witney, for £11 15s., made up of two sums of £3 each, alleged balance on two straw ricks sold by plaintiff when living at Fairford, and other items, inclusive of sums for cartage, trap hire, and liquors supplied, &c. Defendant admitted only the beer and other items to the amount of £1 12s. 5d., and the judge remarking that the plaintiff had a very bad memory, gave judgment for that amount only.'

Witney Gazette and West Oxfordshire Advertiser – Saturday 23 September 1905
'THE NEW INN, CORN STREET, WITNEY. JOHN HADGOOD & SON will Sell by Auction, on the premises on WEDNESDAY 27th SEPTEMBER, 1905, at 2 o'clock punctually, under an execution, and by order of the High Sheriff of Oxfordshire, the HOUSEHOLD FURNIIURE And general effects.'

Witney Gazette and West Oxfordshire Advertiser – Saturday 21 August 1909
'WITNEY HARRIERS F.C. The annual general meeting of the Witney Harriers F.C. was held on Thursday, August 12, at their head quarters (the New Inn) where a good number of supporters assembled. The annual report and balance sheet showed that the club had had a fairly successful season. Votes of thanks were unanimously carried to all those who had generously supported the club, and those who had been so keenly interested in the doings of the club, and their help solicited again for the coming season...'

Faringdon Advertiser and Vale of the White Horse Gazette – Saturday 27 August 1921
'Swifts' Football Club. The annual general meeting of the above club was held

on Thursday evening, at the "New Inn," Mr H. G. Sharpe presiding, A satisfactory report and balance sheet was presented..."

Licensees:

1840	Public House, Outbuildings & Garden owned by James Clinch
1840–1864	Thomas Pumfrey
	Age 41, wife Mary age 35 (1841 Census)
	Age 56, born in Burdrop, Glos. Wife Mary age 50 (1851 Census)
	Age 66, wife Mary age 61 (1861 Census)
1864	The Waggon and Horses was to let in December
1865	Frederick Lyford
1865–1866	William Thornton
1867	William Thornton died in October aged 59
1868	Mary Carpenter
1868–1869	Michael Carpenter
1871–1874	James Porter
	Age 36, born in Fyfield, Glos. Licenced Lodging House. Wife Elizabeth age 33 (1871 Census)
1875	James Porter died in February aged 41
1875–1876	Mrs. Porter
1877–1885	Thomas Collis
1885	Thomas Collis died at end of year age 68
1886–1898	Elizabeth Collis (Mrs.)
	Age 53, born in Kidlington, Oxon. Widow (1891 Census)
1899–1906	Hariph Fowler
	Age 45, born in Witney, Oxon. Wife Elizabeth age 42 (1901 Census)
1907–1926	Ralph Busby
	Age 36, born in Worcester. Wife Emily Florence age 44 (1911 Census)
1925	Owned by Hall & Co
1927–1965	James Garner
	DOB 13 Jul 1890 Licensed Victualler. Wife Florence dob 13 Jul 1892 Unpaid Domestic Duties (1939 Register)
1966–1980	William G. Leach
1997–2002	Beryl Wilmore
2003–2018	Martin Cornish

Rocket (Red Lion), 1 Corn St (1764–present)

(Currently trading, owned by Greene King Retailing)
(1840 Tithe Awards Map ref 53)

From the newspapers:

Oxford Journal – Saturday 13 December 1817
'NOTICE to DEBTORS and CREDTORS of Mr. LEECH, Attorney, Witney, WHEREAS the said Mr. LEECH having lately assigned all his Estate and Effects to Mr. William Quarterman, of the City of Oxford, breeches-maker, and J. Haines, of Charlbury, attorney at law, in trust, for the benefit of his Creditors; Notice is hereby given That the Deed of Assignment is left with Mr. John Wells, Red Lion, Witney, for signature of the Creditors; ...'

Oxford Chronicle and Reading Gazette – Saturday 11 May 1839
'Red Lion Inn, Witney. THE GOOD WILL, STOCK, FURNITURE, BREWING UTENSILS, and FIXTURES, of the above Inn to be DISPOSED OF. No person need apply, who, on taking possession, will not put down £300. It is a concern well worthy of the notice of any attentive man, and presents an opportunity not often to be met with.'

Oxford Chronicle and Reading Gazette – Saturday 26 September 1840
"TO be LET or SOLD, with immediate possession - ... For further particulars apply Mr. Henry Wm. Clark, Red Lion, Witney.'

Banbury Guardian – Thursday 14 September 1843
'DREADFUL SUICIDE. – On Saturday last, on Inquest was held at the Red Lion Inn, in this Town, by James Westell, Esq., Coroner, on view of the body of Mr. Robert Spittle, the landlord of the above inn, who put a period to his existence the night before, by shooting himself through the body. It appeared in evidence that the deceased, who was about 44 years of age, at about half-past 11 on the night of Friday, retired to his bed room with his wife; that there was a single-barrel gun in the next room, in which the daughter of the deceased slept; that the deceased brought the gun from his daughter's room to his own, and commenced loading it, and on his wife asking him for what he was loading it, he replied that he was going out early in the morning, and wished to load it in readiness: when he had completed it, he deliberately placed the but of the gun on the floor, and directing the muzzle in a sloping direction towards his left side, and leaning over it, he discharged it by forcing the trigger back with the ramrod which he held in his right hand. His wife was standing by him the whole time, but was so frightened as to be incapable of preventing the rash act. The deceased fell immediately, and was heard to groan once or twice only. Several persons were immediately on the spot, and Mr. Batt, Surgeon, was directly in attendance, but of course no assistance could be rendered him as his death must have been instantaneous, the shot passing directly through the heart, and quite through the body, and were found scattered in considerable quantity about the room. The deceased had, it appeared, been in a desponding state of mind for the last month, and has before attempted to destroy himself, – once by drinking a bottle of brandy, but he was then prevented by his wife dashing it from his hand. He has within that time more than once told his wife that he had determined to destroy himself within three weeks, and asked her which she thought the most easy death. A distress levied on the day of the fatal occurrence on some potatoe crops, for rent due, seems to have determined the unhappy man in his fatal purpose; this latter occurrence seems to have preyed much on his mind, as he repeatedly expressed unwillingness to see his acquaintances, and wished he was out of his trouble. After a patient investigation, a verdict was returned of "Destroyed himself, being at the time of unsound mind." On Monday morning last, his remains were interred in our church-yard, followed by a great number of spectators. He was much respected, and his untimely end greatly regretted. He has left a wife and one child, the former, as may be supposed, in a distressed state of mind.'

Oxford Chronicle and Reading Gazette – Saturday 07 October 1865
'J. P. LAMBERT, RED LION INN, WITNEY, GRATEFUL to his numerous
Friends and the Public for the patronage shown to him during his residence
in Corn Street, respectfully informs them that he has removed to that old-
established House, THE CROSS KEYS INN, WITNEY, where he hopes to
receive a continuance of those favours and that kind preference which have been
so liberally conferred upon him at his former residence, and which he promises
no effort will be left untried to deserve. Good and carefully aired Beds, excellent
Stabling, and Coach House. Flys, Gigs, and Horses on Hire, with Careful Drivers.
A MARKET ORDINARY EVERY THURSDAY. Sept. 29, 1865.'

Witney Gazette and West Oxfordshire Advertiser – Saturday 25 March
1905
'PETTY SESSIONS. – There was no criminal business at the Petty Sessions on
Thursday. The licence of the "Red Lion," Witney was transferred from Mrs. Jones
to Mr. W. J. Hobbs.'

Faringdon Advertiser and Vale of the White Horse Gazette – Saturday 04
April 1914
'BOWLING CLUB.-The annual meeting of the above club was held at the Red Lion
Hotel on Thursday evening, under the presidency of Mr. J. W. Abraham...'

Licensees:

1764–1830	John Wells (snr & jnr)
1799	John Wells snr was buried 9 September
1832–1840	Henry William Clarke
1840	Public House Outbuildings &c. owned by Thomas Dix
1840	Red Lion was to let or sold
1841–1843	Robert Spittle (from the Butcher's Arms)
	Age 40, wife Harriet age 40 (1841 Census)
1843	Robert Spittle committed suicide in September
1844–1854	Harriet Spittle (Mrs.)
	Age 59, born in Witney, Oxon. Widow (1851 Census)
1861	William Phillips
	Age 24, born in Stourton Caundle, Dorset. Wife Mary age 26 (1861 Census)
1863–1865	John Lambert
1865	John Lambert moved to the Cross Keys in October
1869–1903	John Jones
	Age 42, born in Langyniell (?), Monmouthshire. Wife Hannah age 32 (1871 Census)
	Age 50, born in Montgomershire. Wife Hannah age 42 (1881 Census)
	Age 61, born in Wales. Wife Hannah age 52 (1891 Census)
	Age 70, born in Montgomery. Wife Harriet age 60 (1901 Census)
1903	John Jones died middle of the year age 71
1903–1905	Mary Jones
1905–1925	William John Hobbs
	Age 52, born in Middleton, Glos. Wife Mary Ann age 54 (1911 Census)
1925	Owned by William John Hobbs

1926	Owned by Flowers & Son, Stratford upon Avon
1926–1927	Albert Ernest Victor King
1928–1960	Charles Herbert Holt
	DOB 18 Jul 1876 Licensee. Wife Norah dob 24 Aug 1888 Unpaid Domestic Duties (1939 Register)
1961–1962	Leonard Franklin
1963–1980	Walter Broadbent
1988	Roy & Isabelle Tams
1986–1991	Roy Tams
1991–2004	Ian Payne – moved to the Eagle Tavern
2005	Pub owned by Greene King Brewing & Retailing Ltd
2005–2007	Paul Wakefield
2008–2011	Joan Cove
2012–2014	Thomas Pauling
2015–present	Eluned Sain Ogden

Star Inn (Rocket Tavern), 152 Corn St (1753–1971)

(Currently a Chinese Takeaway)
(1840 Tithe Awards Map ref 249)

From the newspapers:

Oxford Times – Saturday 10 September 1870
'SUDDEN DEATH – An inquest was held at the "Star" Inn, Corn-street, on Monday last, before F. Westell, Esq., coroner, on the body of Mrs. Sarah Brown, wife of Mr. Richard Brown, stonemason, who died suddenly on Saturday night. – Mr. Francis Rawle, of Witney, surgeon, believed that she died from serious apoplexy. – The Jury returned a verdict in accordance with the medical testimony.'

Witney Gazette and West Oxfordshire Advertiser – Saturday 18 January 1890
'ANOTHER FIRE. – On Sunday evening last, about 9 o'clock a fire, which might have proved a serious one, was discovered at the "Star" Inn, Corn Street. It appears Mr. Wright, the landlord, fancied he smelt something burning, and on going into the bar he found the mantle-shelf, which is entirely built of wood, all alight. With great promptitude he fetched buckets of water and dashed over it, which had the desired effect of putting it out. It was most fortunate the fire was discovered at the time it was, for had they gone to bed without discovering it, doubtless the whole place would have been in flames in a short space of time. In addition to there being the usual furniture some few gallons of spirits were stored in the cupboard not many inches from the part that was on fire. The house belongs to Messrs. Clinch & Co., Eagle Brewery, and is insured in the Liverpool, London and Globe Insurance Co., through their Witney Agent, Mr. F. M. Green.'

Faringdon Advertiser and Vale of the White Horse Gazette – Saturday 30 May 1908
'LICENSING. A holdover of the license of the "Star" Inn, Corn-street, Witney, was granted from George James Carr to Charles Garner. ...'

Faringdon Advertiser and Vale of the White Horse Gazette – Saturday 14 March 1914
'PETTY SESSIONS. – There were no cases for hearing at these sessions on Thursday. The following licenses were transferred. – Star Inn, Witney, From Chas. Garner to E. J. Conway; ...'

Licensees:

1753–1770	William Day
1770	Buried on 7 Oct.
1771–1779	Ann Day
1781	John Jeffrey
1840	Rocket Tavern House Yard &c. owned by John Pritchard
1840	Rocket Tavern was void
1852–1854	James Crosswell
1861–1868	William Harman
	Age 65, born in Curbridge, Oxon. Foreign Fruit Dealer. Widower (1861 Census)
1869–1877	Frederick Harman
	Age 33, born in Witney, Oxon. Dealer. (1871 Census)
1883–1895	Walter Wright
	Age 33, born in Hailey, Oxon. Wife Mary age 34 (1891 Census)
1899–1908	George James Carr
	Age 32, born in Marsh Baldon, Oxon. Carter on Farm. Wife Maria age 31. (1901 Census)
1908–1913	Charles Garner
	Age 47, born in Witney, Oxon. Wife Harriett age 44 (1911 Census)
1914–1925	Edward George Conway
1925	Owned by Clinch & Co
1926	Edward Hughes
1927–1933	Charles George Strong
1934–1944	Charles William Garner
	DOB 31 Aug 1887 Inn Keeper Licensee. Wife Florence dob 7 Oct 1887 Inn Keeper Licenses Wife (1939 Register)
1945–1961	Reginald Christopher Garner
1962	Raymond Rea
1963	Peter Egerton Hammond
1964	Reginald Christopher Garner
1965–1967	Charles L. De'arth
1968–1971	John B. C. Butcher

Three Horse Shoes (aka Horse Shoes), 78 Corn St (1770–present)

(Currently trading, owned by Admiral Taverns)
(1840 Tithe Awards Map ref 343)

From the newspapers:

Oxford Journal – Saturday 06 October 1855
'AMICABLE TRADESMAN'S SOCIETY.-The members of this Society will

meet on Tuesday next, at Mr. Andrews's, the Three Horse Shoes, to celebrate the taking of Sebastopol. There will be an abundance of good old English fare, and we doubt not that cordial success will be drunk to the future prosperity of our army and navy, and to our brave allies, who so highly distinguished themselves on the ever memorable 8th of September.

The hop picking in this neighbourhood is finished, and we are glad to hear that the crops are good.'

Oxford Chronicle and Reading Gazette – Saturday 21 August 1858
'WITNEY and HAILEY, Oxon. A VALUABLE FREEHOLD PUBLIC HOUSE Known as "THE THREE HORSE SHOES," And a Convenient Private DWELLING HOUSE, with Garden and MALTHOUSE, in the Town of Witney; also an Inclosure of first-class MEADOW LAND, at Hailey, near Witney; TO BE SOLD BY AUCTION By Messrs. JONAS & THOS. PAXTON, At the Marlborough Arms Inn, Witney, on Tuesday, Aug. 31st, 1858, three o'clock, by direction of Mr. Thomas Waine, –

Lot 1. – A stone-built and slated FREEHOLD PUBLIC HOUSE, situate in Corn Street, Witney, known by the sign of "The Three Horse Shoes," and containing a tap room, parlour, 2 good cellars, brewhouse, and 3 bedrooms, with detached stable and garden, the whole occupied by Mr. John Andrews, at a low annual rent of £15. Quit rent, 6d. ...'

Witney Gazette and West Oxfordshire Advertiser – Saturday 15 March 1902
'PETTY SESSIONS, Thursday. HOLDOVERS. An holdover of the license of the "Three Horse Shoes" Corn Street, Witney, from Maria Moss to James Holland; ...'

Witney Gazette and West Oxfordshire Advertiser – Saturday 24 October 1903
'OCCASIONAL LICENSE. An occasional license was granted to the landlord of the "Three Horse Shoes" Witney, on the occasion of the Oddfellows supper.'

Faringdon Advertiser and Vale of the White Horse Gazette – Saturday 09 January 1904
'PIG CLUB SUPPER – The annual supper in connection with the Witney Working Men's Pig Club was held at the Three Horse Shoes Inn, on Tuesday evening, and was presided over by the secretary (Mr Albert Horne). The business took place afterwards. The balance sheet showed a balance in hand of £15 2s 1½d. There were now 27 members, and 86 pigs were now covered, upwards of 400 having been insured during the past year. A committee and officers were elected for the ensuing year, and songs were sung at intervals.'

Faringdon Advertiser and Vale of the White Horse Gazette – Saturday 01 February 1919
'PETTY SESSIONS, Thursday. HOLDOVER. A holdover of the license of the "Three Horse Shoes" Inn, Witney was granted to Thomas Conway, from Joseph Moss Holland.'

Licensees:

1770–1782	George Brown
1782	Buried on 21 February
1782–1788	Widow Brown
1789–1790	Henry Gadfield
1791–1820	Thomas Fowler
1840	Public House Garden &c. owned by Mary Ann Waine
1821–1863	John Andrews
	Age 45, wife Catherine age 40 (1841 Census)
	Age 60, born in Witney, Oxon. Maltster. Wife Catherine age 58 (1851 Census)
	Age 70, born in Witney, Oxon. Widower (1861 Census)
1858	The Three Horse Shoes was for sale by auction
1864	Frederick Smith
1869–1874	Edward Brown
	Age 69, born in Witney, Oxon. Wife Mary age 67 (1871 Census)
1876–1880	William Moss jnr
1880	William Moss died in October age 47
1881–1902	Maria Moss (Mrs.)
	Age 36, born in Chesterton, Oxon. Widow (1881 Census)
	Age 46, born in Chesterton, Oxon. Widow (1891 Census)
	Age 56, born in Chesterton, Oxon. Widow (1901 Census)
1902–1918	Joseph Moss Holland
	Age 37, born in Witney, Oxon. Haulier. Wife Helen Moss age 37. (1911 Census)
1919–1925	Owned by clinch & Co
1919–1934	Thomas Conway
1935–1972	Edward Samuel Middleton
	DOB 14 Jun 1899 Inn Keeper. Wife Ellen dob 10 Apr 1900 Licence Keeping in Bar (1939 Register)
1973–1980	John F. Kempton
1991–1994	Ben & Libby Salter
2005	Pub owned by Greene King Brewing & Retailing Ltd
2005–2008	Peter Wheeler
2008	Ann Champion
2009–2012	Luke Champion
2012	Pub owned by Admiral Taverns
2013–2015	Sarah Bullwinkel
2016–present	Ann Champion

High Street

Britannia, 53 High St (behind the shops) (1839–1868)

(Currently a private residence)
(1840 Tithe Awards Map ref 479)

From the newspapers:

Oxford Chronicle and Reading Gazette – Saturday 09 November 1839
'CRAWLEY, NEAR WITNEY. TO be LET, with immediate possession, – The Old-established LAMB PUBLIC HOUSE, coming in about Fifty Pounds. For particulars apply personally to the occupier, or to Joseph Clarke, cooper, licensed in spirits. &c. at the Britannia, Witney.'

Oxford Chronicle and Reading Gazette – Saturday 02 January 1841
'On Saturday last was married, by the Rev. R. Shirlock, Mr. Wm. Nunney, of the White Hart, Burford, To Ann, eldest daughter of Mr. J. Clarke, of the Britannia, Witney.'

Oxford Chronicle and Reading Gazette – Saturday 05 April 1845
'TO be LET, and entered upon immediately, – All that established and well-accustomed PUBLIC HOUSE, called THE BRITANNIA, with the Brewhouse, Out-buildings and Premises, and capital Cellaring, situate in the High-street of WITNEY, in the county of Oxford, now in the occupation of the Proprietor, Mr. Joseph Clarke, who is declining the Public Business in consequence of the misconduct of his Sons. The Stock in Trade, Brewing Utensils and Apparatus, and other Fixtures on the premises, to be taken to at a valuation. – For further particulars apply to the Proprietor, on the premises. N.B. A Journeyman COOPER may meet with immediate employment on application to Mr. Clarke, as above; if by letter, pre-paid. None but a good workman need apply.'

Oxford Chronicle and Reading Gazette – Saturday 18 April 1846
'County Court – Wednesday. CLARKE V. GAMBIDGE.
Mr. Tomes, at considerable length, stated the case to the jury. In fact the whole amount claimed was 3s. the balance of an account contracted in 1838 or 1839, for a barrel of ale and half a gross of pipes, 43s.

The defence set up by Mr. Brunner, on the part of the defendant was, first, non-liability, and secondly, limitation the by statute.

Mr. Tomes called Shaler Clarke, and William Clarke, sons of the plaintiff, who both stated that a person named Thos. Humphries applied to their father who kept the Britannia public-house at Witney, on the Friday previous to Witney Races in 1839, to trust him for a barrel of ale for sale on the racecourse on the Monday. That Mr. Gambidge came with Humphries. The father said he did not know Humphries, but would trust Mr. Gambidge with two or three barrels. Afterwards samples were brought, and it was settled that a barrel at 42s. should be supplied. The Monday of the races, Mr. Gambidge called on Mr. Clarke, and directed him to send the barrel to the Downs. Shaler Clarke took the barrel to the downs and delivered it to

Humphries. He did not see Gambidge there, but met him as he returned with half a gross of pipes on his arm in a basket, which witness said his Father had supplied him for Humphries for 1s. In a few days after some person called and paid 2*l*. on account, but the witness could not say who paid it. Both witnesses swore that it was on Monday, September 16, 1839, and they knew it was 1839, because that year was the last of the races, the downs having been inclosed the next year.

Mr. Brunner cross-examined these witnesses very closely. Both were quite sure it was in 1839, because it was the last year of the races.

Mr. Whitlock, of Witney, was then called by Mr. Tomes. He merely stated that the last Witney races were held in 1839, and that he served defendant with a summons for the 3s. September 2, 1845.

Mr. Brunner then rose, and said there never was a more paltry action brought into court. Defendant might, by paying 3s. have prevented its coming there, but he might thus have opened the way for demands of a large amount. He considered this to be a wanton waste of time and money. He called five witnesses, who all deposed that Humphries had no stall at Witney races in 1839, that he never had a booth but in 1841, the last year but one the races. The jury found for the plaintiff, 3s. We understand this case will be carried further.'

Cheltenham Chronicle – Thursday 24 August 1848
'... For a view of the Premises apply to the Tenant; and for other particulars to Mr. Joseph Clarke, Britannia, Witney; or the Auctioneer, Burford, Oxon.'

Licensees:

1839–1848	Joseph Clarke
1840	Public House Outbuildings and Yard owned by Joseph Clarke
1845	The Britannia was to be let in April
1861–1868	John Bowerman
	Age 56, born in Great Milton, Oxon. Wife Sarah age 53 (1861 Census)

Jolly Waggoner, 78 High St

(Currently Retail Premises)
(1840 Tithe Awards Map ref 798)

Licensees:

1840	Public House Garden &c. owned by William Thorley
1839–1842	Thomas Lindsey
	Age 35, wife Jane age 35 (1841 Census)

King's Arms Inn, 106 High St (1761–1955)

(Currently The Windrush Club & Retail Premises)
(1840 Tithe Awards Map ref 778)

From the newspapers:

Oxford Chronicle and Reading Gazette – Saturday 22 February 1840
'On Monday last was married by the Rev. C. Jerram, Mr. Charles Hyett, to Miss Payne, daughter of Mrs. Payne, of the King's Arms Inn.'

Oxford Chronicle and Reading Gazette – Saturday 04 December 1841
'DEATHS. On Thursday last, aged 61, much respected and greatly regretted by her family and friends, Jane Payne, for upwards of thirty years landlady of the King's Arms Inn, Witney.'

Oxford Journal – Saturday 18 December 1841
'The King's Arms Freehold Public House, COMMERCIAL INN, AND PREMISES, WITNEY, OXON. TO BE SOLD BY AUCTION, By Mr. LONG, On the premises in Witney on Wednesday the 29th of December, at Three o'clock (by direction of the Trustees under the will of the late Mr. Payne, and under such conditions as will then be produced). – That capital FREEHOLD, long-established, and well accustomed INN and COMMERCIAL HOUSE, known as "The King's Arms," situate in the High-street, in Witney, for many Years in the occupation of Mrs. Payne.

The Premises comprise a substantial fronted Building, with a carriage entrance, commercial room, back parlour, kitchen, bar, sitting room, six capital bed rooms, and other domestic offices; also excellent brew-house, cellaring, store-houses, stabling for 16 horses, sheds, large warehouse, and a good kitchen garden attached, the whole well supplied with water.

There is a good Retail Wine and Spirit Trade, and the Inn ranks with commercial gentlemen as one of the most comfortable establishments in the country. From the large manufacturing population, and good weekly markets, the consumption of beer is considerable.

Particulars may be had of Mr. Cooper, Wheatley, Oxon; of Mr. John Cocks, Reading, Berks; on the premises; and of the auctioneer, Witney.'

Oxford Journal – Saturday 07 August 1847
'WITNEY, Aug. 5. ODD FELLOWS.-On Tuesday last the fourth anniversary of the opening of the Bud of Friendship Lodge was celebrated at the King's Arms Inn, in this town; the weather, which upon all former occasions had been more than usually unpropitious, was this year as fine as could be wished...'

Oxford Chronicle and Reading Gazette – Saturday 04 February 1854
'EXTRAORDINARY RUN WITH A DEER. – On Monday last, a small spaniel bitch, the properly of Mr. John Bowerman, of the King's Arms Inn, Witney, while with some gentleman shooting in the Chase Woods, near Whichwood Forest, found a deer, which, after a run of nearly three hours, she succeeded in killing, having ran it to death. This is considered extraordinary, there having been no other dog to assist, and the bitch herself not being more than 11 inches high.'

Oxford Chronicle and Reading Gazette – Saturday 11 December 1858
'DEATHS. In the 44th year of her age, Anne, the beloved wife of George Hedges, ostler at the King's Arms Hotel, in this city.'

Oxford Journal – Saturday 06 August 1859
'Re Druce.-In Bankruptcy. KING'S ARMS INN, WITNEY. WINES, SPIRITS, BEER, AND STOUT, Brewing Plant, Casks, Hops, HOUSEHOLD

FURNITURE, &c., TO BE SOLD BY AUCTION, By Mr. LONG, On the premises at the King's Arms Inn, Witney, on Tuesday the 16th and Wednesday the 17th days of August, 1859, at Eleven o'clock each day (by order of the Assignee).

The first day's sale, Tuesday the 16th, will include the whole of the STOCK; comprising about 700 gallons of home-brewed beer, 6 barrels of prime stout and pale ale, 16 dozen of port and sherry wine, 7 dozen of home-made wine, 22 dozen bottles of brandy, about 80 gallons of raw gin, 15 gallons of liquors, 6 dozen of stout, 2 dozen of lemonade, 8lbs. of cigars, 3 pockets of hops, &c. &c.; the Brewing Plant, and 36 sound and sweet casks (from 180 to 36 gallons); a new 6-pull Beer Engine and pipes; excellent; 9-pull Liquor Engine (also new), with dresser and waste, taps, pipes, and 9 liquor casks to ditto; the Furniture of the Club room, and several lots in the yard and garden.

On Wednesday the 17th, the nearly-new HOUSEHOLD FURNITURE, BEDS, &c. (in about 170 lots).

Catalogues may be had on the premises, of the auctioneer, Witney, and at the inns in the neighbourhood.

N.B. The House to be Let, with immediate possession.'

Oxford Journal – Saturday 21 March 1863
'WITNEY STEEPLE CHASES. KING'S ARMS INN. VISITORS to these Races are respectfully informed there is every accommodation to be had at the above Inn. Private Sitting, Dining, and Bed Rooms. Excellent Stabling, Loose Boxes, &c. First-rate Wines and Spirits, Ales, &c. A DINNER will be provided at the close of the Races. THOMAS WELLS, *Proprietor.*'

Oxford Journal – Saturday 29 August 1863
'KING'S ARMS INN, WITNEY. Excellent HOUSEHOLD FURNITURE, and the remaining portion of the Stock of WINE, SPIRITS, BEER, &c., TO BE SOLD BY AUCTION, By Mr. LONG, On the premises at the King's Arms, Witney, on Wednesday the 9th of September, at Twelve o'clock, the property of Mr. Smith, who is retiring from business; the Stock comprises port and sherry wines, British wines, brandy, rum, gin, and other liqueurs, and about 100 gallons of sound home-brewed ale; the capital Furniture includes mahogany, dining, Pembroke, and other tables, Windsor and cane-seat chairs, bagatelle board and stand and marking board, a few prints and paintings, china dinner and tea services, hair sofa in mahogany frame, chimney and pier glasses, several wine and liquor casks; also four-post, tent, and other bedsteads, eight feather beds, flock mattresses and bedding, chests of drawers, wash stands and ware, swing dressing glasses, carpets, &c.; also kitchen utensils and a variety of other articles, all nearly new. Catalogues may be had at the place of sale, and of the auctioneer, Witney.'

Oxford Times – Saturday 03 March 1866
'PETTY SESSIONS, March 1. ALEHOUSE LICENCES.- At this special session the following transfers were made:- ... and Wm. Hollis to James Thomas Luckett, the King's Arms, Witney.'

Oxford Journal – Saturday 07 March 1868

'NISI PRIUS COURT. – MONDAY. (Before Mr. Justice Keating.) His Lordship took his seat on the bench at ten o'clock. LONG V. LINDSAY. The action was brought to recover possession of some goods seized by the defendant.

Mr. Huddlestone, Q.C., in stating the case to the Jury, said the real object of the action was to obtain distribution of the goods of a bankrupt amongst the general body of his creditors, and to prevent his brother-in-law appropriating them to himself. In the year 1865, James Thomas Luckett, who was a painter and glazier, became the landlord of the King's Arms, Witney, which he rented from Mr. Long, brewer, who supplied him with beer. Luckett, however, got into difficulties, and on the 14th of November 1867, he was made bankrupt, on his own petition, and the plaintiff was appointed assignee. On the 27th of December a brother-in-law of the bankrupt, named Lindsay, seized the whole of the goods of Luckett for a debt of £100, and the question for the Jury to decide was whether this was a *bona fide* transaction, or whether it was a voluntary preference and friendly arrangement between Luckett and his brother-in-law for the purpose of defrauding the whole body of creditors.

... The Jury found a verdict for the plaintiff. Leave was given to move the Court above on a point of law.'

Oxford Times – Saturday 28 February 1880

'KING'S ARMS ANNUAL SUPPER. – On Tuesday evening last the supper annually held at the King's Arms Inn took place as usual. Mr. and Mrs. Winslett put a substantial bill of fare, well served, before the company, and under the presidency of Mr. John Coles several hours of pleasant social intercourse were passed.'

Witney Gazette and West Oxfordshire Advertiser – Saturday 14 June 1884

'"KING'S ARMS" INN, High Street, WITNEY, OXON. MESSRS. JOHN & WILLIAM SCROGGS have received instructions from Mr. W. M. Banwell, who is leaving, (in consequence of ill-health). TO SELL BY AUCTION, on Monday, June 23rd, on the above-named premises, the Neat, Clean, and Modern HOUSEHOLD FURNITURE, ...'

Faringdon Advertiser and Vale of the White Horse Gazette – Saturday 31 March 1888

'Found Drowned – On Tuesday morning, the body of a man named William Bussell, was found in the River Windrush, near Witney Mills. An inquest was held in the evening, at the King's Arms Inn, and from the evidence given by deceased's wife and others, it appears that deceased had not been in good health lately, and had been in low spirits. He ate no breakfast on Tuesday morning, but went for walk. He was seen going towards the mill, and later on his body was found in the river. The jury returned a verdict of 'Found drowned."

Witney Gazette and West Oxfordshire Advertiser – Saturday 03 April 1909

'WITNEY AMATEUR ATHLETIC SPORTS, Horse, Galloway and Pony Races, Driving Competition and Bicycle Races, EASTER MONDAY, APRIL 12th,

1909. SPORTS TO COMMENCE AT 1-15. TWO SILVER CUPS AND £65 IN PRIZES. For Special Railway Arrangements see posters and Company's bills, and for Particulars and Entry Forms apply to-. H. H. HINTON and F. MOORE, Hon. Secs. "King's Arms," 106, High Street, Witney.'

Faringdon Advertiser and Vale of the White Horse Gazette – Saturday 27 May 1916
'PETTY SESSIONS, May 18th. LICENSING. A holdover of the license of the King's Arms Hotel, Witney, was transferred from the late Thomas Haines to his widow.'

Faringdon Advertiser and Vale of the White Horse Gazette – Saturday 30 September 1916
'PETTY SESSIONS, Thursday, SEPT. 21st. LICENSING. The license of the King's Arms Hotel, Witney, was transferred to J. W. Staines.'

Faringdon Advertiser and Vale of the White Horse Gazette – Saturday 23 November 1918
'PETTY SESSIONS, Thursday. LICENSING. The license of the "Jolly Sportsman," Eynsham, was transferred to G. B. Jennings, and that of the "King's Arms," Witney, to Arthur Clayson.'

Licensees:

1761–1782	Richard Reeves
1785–1799	Thomas Marriott
1800	John Smith
1801–1808	John Hewer
1809	Patience Hewer
1810–1821	John Pain
1822–1841	Joan Payne
	Age 60 (1841 Census)
1840	Public House Outbuildings Garden Yard &c. owned by Joan Payne
1841	Joan Payne died in December aged 61
1841	King's Arms was to be sold by auction in December
1842–1844	Charlotte Payne
1847–1854	John Bowerman
	Age 45, born in Great Milton, Oxon. Wife Sarah age 44 (1851 Census)
1859	The King's Arms was to let in August
1861–1863	Thomas Smith
	Age 49, born in Oxhill, Warks. Wife Emlin age 47 (1861 Census)
1864–1865	William Hollis
1866–1867	James Thomas Luckett
1868	James Luckett was bankrupt in March
1869–1879	Charles Winslet
	Age 35, born in Richmond, Surrey. Wife Jane age 35 (1871 Census)
1883–1884	William Martin Banwell
1887–1899	Thomas Hinton
	Age 53, born in Eynsham, Oxon. Wife Ellen age 53 (1891 Census)
1900	Thomas Hinton died at the beginning of the year age 62
1900–1910	Ellen Hinton (Mrs.)
	Age 63, born in Shipton on Stour, Glos. Widow (1901 Census)
1911–1915	Thomas Haynes
	Age 52, born in Stanton Harcourt, Oxon. Wife Laura age 43 (1911 Census)

1916	Haynes Thomas of 106 High-street Witney Oxfordshire licensed victualler died 14 May 1916 Probate Oxford 14 June to Laura Haynes widow. Effects £26103 9s 4d.
1916	Mrs. Haines
1916–1918	James William Staines
1919–1920	Arthur Henry Clayson
1925	Owned by Clinch & Co
1924–1941	John Morgan DOB 17 Feb 1857 Publican. Widower. (1939 Register)
1942	John Morgan died in March age 85
1941–1955	Ivy Annie Ashton Pub closed

King's Head (Blackmore's Head), 74 High St (1753–1924)

(Currently an Indian Restaurant)
(1840 Tithe Awards Map ref 800)

From the newspapers:

Oxford Journal – Saturday 08 January 1757
'LOST, ... Whoever will bring the same, either to the Publishers of this Journal, or to the Blackmore's-Head in Witney, shall receive Half a Guinea reward.'

Oxford Journal – Saturday 13 June 1767
'TO be LETT, and entered upon at Michaelmas next or sooner if required, now upon a Lease for nine Years certain, of which Term seven Years were unexpired at Lady-Day last- The BLACKMORE's HEAD in Witney, in the County of Oxford, being an old established and well accustomed Inn; situate and being on the great Road from London to Gloucester, Hereford, Monmouth and Wales; together with a Piece of inclosed Meadow Ground thereto adjoining, and a Piece of Meadow Ground inclosed lying near the said Inn; with Stabling, Lofts, Warehouses, Granaries, Brewhouse, and every Thing necessary and commodious adjoining to the said Inn: – For further Particulars enquire of Mr. Henry Townsend, now living on the Premises.'

Oxford Journal – Saturday 11 April 1772
'WILLIAM GEARING, from the King's-Head Inn, in the Corn-Market, Oxford, humbly begs Leave to inform his Friends and the Public, that he is removed to the King's-Head Inn, near the Bridge, at WITNEY, (formerly the Black's-Head) where all those who are so obliging as to honour him with their Company, may be assured of meeting with civil Treatment, and the best Accommodations of every Kind: The House is now fitted up with the utmost Dispatch, in order to render it in every Way commodious for their Reception, by their most obliged Servant, W. GEARING.'

Oxford Journal – Saturday 21 May 1774
'Witney, Oxford, Thame, *and* Aylesbury FLY, (By Way of Tring, Berkhamstead, and Watford) WILL continue flying from the King's Head Inn at Witney, every Monday, Wednesday, and Friday Morning, at Four o'clock, to the Swan and Two Necks, in Lad-lane, London: Returns from London every Tuesday, Thursday, and

Saturday Morning at Six o'clock. Calls at Jenkins's Green Man and Still in Oxford-Street, both in going up and coming down...'

Stamford Mercury – Thursday 18 March 1779

'WILLIAM BARNETT, at the King's Head Inn in Witney, Oxfordshire, hath fitted up large and convenient Warehouses for the Reception of Wools to be sold per Commission, in which Business he will pay the strictest Attention to the Interest of his Employers: And as a further Recommendation, he is promised the Assistance of a Person of Judgment and Property, who is desirous to establish a Wool Market at said Inn; where Nobility, Gentry, Tradesmen, and Public in general, may depend on meeting with the best Accommodations of every Kind, from their humble Servant, WILLIAM BARNETT. Post-Chaise and able horses.'

Oxford Journal – Saturday 18 May 1805

'TO be SOLD by AUCTION, on Tuesday the 4th Day of June, 1805, if not before disposed of by Private Contract, of which Notice will be given, - that Old-established PUBLIC HOUSE, called the King's Head, in the High Street, Witney, in the County of Oxford, now in the Occupation of JOHN SHORTER, with every Convenience suitable to the Business. For further Particulars enquire of Mr. Attwood, Solicitor, Ensham; or of Wm. Smith, at the Crown Inn, Witney aforesaid.'

Oxford Chronicle and Reading Gazette – Saturday 07 April 1838

'On Friday the 30th ult. died, much respected, Mr. Henry East, landlord of the King's Head Inn, aged 35.'

Oxford Chronicle and Reading Gazette – Saturday 10 February 1866

'PIGEON SHOOTING,- The King's Head annual pigeon shooting match for sweepstakes came off Tuesday last in Mr. Marriott's close, the day was very windy and the shooting was consequently not so good as it otherwise would have been. After the day's sport the party adjourned to the above inn and dined together, when a very pleasant evening was spent.'

Oxford Journal – Saturday 04 April 1868

'DIED. March 29, Harriett, wife of Mr. Dale, of the King's Head, High-street, Witney, aged 43 years.'

Oxford Journal – Saturday 17 April 1869

'Married. – April 14, at St. Mary's Church, Witney, Mr. Dale, of the King's Head Inn, to Elizabeth, daughter of the late Mr. W. Berry, fellmonger, Witney.'

Oxford Journal – Saturday 15 January 1870

'BIRTHS. – Jan. 9, the wife of Mr. Dale, of the King's Head Inn, High-street, of a daughter.'

Oxford Times – Saturday 12 April 1873

'Inquest. – An inquest was held at the King's Head Inn, on the 7th inst, on the body of Elizabeth Holland, Witney, widow, aged 72. – Mr. Rawle, surgeon, gave it as his opinion that the deceased died from concussion of the brain. – Verdict accordingly.'

Oxford Journal – Saturday 19 January 1878
'RETIRING SUPPER.-A supper was given to his old customers on Friday evening by Mr. Dale, on his retirement from the King's Head Inn, the business of which he has carried on during the last quarter of a century. The proceedings were of the most harmonious and friendly character, and Mr. Dale was highly complimented for the manner in which he had conducted the house for so many years, Mr. George Shepherd succeeds him...'

Oxford Times – Saturday 22 June 1878
'PETTY SESSIONS – JUNE 20th. Stephen Batts, minister, was charged with refusing to quit the King's Head, Witney, when requested. – Fined £3 1s. 6d.'

Faringdon Advertiser and Vale of the White Horse Gazette – Saturday 06 October 1906
'PETTY SESSIONS, Thursday. LICENSING. Holdovers of the following licenses were granted; ... "King's Head," Witney, from T. Dale to J. Robbins; ...'

Faringdon Advertiser and Vale of the White Horse Gazette – Saturday 13 May 1911
'PETTY SESSIONS, Thursday. LICENSING. ...and a holdover of the license of the "King's Head," Witney, was granted from Charles Leonard Puryer to John Edward Rogers, of Adderbury.'

Faringdon Advertiser and Vale of the White Horse Gazette – Saturday 18 March 1916
'PETTY SESSIONS, Thursday. TRANFERS. The following licenses were transferred:- ... "King's Head," Witney, from John Edward Rogers to John Davis; ...'

Licensees:

1753–1772	William Smith
1767	The Blackmore's Head was to let in June
1772–1778	William Gearing
1779	William Barnett
1788–1802	Joseph Bolton
1804–1805	John Shorter
1805	The King's Head was to be sold by auction in May
1806–1808	Mary Smith
1809–1810	William Smith
1811–1812	John Millett
1814	John William Clinch
1821–1830	Thomas Causby
1832–1838	Henry East
1838	Henry East died in March aged 35
1838–1844	Hannah East
	Age 45 (1841 Census)
1840	Public House Garden &c. owned by John Williams Clinch
1847–1850	John Simmonds
1851–1854	Ann Simmonds
	Age 64, born in Crawley, Oxon. Widow (1851 Census)

1855–1906	Thomas Dale
	Age 31, born in Middleton Stoney, Oxon. Wife Harriet age 36 (1861 Census)
1868	Harriett Dale died in January aged 43
1869	Thomas Dale married Elizabeth Berry in April
	Age 41, born in Middleton Stoney, Oxon. Wife Elizabeth age 25 (1871 Census)
1877	Elizabeth Dale died in October aged 32
	Age 51, born in Middleton Stoney, Oxon. Widower (1881 Census)
	Age 61, born in Middleton Stoney, Oxon. Widower (1891 Census)
	Age 71, born in Stoney Middleton, Oxon. Widower (1901 Census)
1907	J. Robbins
1911	Charles Leonard Puryer
	Age 42, born in Stantonbury, Bucks. Army Pensioner. Wife Sarah age 40. (1911 Census)
1913–1915	John Edward Rogers
1916	John Davis
1918–1924	William Charles Bull

New Inn, 101 High St (1840–1877)

(Currently Retail Premises)
(1840 Tithe Awards Map ref 542)

From the newspapers:

Oxford Chronicle and Reading Gazette – Saturday 28 July 1860
'JUSTICE ROOM, July 26. John Cripps, publican, Cross Keys, Witney, was charged with assaulting Eliza Rouse, of the New Inn, Witney, on the 19th inst. Fined 5s., and costs 17s.; in default to be committed for 7 days. Paid.'

Oxford Chronicle and Reading Gazette – Saturday 31 October 1863
'DIED. – On the 16th inst., at Harrow Road, Paddington, Mary, wife of Mr. R. Brown, and sister to Mr. C. Rouse, of the New Inn, Witney.'

Oxford Chronicle and Reading Gazette – Saturday 02 September 1865
'MARRIED. August 27, at Burford, Charles, eldest son of Mr. C. Rouse, New Inn, Witney, to Amelia, only daughter of Thos. Johnson, upholsterer, London.'

Oxford Chronicle and Reading Gazette – Saturday 28 September 1867
'MARRIED. - On the 23rd inst. at St. Saviour's Church, in the parish of St. George, Hanover-square, Pimlico, London by the Rev. R. Robson, Mr. Joseph Shorter, upholsterer, West End, Witney, to Eliza, eldest daughter Mr C. Rouse, of the New Inn Witney.'

Oxford Chronicle and Reading Gazette – Saturday 01 May 1869
'ACCIDENT. – Mr. Charles Rouse, jun., of the New Inn, Witney, met with a serious accident in coming from Hailey on Wednesday last. His horse shyed and came in contact with Mr. Smith's (grocer) heavy cart, which turned the lighter vehicle over with great force, precipitating Mr. Rouse and the ostler who accompanied him to

the ground with great force, and the horse freeing himself from the trap galloped towards home. Mr. Rouse is dangerously hurt internally and the ostler very much bruised. E. Hyde, Esq., surgeon, was quickly on the spot, and the sufferers were at once conveyed home in a fly.'

Oxford Journal – Saturday 21 October 1876
'THE NEW INN, WITNEY. HOUSEHOLD FURNITURE, Brewing Plant, Casks, and numerous Effects, and a nearly-new Marquee. TO BE SOLD BY AUCTION, By Mr. LONG, On the premises at the New Inn, High-street, Witney, on Tuesday, Oct. 31st, 1876, at Eleven o'clock, by order of Mr. Charles Rouse, who is retiring from business; comprising a brewing plant, casks of various sizes (from nine gallons to 250 gallons), malt crusher, chaff machine, and bean mill.

The Furniture includes 8 four-post, French, and other bedsteads, flock mattresses, flock & feather beds, blankets, quilts, Chairs, washstands, dressing tables and glasses, a set of mahogany dining tables with circular ends, very superior Windsor chairs, a bagatelle board, a marquee in very excellent condition (38 feet by 18 feet), the effects of the bar, tap room, kitchen, &c., &c.'

Licensees:

1840	Thomas Sylvester
1840	Public House owned by James Clinch
1851	John Weaving
1860	John Cripps
1861–1876	Charles Rouse
	Age 42, born in Chipping Norton, Oxon. Wife Harriet age 43 (1861 Census)
	Age 52, born in Chipping Norton, Oxon. Wife Harriett age 55 (1871 Census)
1876	Charles Rouse retired from business and The New Inn was to be sold by auction in October
1877	Frederick Stead

Plough (Plough & Shuttle, Ball), 98 High St (1800–present)

(Currently trading, owned by Admiral Taverns Ltd)
(1840 Tithe Awards Map ref 782)

From the newspapers:

Oxford Journal – Saturday 15 March 1800
'TO be SOLD by AUCTION, By GEORGE WILKINSON, On the Premises, at Four o'Clock in the Afternoon, on Friday next the 21st of March, 1800, -That old accustomed PUBLIC HOUSE, the Sign of the BALL, situate on the East-Side of the Street, adjoining to the Blanket Hall, in the Town of Witney, Oxfordshire, and in the Occupation of Mr. THOMAS WELLS, as Yearly Tenant. The above comprises a good House, Cellars, a Brew-House, Stable, Yard, Garden, and other Appurtenances.- May be viewed at any Time between this and the Day of Sale, by applying to Mr. Wells the Tenant, or the Auctioneer, Witney.'

Oxford University and City Herald – Saturday 25 June 1814
'TO BE SOLD BY AUCTION, By Mr. JOHN LUCKETT, At the Crown Inn, Witney, at Four o'clock in the Afternoon, on THURSDAY, the 14th of JULY, under such conditions as shall be then and there produced, ... Also, the PLOUGH and SHUTTLE PUBLIC HOUSE, the particulars of which will appear in the next week's Paper. Immediate possession may be had.'

Oxford University and City Herald – Saturday 02 July 1814
'FREEHOLD ESTATES, BLANKET MANUFACTORY, &c. TO BE SOLD BY AUCTION, By Mr. JOHN LUCKETT, At the Crown Inn. Witney, on THURSDAY, the 14th day of JULY instant, between the hours of Three and Five in the Afternoon, under conditions of sale then to be produced, SEVERAL Valuable FREEHOLD ESTATES situate in Witney aforesaid, in the following lots: ...

Lot 4. – All that other well-accustomed and long-established Inn and Public House, now called the Plough and Shuttle, situate in the centre of the High-street, in Witney; comprising kitchen in front, 16 feet by 13, and parlour, 17 feet by 11½, a back parlour, 13½ feet by 9, and excellent cellar, 32 feet by 10½, with three good bed rooms in front, and attics over the same, and capital new built dining room, 33 feet by 14½, stabling for eight horses, brew-house, pigsties, and other convenient out-offices, with a spacious yard, garden, and orchard behind, extending to the River Windrush with the Fishery therein, and the advantage of a river to any business requiring the use of a running stream.

Immediate possession may be had of the two public-houses; and early possession of the other lots. For further particulars apply to Mr. C. Leake, or the Auctioneer, Witney.'

Oxford Chronicle and Reading Gazette – Saturday 26 October 1844
'DIED. On the 23rd inst., Mr. Thomas Collier, of the Plough Inn, Witney.'

Oxford Chronicle and Reading Gazette – Saturday 01 March 1845
'TO be LET, and entered on immediately, - The old-established House, the PLOUGH INN, Witney, with a capital Business, in the occupation of Mr. S. Collier, who is declining business on account of ill health.'

Oxford Journal – Saturday 02 October 1852
'BAMPTON EAST DIVISION. – Witney, Thursday. Oct. 30. Thos. Nevill, of the Plough Inn, Witney, was charged by Chas. White, constable, with keeping a disorderly house, several parties fighting and creating disturbances; fined, with costs, 4*l*. 3s. 6d.'

Wilts and Gloucestershire Standard – Saturday 02 September 1882
'DEATHS. Aug. 24, at Coombe, William John, son of Mr. Joseph Moss, of the Plough Inn, Witney.'

Oxford Journal – Saturday 19 January 1889
'WITNEY AND FIELD ASSARTS, OXON. JOHN HABGOOD & SON HAVE received instructions to SELL by AUCTION, at the Marlborough Hotel, Witney,

on Tuesday, January 22nd, 1889, at Five for Six o'clock in the evening,- Valuable Freehold Property, CONSISTING OF A DWELLING HOUSE and GARDEN, on Church Green, Witney: A FULLY-LICENSED PUBLIC HOUSE, known as a "The Plough," situate in High-street, Witney: A DWELLING HOUSE and GARDEN, known as "Rook House," situate in Witney; and A Fully-licensed PUBLIC HOUSE, known as "The Royal Oak," situate at Field Assarts. Further particulars of N. G. Ravenor, Esq., Solicitor, Witney, or of the Auctioneers, Witney, Oxon, and Faringdon, Berks.'

Oxford Times – Saturday 08 August 1903
'LOCAL LIQUIDATION CASES. Re William Hastings. – The debtor, of the Plough Inn, Witney, lately resided and carried on business as a grocer at 127, Cowley-road, Oxford. ...'

Faringdon Advertiser and Vale of the White Horse Gazette – Saturday 26 October 1918
'PETTY SESSIONS, Thursday. HIGHWAY OFFENCE. John Butler, beer-house keeper, of Hardwick, was summoned for leaving a horse and trap outside the "Plough Inn," High Street, Witney, for 35 minutes on Sept. 25th. P.C. Skidmore gave evidence and defendant pleaded guilty saying he was letting the horse have a rest and some food as he had a long journey of over 30 miles. – Fined 2s 6d.'

Licensees:

1800	Thomas Wells
1800	The Ball is for sale by auction in March
1811	John Wright
1812	William Barnes
1814	Plough & Shuttle was to be sold by auction in July
1814–1816	John Alsop
1819–1830	John Spackman
1839–1844	Thomas Collier
	Age 45, wife Mary age 45 (1841 Census)
1840	Public House Garden &c. owned by John Williams Clinch
1844	Thomas Collier died in October
1845	Mr. S. Collier
1845	Plough was to let in March
1847–1854	Thomas Nevill
	Age 48, born in Witney, Oxon. Wife Esther age 40 (1851 Census)
1855–1869	James Crosswell
	Age 39, born in Witney, Oxon. Wife Priscilla age 39 (1861 Census)
1874–1877	James Prior
1882–1887	Joseph Moss
1889	The Plough is for sale by auction in January
1891–1895	Job Fowler
	Age 38, born in Witney, Oxon. Wife Emma age 33 (1891 Census)
1899–1904	George Thomas Martin
	Age 35, born in Standlake, Oxon. Brewer's Labourer. Wife Lizzie age 31. (1901 Census)

1905–1913	William Hastings
	Age 42, born in Knighton, Radnorshire. Chemist Assistant. Wife Katie Maud age 38. (1911 Census)
1914–1926	Albert Woodbridge
1925	Owned by Clinch & Co
1927	Albert Woodbridge died in March age 68
1927–1928	Hanna Louisa Woodbridge (Mrs.)
1929–1931	Vincent William Ball
1932–1966	Albert William Scarrott
	DOB 18 Jun 1892 Licensed Victualler. Wife Florence dob 7 Jun 1899 Unpaid Domestic Duties (1939 Register)
1967–1969	Florence M. Scarrott
1971	Edmund J. F. Challis
1972–1979	Victor T. Stroud
1980	Vincent H. Parkinson
2005	Pub owned by Admiral Taverns
2005	Paul Roberts
2006	Michael Oates
2007–2010	Guy Ripley
2011	Robert O'Connell
2012	Craig Graddon
2013	Jessica De La Hunty
2014	Nicholas Knott
2015	Daniel Stares
2016–present	Samuel Jenkins

Prince of Wales, 63 High St (1851–1969)

(Currently a Letting Agency)

Licensees:

1851–1863	Robert Nevill
	Age 35, born in Oxford, Oxon. Wife Martha age 32 (1851 Census)
	Age 45, born in Oxford, Oxon. Wife Martha age 43 (1861 Census)
1864–1868	Thomas Fowler
1869	William Miles
1874–1883	George Baker
	Age 34, born in Witney, Oxon. Wife Elizabeth age 32 (1881 Census)
1891–1913	Charles Wright
	Age 30, born in Witney, Oxon. Wife Eleanor age 36 (1891 Census)
	Age 40, born in Witney, Oxon. Wife Eleanor age 46 (1901 Census)
	Age 50, born in Witney, Oxon. Wife Eleanor age 56 (1911 Census)
1913	Charles Wright died age 52
1914–1915	Eleanor Wright (Mrs.)
1916	Eleanor Wright died in June 1916 age 61
1916–1920	Charles William Wright
1921	Charles Wright died in June age 37
	Owned by Clinch & Co
1921–1945	Emily Wright (Mrs.)
	DOB 18 Jun 1882 Landlady of Public House. Widowed (1939 Register)

1946–1954	Charles Frederick Wright
1955–1960	Robert Frederick Townsend
1961–1969	Nicholas Frederick State

Queen's Head, 10 High St (1753–1779)

(Currently Retail Premises)

Licensees:

1753–1771	Josiah Cowell
1772	Buried on 19 May 1772
1772–1776	Mary Cowell
1777	Buried on 6 May 1777
1777–1779	Josiah Cowell

Royal Oak, 17 High St (1753–present)

(Currently trading, Free House)
(1840 Tithe Awards Map ref 458)

From the newspapers:

Oxford Journal – Saturday 28 September 1771
'TO be SOLD by AUCTION, on Saturday the 5th Day of October, 1771, on the Premises ; – A large commodious PUBLICK HOUSE, with a good Close, Garden, Stable, Brewhouse, a small Tenement, and other Out-Buildings adjoining, known by the Sign of The ROYAL OAK; now in the Occupation of Mr. Edney, and well situated in the Market Place, at Witney, in the County of Oxford.

Particulars may be had by applying to Mr. Woods, of Witney, and the present Tenant will shew the Premises.'

Oxford Journal – Saturday 16 January 1836
'To Innkeepers, Publicans, Maltsters, Coal Merchants, Carriers, and others. Valuable Freehold Public Houses, (in full trade,) MALT-HOUSE, Close of fine MEADOW LAND, and other desirable FREEHOLD PROPERTY, and BUSINESS PREMISES, IN WITNEY, OXFORDSHIRE, TO BE SOLD BY AUCTION, By Mr. WILIKINSON, At the Marlborough Arms Inn, Witney, on Wednesday the 10th of February, 1836, at Five o'clock in the afternoon...

Lot 5.-The well-known & desirable PUBLIC HOUSE, called the Royal Oak, situate on the west side of the High-street, in Witney aforesaid, now in the occupation of Mr. Emanuel Lambourne, and carrying on a brisk and thriving trade; with a convenient range of cellarage, and club room over; coal shed, stabling, yard, pigstys, &c.

The Premises may be viewed on application to the respective tenants ; and particulars had of Mr. Charles Henderson, solicitor, Witney; of Mr. Thomas Jones, Fairford, Gloucestershire; of the auctioneer, Witney; and at the principal Inns in Witney, Burford, Chipping-Norton, Woodstock, Ensham, &c.'

Oxford Chronicle and Reading Gazette – Saturday 24 June 1837
'DEATHS. On the 8th inst. Mrs. Fidler, late of the Royal Oak, Witney.'

Oxford Chronicle and Reading Gazette – Saturday 19 April 1845
'DIED. – April 6, aged 64, Mr. Emanuel Lambourne, many years landlord of the Royal Oak, Witney.'

Oxford Chronicle and Reading Gazette – Saturday 17 July 1847
'Oxfordshire Summer Assizes. ... William Lambourn, who keeps the Royal Oak at Witney. He deposed that the prisoner came into his house at half-past eight in the evening in question, and did not leave it till the constable came and took him away. ...'

Oxford Chronicle and Reading Gazette – Saturday 10 October 1868
'SUDDEN DEATH. – On Sunday morning, Mr. G. Heydon, innkeeper and mail contractor, of the Royal Oak Inn, Witney, was found dead in his bed. Deceased was in Oxford in his usual health on Saturday, but he was subject to disease of the heart.'

Witney Gazette and West Oxfordshire Advertiser – Saturday 11 December 1886
'DRUNKENNESS. John Jackson, Junr., of Witney, was charged with being drunk and disorderly at Witney, on the 14th December. Defendant pleaded guilty. P.C. Simmons deposed that he was on duty in the High Street, at about 10-30 p.m. on the 14th, when defendant came up the Street very drunk, and when he got to witness he began blackguarding him. Witness advised him to go home, but he went into the "Royal Oak," where they refused to serve him; he used very bad language. Fines including costs, 15s. Paid.'

Witney Gazette and West Oxfordshire Advertiser – Saturday 13 July 1889
'The "Royal Oak" Inn, HIGH STREET, WITNEY. TO BE SOLD BY AUCTION BY RICHARD GILLETT, On Friday, July 26th, 1889, at 12 for 1 o'clock, on the premises, by order of Mr. John Simpson, who is leaving, the HOUSEHOLD FURNITURE, and effects, ...'

Witney Gazette and West Oxfordshire Advertiser – Saturday 05 May 1900
'DEATHS. BROOKS – May 1st, at the "Royal Oak" Inn, High Street, Witney, Thomas Brooks, aged 68 years.'

Witney Gazette and West Oxfordshire Advertiser – Saturday 09 June 1900
'PETTY SESSIONS, Thursday. TRANSFERS. An application for the transfer of the license of the "Royal Oak," Witney, from the late Thomas Brooks to Ann Brooks, his widow, was granted.'

Faringdon Advertiser and Vale of the White Horse Gazette – Saturday 31 August 1901
'LICENSING. ... and the licence of the "Royal Oak," Witney, was transferred from Ann Brooks to J. C. Weller.'

Witney Gazette and West Oxfordshire Advertiser – Saturday 28 November 1903
'FOUND. – November 19th, at Witney. A PIG. If not claimed within 7 days will be sold to pay expenses. J. Weller, Royal Oak, Witney.'

Oxford Times – Saturday 24 September 1904
'At the petty sessions on Thursday the jury lists for various parishes were allowed and holdover licences were granted as follows:- "Royal Oak," Witney, from Joseph Weller to William C. Moss; ...'

Faringdon Advertiser and Vale of the White Horse Gazette – Saturday 28 February 1914
'PETTY SESSIONS, Thursday. CASE DISMISSED. William Moss, Royal Oak Beerhouse, High Street, Witney, was summoned for permitting drunkenness to take place upon his licensed premises on Jan. 23rd, contrary to section 75 of the Licensing Act, 1910. – The case arose out of proceedings taken at a recent Court, in which an old man named Henry Mumford, was ordered to pay 7s. costs for being found drunk outside the Royal Oak public house. – Mr Andrew Walsh appeared for the defence, and the case was eventually dismissed, at the same time stating the police had acted quite rightly in the case which they regarded as suspicious.'

Licensees:

1753–1769	Richard Edney
1770–1772	Samuel Edney
1771	Royal Oak was to be sold by auction in September
1772–1781	Thomas Fowler
1811–1818	William Fidler
1819–1845	Emmanuel Lambourne
	Age 55 (1841 Census)
1836	Royal Oak was to be sold by auction in February
1840	Public House Yard &c. owned by Francis Spenlove
1841	Francis Spendlove died 02 Jan, intestate
1842	Mary Spendlove buys the Royal Oak for £225 on 11 March
1845	Emmanuel Lambourne died in April aged 64
1847	William Lambourn
1852	James Pratley
1853–1854	William Cox
1864–1868	George Heydon
1868	George Heydon died in October
1881	William Simpson
	Age 48, born in Witney, Oxon. Widower (1881 Census)
1882	William Simpson died in London and leaves the Royal Oak to his brother John
1888	12 Jan. John Simpson 'mason & Innkeeper' sells for £300 to Mary Ann Stone, Dressmaker, of High St., Witney
1895	Royal Oak now in occupation Wm. Clinch & Co
1891–1900	Thomas Brooks
	Age 59, born in Coggs, Oxon. Wife Ann age 50 (1891 Census)
1900	Thomas Brooks died aged 68 in May
1900–1901	Ann Brooks
	Age 60, born in Northleigh, Oxon. Widow (1901 Census)
1901–1904	Joseph Churchill Weller
1910	Mary Ann Stone sells to Clinch & Co for £1,000

1905–1928	William Chester Moss
	Age 52, born in Witney, Oxon. Wife Ellen age 51 (1911 Census)
1925	Owned by Clinch & Co
1929–1940	Francis Theodore Smith
	DOB 20 Nov 1887 Bricklayer & Publican. Wife Elsie dob 14 Mar 1889 Publican's Wife (1939 Register)
1940	Francis Smith died age 52
1941–1951	Elsie Smith
1952–1956	Cyril James Garner
1957	Kenneth Alfonso Calcutt
1958	Raymond George Hicks
1959–1963	William Thomas Thornton
1963	31 Dec. Clinch & Co sell to Courages at valuation £5,250
1964–1965	John J. Doyle
1966–1968	Douglas W. Marsh
1969–1971	Robert N. Tarr
1972–1974	Charles B. Lumsden
1975–1979	Lionel De Ternant
1980	Christopher D. Hitchen or Royston S. N. Randall
1985–1999	Brian Simpson
2000–present	Dean & Leslie Semaine

Market Square

Angel (Greyhound), 42 Market Sq (1753–present)

(Currently trading, Free House)
(1840 Tithe Awards Map ref 50)

'Situated in a prime position on the market square in Witney, the Angel began life as a barber's shop. In the latter part of the seventeenth century the barber, Thomas Heming, leased part of his premises to Richard Lock to run as an Alehouse, at that time known as the Greyhound. By the end of the century Charles Green of Ducklington owned the Greyhound, which now comprised the entire premises. In 1707, his widow Margery agreed to sell an interest in the pub to Robert and William Collier to hold in trust for their nephew William Constable. When Constable attained his majority in 1712 he sold back his interest and the tavern remained in the hands of the Green family until 1795 when it was sold to John Gethyn, a wealthy saddler who owned the house next door. Gethyn's executors included John Clinch, the banker who founded the family's fortune in Witney. In 1809, the Greyhound was sold to Joseph Masters, who changed the name to the Angel Tavern. He became a substantial figure in Witney in the early part of the century, since he also ran Staple Hall, a major coaching inn, from 1812, and ended his life as Witney postmaster. In 1840 he sold the freehold to George Cooper, a maltster, who himself left the tavern to his niece, Ann Walker, for her lifetime. When she died in 1858 the executors, who included Edward Early, blanket baron, offered the tavern for sale at public auction. It was bought by another member of the family, Joseph Early. The family had bought the old premises of the Witney Blanket Company, Blanket Hall, in 1852 and were in the process of setting up a brewery of that to which the Angel was added. For the remainder of the century the tavern came under the umbrella of the Blanket Hall Brewery, but in 1800 negotiations were under way to sell the whole concern to their main rivals, Clinch's Brewery. Thus the Angel became part of a group of over 70 pubs stretching from Swindon to Oxford, until 1962 when the brewery was taken over by Courage's.'
(Reproduced from a picture hanging in the pub.)

From the newspapers:

Oxford University and City Herald – Saturday 23 April 1842
'LOCAL INTELLIGENCE. On the 12th instant was married, at St. Paul's church, in this city *(Oxford, ed.)*, Mr. Warner, of the Angel Inn, Witney, to Mary, youngest daughter of Mr. Johnson, baker, of Hailey.'

Bell's Life in London and Sporting Chronicle – Sunday 21 April 1850
'EDWARD WELCH will run any man in Witney, or within six miles of the town, for from £2 to £5. Money ready at Mr. Smith's, Angel Inn, Witney.'

Oxford Chronicle and Reading Gazette – Saturday 10 July 1858
Refer to page 161 for full article for the sale of three Public Houses in Witney.

Oxford Times – Saturday 06 May 1865
'PETTY SESSIONS, May 4. ALEHOUSE LICENCES. – This being a special session for the transfer of victuallers' licences, the following transfers were made:- Elm Tree, Witney, Mark Knight to Henry Townsend; Waggon and Horses, Witney, Frederick Lyford to William Thornton; The Angel, Henry Paine to Charles Hitchman.'

Oxford Journal – Saturday 26 January 1878
'BAMPTON EAST DIVISION PETTY SESSIONS, January 17. Samuel Groves, of Hailey, was fined 11s., including costs, for being drunk at the Angel Inn, Witney, on the 4th inst.'

Faringdon Advertiser and Vale of the White Horse Gazette – Saturday 02 April 1904
'PETTY SESSIONS, Thursday, March 24th. LICENSING. ... and of the "Angel," Witney, from John Seacole to John Davis were also granted. ...'

Faringdon Advertiser and Vale of the White Horse Gazette – Saturday 29 September 1906
'PETTY SESSIONS, Thursday, Sept. 20th. MALICIOUS DAMAGE. Harry Wright, labourer, of no fixed abode, was summoned for assaulting George Maycock, at the Angel Inn, Witney, on the 10th inst., and further for maliciously damaging a window to the extent of 2s at the same time and place. – He did not appear, and was fined £1 in each case, or a month's hard labour.'

Faringdon Advertiser and Vale of the White Horse Gazette – Saturday 06 October 1906
'PETTY SESSIONS, Thursday. LICENSING. ... "Angel," Witney, from G. Maycock to C. J. Langston.'

Faringdon Advertiser and Vale of the White Horse Gazette – Saturday 26 October 1907
'PETTY SESSIONS, Thursday. LICENSING. A holdover of the license of the Angel Inn, Witney, was granted from John Davis to Charles Ernest Westall. ...'

Faringdon Advertiser and Vale of the White Horse Gazette – Saturday 07 May 1910
'PETTY SESSIONS, Thursday. HOLDOVER. A holdover of the license of the "Angel Inn," Witney, was granted from Arthur Smith to George Hudson.'

Faringdon Advertiser and Vale of the White Horse Gazette – Saturday 14 September 1912
'PETTY SESSIONS, Thursday. CHARGE AGAINST AN INNKEEPER. George Hudson, "Angel" Inn, Witney, was summoned for unlawfully permitting drunkenness to take place on his licensed premises called the "Angel" Inn, Witney, on August 10th. – Mr Andrew Walsh, of Oxford, appeared for the defence. – The case was dismissed.'

Faringdon Advertiser and Vale of the White Horse Gazette – Saturday 29 March 1913
'PETTY SESSIONS, Thursday. WILFUL DAMAGE AT WITNEY. Alfred David, described on the charge sheet as a fitter, but who now said he was on the way

to Swansea in search of work as a watch-maker, was charged with wilfully and maliciously damaging certain glass windows at the "Angel" Inn, Witney, on the 23rd inst., the property of George Hudson, to the amount of 6s.. – He pleaded guilty, and was discharged on promising to leave the town at once, having been in prison for five days.'

Licensees:

1753–1776	John Hunt
1777–1783	James Rudge
1796	Thomas Collier (at the Greyhound)
1808–1811	John Green
1809	The Greyhound was sold to Joseph Masters who changed its name to the Angel Tavern
1812	Stephen Brice
1814–1816	William Hollis
1830	William Harwood
1839	John Mourby
1840	Public House Outbuildings and Yard owned by Joseph Masters, who sells the freehold to George Cooper, a maltster
1842	Thomas Warner married Mary Johnson in April
1842–1844	Thomas Warner
1847	David Paish
1852–1858	James Smith
1858	The Angel was for sale by auction in July
1861–1864	Henry Payne
	Age 29, born in Oxford, Oxon. Wife Sarah age 23 (1861 Census)
1865–1876	Charles Hitchman
	Age 55, born in Witney, Oxon. Tailor. Wife Hannah age 51 (1871 Census)
1881–1883	James Busby
	Age 53, born in Curbridge, Oxon. Widower (1881 Census)
1887	George Baker
1891–1895	Alfred Rogers
	Age 37, born in Stow, Glos. Wife Maryan age 37 (1891 Census)
1899	Alexander Merritt
1902	Thomas Talbot
1903	John Seacole
1904	John Davis
1906	George Maycock
1907	Charles James Langstone
1910	Arthur Smith
1910–1925	George Hudson
	Age 60, born in Handborough, Oxon. Bootmaker. Wife Elizabeth age 56. (1911 Census)
1926	Edward James Merchant
1927–1933	Edward John Ealey
1934–1946	Richard Harold Walker
1947	Richard Walker died age 56
1947–1954	Gertrude May Walker
1955–1959	Harry Leslie Hyett

1960–1961	Harold Elliot
1962	Henry David Stewart
1963–1965	Peter Eric Turner
1966–1970	Leonard S. Parratt
1971–1975	Peter Goodnight
1976–1980	Thomas E. Crampton
1995	Eric Crampton died aged 71
1992	Pub bought by Steve Thompson & Diana Rose
1992–present	Steve Thompson & Diana Rose

Blue Boar (Marlborough Arms), 28 Market Sq
(1757–present)

(Currently trading, owned by Oakman Inns)
(1840 Tithe Awards Map ref 400)

From the newspapers:

Oxford Journal – Saturday 12 September 1778
'SEPTEMBER 12th, 1778. NOTICE is hereby given, That all Persons who have any Claim or Demand on the Estate or Effects of Henry Gadfield, late of Witney, in the County of Oxford, Victualler, deceased, are desired to send an immediate Account to Mrs. Gadfield, his Widow and Administratrix, or to Mr. Leake, in Witney, in order that the same may be discharged: And all those who are indebted to the said Estate, are requested to pay their respective Debts to Mrs. Gadfield or Mr. Leake, within one Month from the Date hereof, or they will be sued without further Notice.'

Oxford Journal – Saturday 31 May 1788
'To all Gentlemen and Ladies who are afflictted with the Gout and Rheumatism. MR. WILSON is now possest of Medicine which he purchased from an eminent Physician in Bath, who brought the same from the College of Physicians in Paris, in France, and has performed many capital Cures in Bath, several of which Mr. Wilson has seen and been with; and he has now such a Confidence in the Medicine, that he is willing to take any Person in the above Disorders under Hand no Cure no Pay, if a sufficient Number apply to pay him for his Time. He will undertake the Ague on the same Terms. All Letters directed to him at the Blue Boar, Witney, post paid, will be duly attended to. Apply immediately. ...'

Oxford Journal – Saturday 14 July 1792
'By Permission of the Worshipful the Mayor of Woodstock. For the BENEFIT of Mr. TURNER, of Oxford, ON Wednesday the 18th of July Instant, at the Town Hall, Woodstock, will be performed, A CONCERT of Vocal and Instrumental MUSICK. The principal Instrumental Performers are, Messrs. Buckingham, Weaver, Hatton, Shimmev, &c. Tickets to be had at Mr. Hatton's, Mr. Hardy's, and Mr. Firth's Musick Shops; and at Mr. Parr's, Mercer, in the High Street, Oxford; at Mr. Payne's, the King's Arms, Woodstock ; and at Mr. Trundle's, the Blue Boar, Witney. The Concert to begin at Seven o'Clock.'

Reading Mercury – Monday 02 February 1795
'OXFORD, Saturday, Jan. 31. On Wednesday last was married at Witney, Mr. Benjamin Trundell, of the Blue Boar Inn in that town, to Miss Martha Hopkins, late of Standlake in this county.'

Oxford Journal – Saturday 26 March 1796
'Minster and Hanborough Turnpike Gates. The Trustees appointed to put in Execution two several Acts of Parliament made for repairing the Road from the Top of Crickley Hill, in the County of Gloucester, to Campsfield, in the Parish of Kidlington, in this County of Oxford and also the Road from Campsfield to the Turnpike Road at or near Enslow Bridge, in the said County of Oxford, will meet on Tuesday the 12th Day of April next, at Eleven o'Clock in the Forenoon, at the House of Benjamin Trundell, called the Blue Boar, In Witney, in the said County of Oxford, and will then and there LETT by AUCTION to the Best Bidder, on his producing sufficient Sureties for Payment of the Rent, as shall be then and there required by the Trustees, from the 14th Day of May next, ...'

Oxford Journal – Saturday 28 September 1799
'TO be SOLD by AUCTION, By GEORGE WILKINSON, At the Blue Boar Inn, in Witney, in the County of Oxford, on Thursday the 10th Day of October, 1790, at Five o'Clock in the Afternoon, – A large convenient SASHED HOUSE, pleasantly situated on the Hill near the Market Place in Witney aforesaid, and an eligible Situation for a large Family, or any Trade; consisting of two large Cellars; two Shops in Front, three Rooms, two Kitchens, and a Brew-House, on the Ground Floor; seven Bed Rooms on the First Floor, with Closets; four Red Rooms on the Second Floor, and three Attics; a Stable, large Weaving Shop, and Lofts; also large Gardens and other Appurtenances, ...'

Cheltenham Chronicle – Thursday 11 June 1812
'WITNEY, OXON. To be LET, and entered upon at Midsummer next, A VERY desirable long-established INN in Witney, called the Marlborough Arms, (late Blue Boar) situated in the centre of the Market, now in the occupation of Mr. John Dolley, who is going to decline the Public Business on account of his ill state of health. The Stock and furniture may be taken at a fair appraisement. For further particulars and to treat for the same, apply Mr. Thos. Jones, Witney.'

Oxford Chronicle and Reading Gazette – Saturday 26 August 1837
'WITNEY, August 24. The arrangements for the great Tory gathering here last Friday were made by Messrs. James Gillett, of the Marlborough Arms, and Mr. Grace, of the Crown Inn, with considerable judgment. As to the party itself we should say it was but a *Blue go*. Instead of 300, which was first talked of, or 150, for whom tables were laid, only seventy sat down, including members friends, clergy, agents, sub-agents, and poll-clerks. Mr. Pickering of Wilcot, who presided certainly kept up the spirit and cheerfulness of the meeting, although we thought some of his observations on his political opponents unnecessarily severe. Mr. Parker, M. P. addressed the meeting in a style inferior only to that of Burke. We

anticipate great doings when he gets into the House. They say he will take his godmother Ashhurst with him. The Queen's health we hear was drunk in silence. We apprehend the Tories rather miscalculated their strength; many Reformers went with them in this election, entirely from erroneous impressions in the matter of religion and not from any particular relish for the principles of a party which on every other occasion they had opposed.'

Oxford Journal – Saturday 24 June 1843
'MARLBOROUGH ARMS INN, WITNEY, OXON. HOUSEHOLD GOODS and FURNITURE, FOREIGN and BRITISH WINES, LIQUORS, BEER, &c. the celebrated large BEER CASKS, complete STEAM-COOKING APPARATUS, and other valuable Effects, of the above well-known and extensive Commercial and Market Establishment,

TO BE SOLD BY AUCTION, By W. WILKINSON, On the premises, on Tuesday and Wednesday next the 27th and 28th of June, commencing each day punctually at Ten o'clock; comprising nine handsomely-furnished Bed Rooms; expensively and appropriately furnished Dining and Sitting Rooms; also large Market and Smoking Rooms; every necessary and convenient article in the well-arranged Bar and Tap Rooms; the usual Kitchen Requisites for a large establishment; the celebrated stock of fine Beer Casks, four of which contain 4852 gallons, viz. Wellington, Nelson, Wolfe, and - ; about 60 dozen of prime Old Port; 140 gallons of superior Green Gooseberry and Grape Wine, in casks; 16 dozen of Gooseberry and Ginger, in bottles; 460 gallons of Ale; complete Steam-Cooking Apparatus, several Fixtures, and other valuable effects, of the late Mr. James Gillett.

The lots may be viewed the mornings of sale prior to the commencement. Catalogues may be had at the Cross and Roebuck Inns, Oxford; Bear Inn, Woodstock; Red Lion, Ensham; Bell Inn, Faringdon; Ball Inn, Burford; Printing Office, Bampton; place of sale; and of the auctioneer, Witney.'

Oxford Chronicle and Reading Gazette – Saturday 15 June 1850
'Commercial Inn, Witney. MARY GILLETT respectfully informs Commercial Gentlemen and the Public in general that, in consequence of the Crown Hotel being closed as an inn, she has taken to the POST HORSES, FLYS, &c. and is making extensive alterations on the premises where she resides, in order to enable her to offer more improved accommodation to Commercial Gentlemen and Travellers than it has hitherto been in her power to afford; she humbly begs, therefore, to solicit a share of their patronage and support, which she assures them it will always her endeavour to merit, by the strictest attention to their comforts, and by a readiness at all times to meet their requirements with punctuality and despatch.

M. G. takes this opportunity of returning her warmest thanks to those friends whose past favours she has to acknowledge, and trusts they will continue to bestow on her the liberal patronage she has hitherto received from them. MARLBOROUGH ARMS INN, WITNEY, June 13th 1853.'

Oxford Chronicle and Reading Gazette – Saturday 04 February 1854
'An inquest was held on the 1st inst., at the Marlborough Arms Inn, in this town, by James Westell, Esq., Coroner, on the body of Charles, son of Thomas Bolton, of Glympton, Oxon, yeoman, aged 10 years. Deceased had been an idiot ever since his birth, and died from congestion of brain. – Verdict accordingly.'

Oxford Chronicle and Reading Gazette – Saturday 17 March 1855
'On Friday last, the 9th inst., the members of the E. Troop of the Q.O.R., O.Y.C., assembled at the Marlborough Arms Inn, Witney, for the purpose of presenting a silver cup to Serjeant Major J. W. Burden. They partook of an excellent dinner provided by the hostess, Mrs. Gillett, and after the removal of the cloth, Sergeant Robert Sheppard was called to the chair; Sergeant Thomas Lea filling the Vice-chair...'

Oxford Chronicle and Reading Gazette – Saturday 03 July 1858
'MARRIAGES. June 30th, at the parish church, Witney, by the Rev. R. Sankey, Mr. Philip Richards, of Rugby, to Mary, third daughter of the late Mr. James Gillett, of the Marlborough Arms, Witney.'

Oxford Chronicle and Reading Gazette – Saturday 18 August 1860
'THE WITNEY RAILWAY COMPANY. NOTICE is hereby Given, that the Ordinary HALF-YEARLY MEETING of the SHAREHOLDERS of the WITNEY RAILWAY COMPANY will be held at the Marlborough Arms, Witney, on Friday, the 24th of August instant, at two o'clock in the afternoon precisely, for the general purposes of the Company. ...'

Oxford Chronicle and Reading Gazette – Saturday 20 April 1861
'WITNEY RAILWAY. – On Saturday, the 13th instant, a special general meeting of the proprietors was held at the Marlborough Arms, "for the purpose of approving, or otherwise, an act to enable the Witney Railway Company to make a road to their station at Witney." The meeting was largely attended, and their approval was unanimously accorded to the resolution.'

Oxford Chronicle and Reading Gazette – Saturday 05 April 1862
'RAILWAY CHARGES. – The adjourned meeting respecting the Railway Goods Charges, was held at the Marlborough Arms Hotel, on Tuesday last, at 4 p.m., according to notice, when the interest in the matter was shown, by seeing all the principal manufacturers and tradesmen of the town present. James Clinch, Esq., was voted to the chair. ...'

Oxford Times – Saturday 26 March 1864
'ELECTRIC TELEGRAPH COMPANY. – A public meeting was held on Monday evening, at the Marlborough Arms Hotel, Mr. C. Early in the chair, to take into consideration an offer made by the United Kingdom Electric Telegraph Company to establish a station at Witney on one of two conditions, viz., either that £500 debenture should be subscribed bearing interest at seven and a half per cent., paid by franked orders for telegraphic messages, or the sum of £50 per annum should be granted. It was agreed to adopt the latter offer, and half the money, £25, was guaranteed in the room.'

Oxford Times – Saturday 02 July 1864
'CHRISTIAN KNOWLEDGE SOCIETY. – On Tuesday last a sermon was preached in the parish church on behalf of this Society, by the Rev. D. Adams, rural dean, and the friends of the Society, connected with the Witney Association, afterwards dined together at the Marlborough Arms, when the business of the Association was transacted, and new members elected.'

Oxford Times – Saturday 08 October 1864
'WITNEY RAILWAY COMPANY. The half-yearly meeting of this company was held at the Marlborough Arms Inn on Friday last, Mr. Locock Webb in the chair. The secretary read the notice convening the meeting. The Chairman then said that the Directors had not received the accounts from the Great Western Railway, and this company's receipts could not therefore be ascertained, he would move that the meeting be adjourned until the 28th of October, at three o'clock. It was hoped the Great Western would render their accounts within a few days. Mr. Akers having seconded the motion, it was put and carried unanimously.'

Oxford Times – Saturday 28 October 1865
'RAILWAY COMPANY. – The half-yearly ordinary meeting of the Witney Railway Company will be held at the Marlborough Arms this day (Saturday) at three o'clock.'

Oxford Chronicle and Reading Gazette – Saturday 07 July 1866
'CRICKET. – A meeting was held at the Marlborough Arms Hotel on Saturday last, for the purpose of reorganising the Witney Cricket Club. Mr. Charles Jones occupied the chair...'

Oxford Journal – Saturday 23 May 1868
'VISITATION.- Archdeacon Clerke held his annual Visitation at St. Mary's on Monday last, and in his Charge (which was largely devoted to a review of the law as it affected burials in churchyards) he spoke of the present condition of the Church, and of her stability as being founded on the "Rock of Ages;" ... There was a considerable attendance of the Clergy, several of whom afterwards lunched with the Archdeacon at the Marlborough Arms.'

Oxford Chronicle and Reading Gazette – Saturday 01 August 1868
'FOR SALE, - A BAY MARE, in good condition, 15 hands, rising 6 years, quiet in harness. – Enquire of Mr. Elms, Marlborough Arms, Witney.'

Oxford Journal – Saturday 06 August 1870
'WITNEY RAILWAY SHARES. Five shares in the Witney Railway Company were sold by auction on Wednesday the 27th of July, at the Marlborough Arms, Witney, and were knocked down at 4*l*., or 16s. per 10*l*. share.'

Oxford Journal – Saturday 24 February 1872
'WITNEY RAILWAY COMPANY. A special meeting of the Proprietors of this Company took place at the Marlborough Arms Hotel on Wednesday last. Present, C. E. Thornhill, Esq., the Chairman of the Company, Messrs. J. Druce, H. Akers. and E. Early, Directors, the Solicitor and Secretary of the Company, and several

Shareholders. The Chairman said that the business before the meeting was, to consider three Bills which were at this time before Parliament, viz.: ...'

Oxford Times – Saturday 04 May 1872
'WITNEY RAILWAY COMPANY. The 24th half-yearly ordinary general meeting of the above company, was held at the "Marlborough Arms" Hotel, on Monday last, C. E. Thornhill, Esq., in the chair... In reply to a shareholder Mr. Akers said the East Gloucestershire Works were being pushed on with all speed. The Witney station was the most backward. He believed the line would be opened in the Autumn. The meeting then broke up.'

Oxford Journal – Saturday 25 October 1873
'A meeting was held at the Marlborough Arms on Tuesday last, the Vicar of Coggs in the chair, for the purpose of taking into consideration the formation of a Football Club. Some suggestions were brought forward, but the meeting was adjourned till Tuesday next.'

Oxford Journal – Saturday 23 October 1875
'GARDNER'S MANURE COMPANY,- On Thursday the 14th instant a meeting of shareholders in Gardner's Manure Company (Limited) was held at the Marlborough Arms Hotel, Witney. The meeting was well represented, some 13 or 14 of the principal investors being present. The report was read and unanimously adopted, and a dividend of 12½ per cent. declared. It was considered necessary to issue more shares.'

Oxford Journal – Saturday 08 June 1878
'Mr. E. W. Harcourt, M.P., at Witney. Mr. Harcourt, the recently elected Member for this County, attended the market ordinary at the Marlborough Arms Hotel, Witney, on Thursday last, for the purpose of delivering an address to the electors of that part of the county. There was a numerous attendance ... At the conclusion of the capital repast provided by Host Elms, ...'

Witney Gazette and West Oxfordshire Advertiser – Saturday 06 September 1890
'THE WITNEY RAILWAY COMPANY. NOTICE IS HEREBY GIVEN that in compliance with the provisions of the Great Western Railway Act, 1890, an Extraordinary General Meeting of the Witney Railway Company, will be held at the "Marlborough Arms" Hotel, Witney, in the County of Oxford, on Tuesday the 30th day of September, 1890, at half-past two o'clock in the afternoon, for the purpose of considering, and if thought fit, passing the subjoined resolution.
RESOLUTION :-
   "That the Company be wound up voluntarily under the provisions of the Companies' Acts, 1862 and 1867, and that Charles Edward Thornhill, of Seven Springs, in the County of Oxford, Esq., be, and he is hereby appointed Liquidator for the purposes of such winding up."
   Dated this 4th day of September, 1890. By order of the Board, GEORGE BROOM, Secretary.'

Faringdon Advertiser and Vale of the White Horse Gazette – Saturday 15 July 1922

'PROPERTY SALE. – Acting under instructions from Sir George Granville Leveson Gower, K.B.E., Messrs. Habgood and Innocent offered for sale by public auction at the Marlborough Arms Hotel on Thursday in last week, a freehold dwelling house and about 2 acres of land, being Crown property, situated at Carterton. The lot was knocked down to Mr J. W. Blake, of Carterton, for £320.'

Licensees:

1757–1778	Henry Gadfield
1778	Henry Gadfield died
1779	Susannah Gadfield
1781–1798	Benjamin Trundle
1799–1800	John Gythin
1801	Elizabeth ?
1802	James Masters
1804–1811	John Jackson
1812	The Marlborough Arms was to be let in June
1812–1821	George Jones
1822–1830	Charles Jones
1838–1844	James Gillet
	Age 40, wife Mary age 35 (1841 Census)
1840	Public House Garden &c. owned by John Williams Clinch
1847–1852	Mary Gillet (Mrs.)
	Age 46, born in Redditch, Worcs. Widow (1851 Census)
1853	James Gillet
1854–1861	Mrs. Mary Gillet & James Gillet
	Age 58, born in Redditch, Worcs, Widow. Son James age 35, born in Brize Norton, Oxon (1861 Census)
1862–1867	James Gillet
1868–1898	Edward Elms
	Age 44, born in Oxford, Oxon. Wife Marian age 39 (1871 Census)
	Age 32, born in Merton, Oxon. Wife Annie age 36 (1881 Census)
	Age 63, born in Oxford, Oxon. Wife Annie age 48 (1891 Census)
1899–1908	Annie Hadley (Mrs.)
	Age 28, born in Newtown, Montgomeryshire, Wales. Widow (1901 Census)
1911–1915	William Blunt
	Age 42, born in Chipping Norton, Oxon. Wife Annie age 38 (1911 Census)
1918–1929	Samuel Herbert Cruley
1925	Owned by Hall & Co
1930–1954	Lewis Percival Collett
	DOB 13 Dec 1895 Hotel Proprietor. Married (1939 Register)
1955	Anthony James Preston Parker
1956–1957	Basil John New
1958–1961	J. E. H. R. Bosman
1962–1968	Kenneth Frederick Cyril Lintott

1969	Michael J. Ostler
1970–1972	Barry A. Parkes
1973	Edward J. Clark
1974	Gordon A. R. Kemp
1976–1980	Jeffrey Lilleman
2005–2010	Rebekah Ellis
2011	Marlborough Arms bought by Oakman Inns & Restaurants and name changed to Blue Boar Hotel
2011	Heide-Michelle Noble
	Stephanie Fisher
2012	Ross Phillips
2013	Andrew Palfreyman
	Paul Brown
	Cian McMonagle
2014–2015	Rebekah Ellis
2016	Paul Wicker
2017	Emily Hobday
2018–present	Richard Batchelor

Bull Inn (Boar's Head), 46 Market Sq (1762–1969)
(known as Pig Market in 1839)

(Currently a Book Shop & Care Agency)
(1840 Tithe Awards Map ref 47)

From the newspapers:

Oxford Journal – Saturday 06 August 1768
'THE BULL INN in WITNEY, a very good and well accustomed House, situate very near the Market Place, is to let at Michaelmas next. – Enquire of Mr. Leverett, of the same Place.'

Oxford University and City Herald – Saturday 07 August 1841
'On the 29th ult. died, after a short illness, much respected, Mr. John Ellis, tailor, many years landlord of the Boar's Head, Witney, aged 69.'

Oxford Journal – Saturday 28 September 1867
'MARRIED. Sept. 24, at St. Mary's Church, Witney, Mr. G. Luckett, of Coombe, to Mary, eldest daughter of Mr. Phipps, of the Bull Inn, Witney.'

Oxford Chronicle and Reading Gazette – Saturday 15 August 1868
'JUSTICE ROOM, Aug. 13. Stephen Hodgkins, of Ramsden, who did not appear, was fined, including costs, £1 6s. 6d., or 21 days' imprisonment, for being drunk and refusing to quit the Bull Inn, Witney, on the 7th inst. Warrant granted.'

Faringdon Advertiser and Vale of the White Horse Gazette - Saturday 05 September 1903
'Two Sad Occurrences. – Quite a gloom has been cast over the town by the death, within a day of each other, of two of the most respected licensed victuallers in the town. ... Last Friday week, Mr Charles Howell, landlord of the "Bull" Inn, Market Place, who had for the previous three weeks complained of feeling unwell,

was also taken with violent pains, and was assisted to bed medically attended. His condition rapidly grew worse, however, and on Sunday an operation was performed by Dr. Whitelock, of Oxford, but the case was regarded from the first as almost hopeless, and the patient passed away early on Saturday morning from abscess of the liver, peritonitis, and gangrene. Mr. Howell, who was 38 years of age, had been at the "Bull" for five years, and treasurer of the Court Windrush A.O.F. He leaves a widow and two children.'

Witney Gazette and West Oxfordshire Advertiser – Saturday 05 September 1903
'DEATHS. HOWELL. – Aug 29th, at the "Bull" Inn, Witney, Charles Howell, aged 38 years.'

Witney Gazette and West Oxfordshire Advertiser – Saturday 12 September 1903
'PETTY SESSIONS, Thursday. HOLDOVERS. Applications for the holdover of the license of the ... "Bull" Inn, Witney, from Charles Howell, deceased, to Ann Howell; ...'

Oxford Times – Saturday 26 September 1903
'PETTY SESSIONS, Thursday. TRANSFER. – The licence of the ... "Bull" Inn, Witney, from the late Charles Howell to his widow, Ann Howell; ...'

Licensees:

1762–1764	Robert Taylor
1764	Buried on 17 Oct.
1765–1768	Mary Taylor (widow)
1768	The Bull Inn was to let in August
1772–1782	Stephen Taylor
1784	Thomas Bolton
1785–1790	John Sheppard
1791–1792	Ann Sheppard
1793–1795	John Gethyn
1796	Thomas Trinder
1797–1801	William Sheppard
1804–1811	George Bolton
1830–1841	John Ellis
	Age 65, wife Elizabeth age 60 (1841 Census)
1841	John Ellis died in July aged 69
1840	Public House outbuildings &c. owned by John Williams Clinch
1847–1877	John Phipps
	Age 32, born in Northleigh, Oxon. Wife Elizabeth age 33 (1851 Census)
	Age 42, born in Northleigh, Oxon. Wife Elizabeth age 42 (1861 Census)
	Age 52, born in Northleigh, Oxon. Wife Elizabeth age 52 (1871 Census)
1881–1895	Edmund Baker
	Age 28, born in Nuneham, Oxon. Wife Mary Ann age 29 (1881 Census)
	Age 37, born in Abingdon, Berks. Wife Mary age 38 (1891 Census)
1899–1903	Charles Howell
	Age 36, born in Aldburgh, Norfolk. Wife Annie age 37 (1901 Census)

1903	Howell Charles of the "Bull" inn Whitney (sic) Oxfordshire licensed-victualler died 29 August 1903 age 38 Administration Oxford 4 February to Ann Howell widow Effects £197
1903–1913	Ann Howell (Mrs.) Age 47, born in Nuneham, Oxon. Widow (1911 Census)
1915–1924	William George Cubbidge
1925	Cubbidge William George Vincent of The Bull Inn Witney Oxfordshire died 1 October 1925 at The Radcliffe Infirmary Oxford Administration Oxford 3 December to Ethel May Cubbidge widow. Effects £1012 14s 11d.
1925–1931	Edith May Cubbidge (Mrs.)
1932–1940	Roger James Flemans DOB 26 Feb 1886 Licensed Victualler. Wife Mary dob 3 Nov 1885 Unpaid Domestic Duties (1939 Register)
1941–1948	Thomas Henry Hayward
1949–1960	James Brian
1961–1969	Albert Peter Kemp Closed

Company of Weavers, 31 Market Sq (2012–present)

(Currently trading, owned by J. D. Weatherspoons)

Licensees:

2011	Pub opened
2012–2013	David Duppa-Whyte
2013	Joel Dyer
2014–2015	Kirsty Archer
2016–2017	Ervis Kumeta
2018	Niall Mendes-da-Costa

Crown Hotel, 27 Market Sq (1753–1981)

(Demolished in 1981 to make way for Langdale Gate)
(1840 Tithe Awards Map ref 944)

From the newspapers:

Oxford Journal – Saturday 01 November 1755
'THE Trustees appointed to put in Execution an Act of Parliament made in the twenty-fourth Year of his present Majesty's Reign, intitled, An Act for repairing the Road from the Top of Crickley-Hill, in the County of Gloucester, to Frogg-Mill, through the Towns of Northleach, Burford, and Witney, and Parishes of Hanborough and Bladen, to Campsfield in the Parish of Kidlington, in the County of Oxford; and also the Road from Witney through Ensham, Cumnor, and Botley, to the City of Oxford, will meet on Monday the 17th Day of November next at Ten of the Clock in the Forenoon, at the House of John Fisher, called the Crown Inn in Witney, in the County of Oxford, ...'

Oxford Journal – Saturday 04 June 1757
'TO BE SOLD, A Very good Inn, conveniently situated for the Market, at Witney

in the County of Oxford; together with three Tenements thereto belonging: The whole being very convenient for Business. For Particulars enquire of Mr. John Fisher at the Crown Inn in Witney aforesaid.'

Oxford Journal – Saturday 15 March 1760
'DESERTED, From the Thirty-third Regiment of Foot; SAMUEL WOODBURN: ... Whoever secures him shall receive a Guinea Reward, (over and above what is allowed by Act of Parliament) by applying to the Crown Inn in Witney, Oxfordshire.'

Oxford Journal – Saturday 06 September 1760
'CURBRIDGE RACE, Oxfordshire. On Monday the 15th Instant there will be a Race on Curbridge Downs near Witney. To enter at the Crown Inn at Witney, by Nine o'Clock in the Morning of the Day of Running: To start at Eleven; ...'

Oxford Journal – Saturday 08 June 1765
'... will meet on Wednesday the 12th Day of June next, 1765, at Three o'Clock in the Afternoon, at the House of Brian Alder, called the Crown Inn, in Witney, in the County of Oxford; ...'

Oxford Journal – Saturday 24 August 1776
'WITNEY, August 22d, 1776. TO be LETT, on Lease, and entered on at Michaelmas next, – All that well-accustomed INN, called the Crown Inn, situated in Witney, in the County of Oxford, now in the Possession of the Proprietor thereof, Mr. Bryan Alder, who is going to decline Business; consisting of three Parlours, a large Dining-Room, two Bars, seven Chambers, and Garrets over the same, three good Kitchens, Pantries, a very large and convenient Cellar, Stabling for upwards of sixty Horses, Wood-House, and Wool-Loft; a Close, Garden, and Orchard, contiguous to the said Inn, with every other Convenience for the carrying on of the said Business.– – – Persons, inclinable to treat for the taking of the above Inn, may have a View of the same, and be acquainted with the Particulars thereof, by making Application to the said Mr. Bryan Alder. N. B. The Stock in Trade and Furniture to be taken at a fair Appraisement.'

Oxford Journal – Saturday 29 May 1779
'... will meet on Wednesday the second Day of June, 1779, at Eleven of the Clock in the Forenoon, at the House of William Jope, called the Crown Inn, in Witney, in the County of Oxford ; ...'

Oxford Journal – Saturday 22 February 1806
'WITNEY, OXON. TO be LETT,- All that old-established and well-known accustomed INN, in full Trade, called the Crown, with the Malt House, convenient Stall Stables, and Out-Buildings, Gardens, and Close thereto belonging, situate in the Centre of the Market Place, in Witney, Oxon, now, and has been for Eighteen Years past, in the Occupation of WILLIAM SMITH, who wishes to decline Public Business. Possession may be had at Lady Day next. The Stock, Fixtures, and Brewing Utensils to be taken to at an appraised Price. Enquire of William Smith, on the Premises. N. B. Post Chaises are kept at the above Inn.'

Banbury Guardian – Thursday 05 November 1846
'Births November 1, the wife of Mr. John Peake, of the Crown Hotel, Witney, a daughter.'

Oxford Chronicle and Reading Gazette – Saturday 17 April 1847
'DIED. April 11, aged 6 months, Mary Zilpha, daughter of Mr. John Peake, Crown Hotel, Witney.'

Oxford Chronicle and Reading Gazette – Saturday 08 May 1847
'CROWN HOTEL, WITNEY. J. PEAKE respectfully informs his friends and the public, that his OPENING DINNER will take place on Tuesday, the 18th instant, when he will be most happy to meet his friends. N.B. Dinner on the table at Three o'clock. Witney, May 5th, 1847.'

Oxford Chronicle and Reading Gazette – Saturday 15 May 1847
'THE CROWN HOTEL OPENING DINNER. – We perceive, from an advertisement appearing in last week's impression, that our worthy host's opening dinner will take place Tuesday, the 18th instant. Mr. Peake's style of catering being too well known to need any eulogism here, we anticipate accordingly a spread of the most recherché description, and have no doubt but that there will be a large attendance of Mr. P.'s friends and patrons on the occasion.'

Oxford Chronicle and Reading Gazette – Saturday 22 May 1847
'CROWN HOTEL OPENING DINNER. – The opening Dinner at the Crown Hotel, Witney took place on Tuesday. A first-rate spread was provided. The company spent a cheerful evening. "Success to Mr. Peake" was drank in bumpers.'

Licensees:

1753–1763	John Fisher
1757	Crown Hotel was to be sold in June
1764–1776	Brian Alder
1776	Crown Inn was to be let in August
1776–1787	William Jope
1788–1805	William Smith
1806	Crown Inn was to be let in February
1806–1809	Thomas Hudson
1810	Thomas Hudson was buried 6 July
1810–1822	Ann Hudson
1830–1844	William Grace
	Farmer age 40, wife Mary age 35 (1841 Census)
1840	Crown Hotel Houses &c. owned by James Leake
1847	John Peake
1876–1878	Edmund Smith
1879	Edmund Smith died April 1879 age 75
1879–1881	Phœbe Smith
	Age 78, born in Bladon, Oxon. Widow (1881 Census)

Eagle Vaults, 18-22 Market Sq (1899–present)

(Currently trading, owned by Mitchells and Butlers)

From the newspapers:

Faringdon Advertiser and Vale of the White Horse Gazette – Saturday 19 November 1921

'LICENSING HOURS ON MARKET DAYS. Mr Walsh then applied on behalf of Mr Cruly, of the Marlborough Hotel, and Mr Jones, of the "Eagle Vaults," Witney, under section 55, of the Licensing Act, 1910, which was confirmed by the 1921 Act for an extra hours exemption from 4 to 5 p.m on big market days, and for exemption from 2 to 5 pm. on small market days. Evidence in support of the application was given by Mr Cruly; Mr Jones; Mr C. Walker, C.C., Alvescott; Mr C W. List, butcher, Witney; Mr R. T. Rose, C.C. Bampton; and Mr J. Holloway, dealer, Taston After a lengthy hearing and consultation in private, the Chairman said this question was carefully gone into by a full Bench six weeks ago, and they did not now propose to give any further exemption on big market days than at present allowed - namely till 4 o'clock. They would, however, give exemption on small market days from 2 to 4 p.m.'

Licensees:

1899–1919	William Thomas Felton
	Age 42, born in Ackleton, Salop. Wine Agent. Wife Mary age 48. (1901 Census)
	Age 52, born in Ackleton, Salop. Wife Mary Elizabeth age 58 (1911 Census)
1920–1921	George Frederick Jones
1925	Owned by Hunt Edmunds & Co
1923–1937	Bernard Charles Heath
1938–1966	Walter Ernest Barnes
1967–1975	William H. Barker
1978–1980	Edward V. Trowbridge
2005	Pub owned by Mitchells & Butlers Leisure Retail
2005–2006	John Davies
2007–2009	David Thomas
2010–2011	Eleanor Foster
2011–2012	Kerrinne Tracey
2012–2014	Danna Hamilton
2015–2016	Alexander Doust
2017	Kieran Nirum
2018	Steven Mulholland

George Inn, 44 Market Sq (1771–1854)

(Currently a Restaurant)
(1840 Tithe Awards Map ref 48)

From the newspapers:

Oxford Journal – Saturday 07 January 1832

'GEORGE INN, CHURCH GREEN, WITNEY. TO be LET, and may be entered on immediately, -The GEORGE INN, in full trade, with extensive Premises, two good Gardens, Stabling, and Pigstys. The situation is good. For further particulars enquire of Mr. Thomas East, at the Lamb Inn, who begs respectfully to return his most grateful thanks to his friends at Witney, and the public in general, for the liberal support he has received from them, and hopes to receive the same at his New Establishment. N. B. Good stabling, with every accommodation for cattle dealers.

Oxford Chronicle and Reading Gazette – Saturday 21 March 1840

'TO BREWERS AND MALTSTERS, FREEHOLD PUBLIC HOUSE, In the MARKET, at WITNEY, with a malt-house and premises, TO BE SOLD BY AUCTION, By Mr. LONG, On the premises, on Tuesday 31st of March, 1840 at Four o'clock, (in two lots,) by direction the Mortgagee under a power of Sale and subject to such conditions as will be then produced :-

Lot 1. A capital Stone-built and Slated Eight-quarter MALT-HOUSE, newly erected, with excellent kiln, cistern, and two floors ; the whole well timbered and constructed. Also a Piece of Garden Ground, and a Hovel thereon, with a gateway entrance to the premises, the whole situate at the back of the George public house, in Witney.

Lot 2 – That well-accustomed PUBLIC HOUSE, situate in the Market-place, Witney, and known as THE GEORGE; comprising a bar, kitchen, back parlour, market room, and four bed rooms; also a dairy, brewhouse, cellars and other out-buildings, stabling, pig-shed, garden, and appurtenances thereto belonging.

This Property, from its eligible situation in the Market, and the great manufacturing population, commands very considerable consumption of beer, and would be a valuable acquisition to a Brewer or Maltster.

Particulars describing the extent of the Premises, may be had at Mr. Leake's Office, in Witney; at the place of sale; and of the Auctioneer.'

Oxford Chronicle and Reading Gazette – Saturday 24 May 1851

'The licence of the George and Dragon Inn was transferred from William Horley to Richard Rose.'

Oxford Chronicle and Reading Gazette – Saturday 28 June 1856

'The "GEORGE" Public House, In the MARKET PLACE. WITNEY, OXON, TO BE SOLD BY AUCTION By Mr. LONG, At the King's Arms Inn, in Witney, on Friday next, July 4, at Four o'clock : The above well-accustomed PUBLIC HOUSE, being situate in the Pig Market, and having constantly commanded a good business; the premises include every requisite and convenience as a market house. The property is freehold, with an unexceptionable title, and immediate possession may be had.

Also will offer, at the same Auction, several COTTAGES, at Leafield, Finstock, and Ramsden.

Particulars and conditions of sale may be had of Messrs. Goodwin and Co., 3, Lancaster Place, London, or of the Auctioneer, Witney.'

Licensees:

1771–1785	Samuel Wright
1786–1797	James Hunt
1798–1814	Thomas Smith
1830	Thomas Clack
1832	The George Inn was to be let in January
1839–1841	Charles Fisher
	Age 30, Cabinet Maker. Wife Anne age 25 (1841 Census)
1840	Public House Garden &c. owned by Thomas Smith
1840	The George was for sale by auction in March
1842–1844	Harriet Mourby
1846	The Vale of White Horse Brewery of Faringdon was selling the complete brewing plant
1847	John Adams
1850–1851	William Horley
1851–1854	Richard Rose
1856	The George was for sale by auction in June

Lamb Inn, 34 Market Sq (1753–1844)

(Demolished in the 1890s, rebuilt, currently a Charity Shop & Café Bar)
(1840 Tithe Awards Map ref 397)

From the newspapers:

Oxford Journal – Saturday 19 November 1757
'...This being positively the last Day the Sculptures will be shewn in Burford – on Monday they will be shewn at the Lamb Inn in Witney, (Prices for Gentlemen or Ladies One Shilling each, Servants 6d.) ...'

Oxford Journal – Saturday 17 October 1772
'THE Trustees for putting in Execution an Act of Parliament made in the Eleventh Year of the Reign of his present Majesty King George the Third, for amending, widening, turning, and altering the Road from the Bottom of Galley-Hill near the Town of Witney, to the Cross in Clanfield, in the County of Oxford, are appointed to meet on Friday the 23rd Day of October, 1772, at Eleven o'Clock in the Forenoon, at the House of Robert Trotman, called the Lamb Inn, in Witney, in the County of Oxford, ...'

Oxford Journal – Saturday 14 October 1775
'LAMB INN, Witney, October 13, 1775. Robert Andrews, late Waiter at the Cross Inn, in Oxford, begs leave to inform the Public, That he has taken and entered upon the above Inn, lately occupied Mr. Trotman; where he humbly hopes for the countenance of the former customers to the said House in general, and of his friends in particular, as no pains or assiduity will be spared to render their accommodations perfectly satisfactory; and their favours will be gratefully acknowledged, by Their most obedient Servant, ROBERT ANDREWS. N. B. A good Ordinary every market-day.'

Oxford Chronicle and Reading Gazette – Saturday 13 October 1838
'Valuable FREEHOLD PROPERTY, The Lamb Inn, Witney, Oxon. TO BE
SOLD BY AUCTION, By Mr. COLLIER, On Thursday the 25th day of Oct.
1838, on the premises, at Four o'clock in the afternoon, – All that old-established
and well-accustomed INN, known as "THE LAMB," most eligibly situate in the
Market-place, Witney; with its extensive and well-arranged outbuildings, stables,
and coach house, now in the occupation of Mr. Gilbert; together with a range of
Buildings adjoining and fronting the Corn-street, let present as a dwelling house
and warehouse. The situation of this property, in the centre of the Market and the
respectable and increasing trade which it enjoys, renders it particularly desirable
for purchase. Conditions will be produced at the sale. Particulars may obtained of
Mr. Edgington, Solicitor, or the Auctioneer, Witney.'

Licensees:

1754–1775	Robert Trotman
1776–1788	Robert Andrews
1788	Buried on 8 September
1788–1796	Isabel Andrews
1797–1798	Jacob Andrews
1799–1801	William Osman
1802	John Holton
1804–1808	Joseph Masters
1809–1814	Benjamin Weston
1830	Thomas Fletcher
1838	The Lamb was to be sold by auction in October
1839–1840	Richard Gilbert
1840	Public House Outbuildings &c. owned by Thomas East
1841–1844	John Edwards
	Age 25 (1841 Census)

Old White Hart, 13-15 Market Place (1771–1782)

(Demolished, rebuilt currently a Building Society and Retail Premises)

In A History of the County of Oxford: Volume 14 it states '"The White Hart," a
'chief inn of the town' visited by Charles I, stood probably on or near the site of
the later Corn Exchange on the east side of the market place, ...'

'Under the head of Games and Popular Amusements there is, I fear, very little
remaining in Witney to attract the notice of those who are interested in such
matters. The few remnants of our old Sports and Pastimes are rapidly disappearing,
and this is, in my opinion, a change much to be lamented. ...

But, to return from this digression, Witney has little to be recorded in the way
of sports and pastimes. It would seem that it never possessed a public theatre for
the exhibition of dramatic representations, for so long ago as Feb. 3, 1622, I find in
an old register the notice that a comedy was represented at the White Hart Inn,
when five persons were killed by the falling in of the floor. I copy the following
account of it from the Beauties of Oxfordshire.

In the seventeenth century an accident occurred at Witney which was disastrous in itself, and is especially memorable from the publicity it gained through puritanical misrepresentation. The young and the gay of the town assembled, in innocent merriment, to witness the performance of a dramatic piece. The flooring gave way, and several lives were lost in the general downfall. Instead of sympathy the sufferers met with execration. One John Rowe, of the University of Oxford, and "Lecturer in the towne of Witney," published an account of the occurrence entitled "TRAGI-COMŒDIA: being a brief relation of the strange and wonderful hand of God discovered at Witney, in the Comedy acted there, February 3, where there were some slaine, many hurt, with several other remarkable passages: together with what was preached in three sermons on that occasion from Rom. i. 18: both which may serve as some check to the growing Atheisme of the present age. By John Rowe of C. C. C. in Oxford, lecturer in the town of Witney. *Oxf.* 1652." The age must indeed be far gone in enthusiasm, which could be influenced by such imbecile ravings as those of Mr. Rowe; yet we are told that this publication contributed not a little to the suppression of plays at that period. We learn from the pamphlet that the piece performed was "Mucedorus, the king's sonne of Valentia, and Amandine, the king's daughter of Arragon; with the merry conceits of Mouse, &c." The actors were countrymen, and nearly all from Stanton Harcourt. They acted for pecuniary reward, and had performed their comedy in several adjacent places. Denied the use of the town-hall, they fixed on the White Hart, a principal inn at Witney. At seven o'clock in the evening the drum beat and the trumpet sounded, to announce that all was ready. Men, women, and children, to the number of three hundred, attended the summons. The theatre of the night was a large apartment, which had been used as a malting-room, having a part of it covered with earth to that purpose. The play had proceeded for about an hour and a half, when a beam gave way; and the flooring sank. The fall was not quick, and the whole went into a room, where there was a shuffleboard, which was broken to pieces. All for a few dreadful moments was silence. At length such cries and groans arose as furnished the declaimer with several very pertinent allusions in his three sermons to ROM. i. 18; and it was found that five were "slaine outright." The whole of the persons killed on the spot were children; a woman had her leg broken and underwent amputation. Though these were "awful warnings," the sufferers were still few in number: but Mr. Rowe closes the account by informing us "that sixty persons are said to have been much bruised." The old White Hart, in which this calamity happened, was part of an ancient mansion belonging to the family of Yates, and stood in the market place. It is said that a tapestried room of this mansion was occupied by Queen Elizabeth during one of her progresses in these parts.'

'... There is no authentic record of the visit of this Queen to Witney, though it is more than likely that she came to the town. She was frequently at her hunting lodge at Langley, not far away in Wychwood Forest, and it is perfectly certain that she visited the town of Burford. What more likely than that the good Queen honoured Witney in a similar manner? ...'

(Reproduced from History of Witney by J. A. Giles, first published in 1852, pages 58 & 59: see also History of Witney by W. J. Monk, first published in 1894, pages 34-36)

From the newspapers:

Oxford Journal – Saturday 21 March 1772
SARAH JONES, Carrier from Witney to London, intending to leave off that Business, takes this Method of informing the Publick, that she will dispose of her Stock, consisting of two Broad-wheeled Waggons and twelve good Horses.

N. B. To any one whom this may suit, it cannot fail of being a desirable Opportunity of entering into that Business, as it has been a good accustomed Stage for many Years. – For Particulars, apply to the said Mrs. Jones, the Old White Hart in Witney.'

Oxford Journal – Saturday 25 September 1779
The Old White Hart Inn, at Witney, Oxfordshire. TO be SOLD by AUCTION, on the Premises, by Mr. Woods, on Monday the Fourth Day of October, 1779, All that well-accustomed INN known by the Sign of the Old White Hart, situated in the Market-place, at Witney, Oxfordshire, now in the Possession of Mr. John Simms, at the yearly Rent of Eighteen Pounds. The Premises are Freehold, with a good Garden, a large Yard, and very convenient Out-buildings. Conditions will be produced at the Time of Sale, and the Premises may be viewed any Time by applying to the Tenant, and will be put up precisely at Four o'clock in the Afternoon.'

Oxford Journal – Saturday 08 October 1803
'TO be SOLD by AUCTION, by W. SMTH, on Monday the 24th Day of October, 1803, at the Crown Inn, Witney, in the County of Oxford, at Three o'clock in the Afternoon, under such Conditions of Sale as shall be then produced, in 5 Lots,

LOT 1.-All those extensive desirable PREMISSES formerly known by the Sign of the WHITE HART INN, desirably situated near the Market Place, in Witney, comprising a large Stone - built Dwelling House, with spacious Parlours, large Kitchen, two Cellars, five Bed Chambers, Garrets, large Garden, Yard, and convenient Out-Buildings thereon; these Premises are well worth the Attention of any Person desirous of carrying on the Business of a Brewer or Maltster, and may be entered on immediately.'

Licensees:

1771–1776	Sarah Jones
1779	John Simms
1779	Old White Hart was to be sold by auction in September
1781–1782	Edward Saunders

Sun (Sundial), 49 Market Sq (1779–1784)

(Currently a Charity Shop)

Licensees:
1779	Richard Baker
1781	Joseph Perry
1782–1784	William Andrews

Ye Olde Cross Keys (Cross Keys, Salutation),
1 Market Sq (1753–present)

(Currently trading, Spirit Pub Company)
(1840 Tithe Awards Map ref 917)

From the newspapers:

Oxford Journal – Saturday 10 July 1779
'MARGARET BREAKSPEAR, Widow of Robert Breakspear, of Witney, in Oxfordshire, Slater and Plaisterer, begs Leave to give Notice, That for the Support of herself and a Family of small Children, she purposes to continue the Business of her late Husband in all its Branches, and hereby humbly solicits Continuance of the Favours of all her Friends.'

Oxford Journal – Saturday 17 December 1803
'TO be LETT, and entered on immediately, Two PUBLIC HOUSES, in good Repair, situate in Witney, in the County of Oxford, called the White Lion, which has a large Garden, and good Stabling, and the CROSS KEYS, each of them having good Custom. – For Particulars apply to Mr. Leake, Brewer, of Witney, aforesaid.'

Cheltenham Chronicle – Thursday 04 May 1809
'TO BE SOLD BY AUCTION, By THOMAS FOX, On Thursday next, the Eleventh May, 1809, at the Crown Inn, in Witney, Oxon, at Three o'clock in the afternoon, ALL that old established INN, called the CROSS KEYS, situate in the High Street, near the Market-place, in Witney aforesaid, with good Brewhouse, Stables, Lofts, Woodhouse, and other convenient Out-buildings. For further particulars apply to Mr. Leech, Solicitor, or the Auctioneer, Witney.'

Oxford University and City Herald – Saturday 29 June 1811
'CROSS KEYS, WITNEY. In a few Weeks will be SOLD BY AUCTION, ALL that old-established and well-accustomed INN and PUBLIC-HOUSE, called the CROSS KEYS, situated in the High-street, near the Market-place, Witney, Oxon, now in the occupation of William Moulder, with good brew-house, stabling, lofts, wood-house, and other convenient out-buildings. For further particulars apply to Mr. Leech, Solicitor, Witney.'

Oxford Chronicle and Reading Gazette – Saturday 24 May 1856
'CROSS KEYS, WITNEY. C. Rouse begs to inform his Friends that he intends to PROVIDE a DINNER on WEDNESDAY, the 28th May inst., at 2 o'clock to COMMEMORATE the RESTORATION of PEACE. Dinner 1s. 6d. each. 6th May 1856'

Oxford Chronicle and Reading Gazette – Saturday 28 July 1860
'JUSTICE ROOM, July 26. John Cripps, publican, Cross Keys, Witney, was charged with assaulting Eliza Rouse, of the New Inn, Witney, on the 19th inst. Fined 5s., and costs 17s.; in default to be committed for 7 days. Paid.'

Oxford Chronicle and Reading Gazette – Saturday 05 September 1863
'CROSS KEYS INN, WITNEY, MESSSRS. SEELY and BUCKINGHAM have received instructions to SELL BY AUCTION, in the course of the present month, on the premises known as the Cross Keys, in the High Street, Witney, - The Capital BREWING PLANT, CASKS, INNKEEPER'S STOCK-IN TRADE, HOUSEHOLD FURNITURE, HORSES, TRAP, CARTS, FLYS, and other EFFECTS, the property of Mr. John Cripps, who is retiring from business.

Further particulars will appear in future Advertisements. High Street, Witney, Sept 3rd, 1863.'

Oxford Times – Saturday 24 February 1866
'PETTY SESSIONS, February 22. ASSAULTS. John P. Lambert, landlord of the Cross Keys, Witney, was summoned for assaulting George Pratley, at Witney, on the 8th instant. Fined, including costs, 20s. Paid.'

Oxford Journal – Saturday 16 July 1870
'WITNEY. MARRIED. – July 13, at St. Mary's Church, Witney, Mr. Lambert, of the Cross Keys, Witney, to Mrs. Ellis, of Milton-under-Wychwood.'

Oxford Journal – Saturday 18 July 1874
'Notice of Postponement of Sale. The Sale of the "Cross Keys Inn," Witney, advertised to take place on Thursday the 30th of July, 1874, is COUNTERMANDED. J. and W. SCROGGS, Auctioneers.'

Faringdon Advertiser and Vale of the White Horse Gazette – Saturday 13 November 1920
'PETTY SESSIONS, October 28th. HOLDOVERS. Holdovers of the license of the "Golden Ball," Brighthampton, to W. T. Henson, and of the "Cross Keys," Witney, to Spencer Fisher, were granted.'

Faringdon Advertiser and Vale of the White Horse Gazette – Saturday 12 August 1922
'PETTY SESSIONS, Friday. APPLICATION REFUSED. Mr C. Fisher, of the "Cross Keys," Witney, applied on behalf of the licence holders in the vicinity of the Market Place for permission to remain open from 2 to 4p.m. on August Bank Holiday on the occasion of Witney Races. Inspector Hawtin reminded the Bench that an extension on Easter Monday was granted to the whole of the licensed houses in Witney on the understanding that it was to be for the convenience of the public. On passing one licensed house he saw a notice outside that no teas were provided, and thought difficulties were put in the way of persons requiring teas. The Chairman said this was most improper and the Bench refused the application.'

Licensees:

1753–1763	Bartholomew Collingwood
1769–1779	Robert Breakspear
1779	Buried on 7 July
1779–1795	Margaret Breakspear
1796–1806	John Breakspear
1803	Cross Keys was to be let in December
1807–1808	Richard Radbourn
1809	Cross Keys was to be sold by auction in May
1811	Cross Keys was to be sold by auction in June
1809–1822	William Patrick Moulder
1830–1850	John Steptoe
	Age 30, wife Mary age 30 (1841 Census)
1840	Public House Garden &c. owned by Anne Moulder
1851–1856	Charles Rouse
	Age 35, born in Chipping Norton, Oxon. Wife Harriett age 36 (1851 Census)
1860–1865	John Cripps
	Age 45, born in Witney, Oxon. Wife Maria age 45 (1861 Census)
1866–1869	John Price Lambert
1870	John Lambert married Mrs. Ellis in July
1871–1874	Ann Jenkins (Mrs.)
	Age 53, born in Stafford (1871 Census)
1876–1883	George Whitlock
	Age 44, wife Emma age 47 (1881 Census)
1887	George Austin
1891–1904	William John Hobbs
	Age 38, born in Admington, Glos. Wife Mary A age 32 (1891 Census)
	Age 47, born in Admington, Glos. Wife Mary age 45 (1901 Census)
1905–1907	Joseph Bond
1908–1912	Mark Winfield
	Age 45, born in Witney, Oxon. Wife Laura Antonia age 48 (1911 Census)
1915–1920	Frank Harold Sharp
1921–1925	Spencer Charles Fisher
1925	Owned by Clinch & Co
1926–1928	Henry Mills
1929–1932	James Poole
1933–1935	George Rooke Ginn
1936	Walter Robert Sandford
1937–1941	Thomas Frederick Cable
	DOB 23 Mar 1889 Hotel Proprietor. Wife Emily dob 8 Dec 1888 Unpaid Domestic Duties (1939 Register)
1942	Sidney Robert Nash
1943–1944	Maurice William Regan
1945–1948	Cedric Arthur Brown
1949–1955	Leslie Edward Tickner
1956–1966	Morris Wilfred Day
1967–1968	Derek B. Hayne

1969–1972	Gerald M. Dowding
1973	Stephen Wicks
1974	David E. Perfect
1975–1978	Richard D. Wilson
1979	David Newman
1980	Robert H. Avery
2005	Pub owned by Spirit Pub Co
2005–2008	Peta Ashbrook
2009	Tracy Smith
2010	Stacy Lucas
2011	Paul Gibbs
	Steven Bate
	Jessica Craven
2012	Emma Thomas
	Nicholas Hopkins
2013–2016	Gareth Hunter
2017	Jadi Burgess
2018–present	Amy Goulding

West End

Black Horse, 70 West End (1761–1883)

(Currently a private residence)

From the newspapers:

Witney Gazette and West Oxfordshire Advertiser – Saturday 02 May 1885
'DESIRABLE COPYHOLD PROPERTY. WEST END, WITNEY, OXON.
WILLIAM SEELY Of Witney, HAS been favored with instructions from the
Mortgagee to OFFER FOR SALE at an early date, all that Commodious and
Desirable PROPERTY known as the "BLACK HORSE INN," but now as
the SALVATION ARMY BARRACKS, together with all those two well built
COTTAGES or Private Tenements adjoining the same, situate in West End,
Witney, in the county of Oxford, and now in the occupation of Mr. Wm. Brooke,
and his under tenants, the whole producing a net annual rental of £40. Further
particulars will appear in future advertisements, and in the mean time may be
obtained as above, or of G. H. Saunders, Esq., solicitor, &c., Chipping Norton,
Oxon.'

Licensees:

1761	John Seeley
1765–1794	William Seeley (1774 at the Glazier's Arms)
1795	Thomas Collier
1797	William Seeley was buried on 16 July
1797–1809	Daniel Seeley
1853–1867	George Bowerman
	Age 64, born in Ramsden, Oxon. Wife Sarah age 61 (1861 Census)
1869	William Jackson
1876	James Harwood
1877	Charles Harwood
1883	John Frederick Rose
1885	now a Salvation Army Barracks

Elm Tree, 21 West End (1753–present)

(Currently trading, Free House)
(1840 Tithe Awards Map ref 647)

From the newspapers:

Oxford Journal – Saturday 05 August 1826
'To BREWERS, MALTSTERS, &c. Desirable Freehold Public House, Witney.
TO BE SOLD BY AUCTION, By Mr. LONG, On the premises, at the Elm
Tree, in Witney, on Wednesday the 16th of August, 1826, at Three o'clock in the
afternoon, under such conditions as will be then produced.- That very desirable
FREEHOLD and convenient PUBLIC HOUSE, called the Elm Tree, situate
in the centre of West End-street, Witney, carrying on a good trade, and now let

to a responsible tenant. The premises have lately undergone very considerable repair and improvement, and contain large under-ground cellars, a front kitchen, parlour, bar, &c.; 4 bed rooms, a large and convenient brew-house, malt room, stables, pigsties, and garden, a never failing well of water, and other conveniences.

Any person requiring a consumption for malt or beer, or wishing to carry on a retail beer trade, will find this a desirable opportunity.- For particulars apply to the auctioneer, Witney; and to view the premises to Mr. Elsley, the occupier.'

Banbury Guardian – Thursday 12 June 1845
'Deaths. May 26, Mr. Job Baughan, landlord of the Elm Tree, Witney, much respected by all who knew him.'

Oxford Times – Saturday 06 May 1865
'PETTY SESSIONS, May 4. ALEHOUSE LICENCES. – This being a special session for the transfer of victuallers' licences, the following transfers were made:- Elm Tree, Witney, Mark Knight to Henry Townsend; Waggon and Horses, Witney, Frederick Lyford to William Thornton; The Angel, Henry Paine to Charles Hitchman.'

Oxford Chronicle and Reading Gazette – Saturday 15 June 1867
'Clubs. – On Monday the Benefit Societies held their annual feasts at the Elm Tree, Jolly Tucker, Court Inn, and Butchers' Arms, Witney. – On Tuesday the Benefit Club held their annual dinner at the Griffin Inn, New Land, Coggs. The Witney Band were engaged playing through the principal streets, after their return from Coggs Church.'

Oxford Times – Saturday 02 February 1878
'PETTY SESSIONS – Jan. 31. Mary Ann Clements, of the Elm Tree Inn, Witney, was charged with allowing gambling for beer, by boys from 10 years to 15 years of age, on her licensed premises at Witney on the 2nd inst. – Fined including costs 22s. 6d. and license endorsed.'

Witney Gazette and West Oxfordshire Advertiser – Saturday 03 July 1886
'The fully licensed FREEHOLD PUBLIC HOUSE, Known as the "Elm Tree," situate in the West End, Witney, in the occupation of Mr. John Thomas Davis, and let to Messrs. W. Clinch & Co., at £19 per annum.'

Witney Gazette and West Oxfordshire Advertiser – Saturday 03 October 1891
'TO LET. – With possession at Michaelmas, the "ELM TREE," INN, West End, Witney. Apply Phillips & Sons, Tower Brewery, Oxford, or W. H. Gillett, The Stores, Witney.'

Oxford Times – Saturday 26 September 1903
'PETTY SESSIONS, Thursday. TRANSFER. – The licence of the ... "Elm Tree," West End, Witney, was transferred from T. Smith to F. Moore; ...'

The Stage – Thursday 26 January 1933
'WANTED, Jan. 30. Feb. 6. The Great Laughter Show, "Pick o' the Bunch," Revuette, Band. – Wire, Barrat, Elm Tree, Witney, Oxon.'

Oxford Mail – Friday 09 September 1988
'Where the two young lovebirds found their happy home. When Peter and Ann
Dunstan frequented the Elm Tree in West End, Witney, as a courting couple a
quarter of a century ago they never thought that one day they would own the pub.
But when it came on the market two years ago they leapt at the chance to buy it.

Sharing lives. Since then, running the pub has become very much a family
affair with daughters Emma, 19, and Joanne, 20, helping out behind the bar. In fact
it is the female section of the Dunstan family which keeps the Elm Tree in order
while Peter is out at work as a director of Cotswold Motors. "It's hard work – but
we have quite a laugh," said Ann. "The best part is getting to know people and
sharing their lives."

Friendly appeal. The first thing you notice when entering the pub is that the
bar is actually below street level. The low ceiling, dark timber and Cotswold stone
walls add to the Elm Tree's cosy and friendly appeal. It has been a pub for 150 years
though the building is probably older than that. The atmosphere is quiet and relaxed
– and that is how Ann likes it. "We are definitely a locals pub – we see the same
people every day, but it is always nice to meet new people." Familiarity certainly
has its advantages when it comes to applying the 18 card system pioneered by
Witney publicans against under-age drinking. If Ann doubts whether someone
can legally buy a drink she can always find someone in the pub who knows them
and can tell her. "We don't get any trouble – we are quite lucky being on the edge
of the town," she said.

Tiring time. The Elm Tree sells a wide range of bitters, including Cotswold,
Witney, 6X, Simmonds, Tartan and John Smiths, as well as Stella and Castlemaine
lagers, Guinness and Taunton cider. The Dunstans provide a good selection of
cheap lunchtime meals including toasted sandwiches, ploughman's and chilli. The
Elm Tree tried out the new licencing laws on August Bank Holiday Monday by
staying open all day – but Ann admits she found it exhausting and does not plan
to do it again. The pub will stay open to 4 pm on Friday and Saturday lunchtimes,
but beyond that she says there is not the demand. A new pool room was added at
the back at the end of last year and four darts teams complete the sporting picture
keeping the pub busy in the middle of the week.'

Licensees:

1754–1765	Edward Mills
1765	Buried 5 July
1765–1781	Sarah Mills (widow)
1782	Richard Dyer
1784	Sarah Mills was buried on 5 September
1785	Thomas Brooks
1786–1788	William Townsend
1789–1817	William Rowles
1826	Mr. Elsley
1826	The Elm Tree was for sale by auction in August
1830–1845	Job Baugham
	Age 50, wife Phœbe age 35 (1841 Census)

1840	Public House Garden owned by James Ward
1845	Job Baugham died in May
1847	Henry Lambourn
1851–1865	Mark Knight
	Age 38, born in Charlbury, Oxon. Glazier. Wife Elizabeth age 42 (1851 Census)
	Age 48, born in Charlbury, Oxon. Glazier & Plasterer. Wife Elizabeth age 58 (1861 Census)
1865	Henry Townsend
1869	Thomas Haines
1874–1875	Reuben Clements
1876	15 February. Administration of the effects of Reuben Clements late of West End Witney in the County of Oxford Licensed Victualler who died 7 December 1875 at West End Witney was granted at Oxford to Mary Ann Clements of West End Witney Widow the Relict. Age 45
1876–1877	Mary Ann Clements (Mrs.)
1881–1887	John Thomas Davis
	Age 31, born in Witney, Oxon. Coach Painter. Wife Mary Anne age 31 (1881 Census)
1891	William Hicks
	Age 24, born in Ramsden, Oxon. Wife Sarah Jane age 24 (1891 Census)
1891	The Elm Tree was to let in October
1895	William Harding
1899–1903	Thomas Edward Smith
	Age 31, born in Coxwell, Berks. Brewers Drayman. Wife Dora age 29. (1901 Census)
1904–1906	Frederick Moore
1907–1920	Frederick William Sabin
	Age 49, born in Middle Barton, Oxon. Army Pensioner. Wife Lily age 36. (1911 Census)
1925	Owned by Hall & Co
1921–1940	George Price
	DOB 17 Aug 1884 Publican. Wife Lucy dob 31 Dec 1872 Blanket Weaver (1939 Register)
1940	George Price died age 56
1941–1843	Lucy Ann Price
1944–1954	Albert Thomas Charles White
1955	Albert Henry Lewis
1956–1961	George Dennis Neale
1962–1969	Thomas Frank Bird
1970–1979	Freda E. Bird
1980	Angus McMartin
1981–1983	Peter & Judith Henderson
1984–2011	Peter & Annie Dunstan
2011–2014	Emma Wadlsey
2014–present	Neilson McDermott

Harriers (Duke's Head), 15 West End (1757–1978)

(Currently a private residence)
(1840 Tithe Awards Map ref 642)

From the newspapers:

Oxford Journal – Saturday 15 July 1786
'TO be SOLD by AUCTION, By Mr. WOODS, On Friday the 28th Day of July instant, at the House of Mr. Henry Bolton, called the Duke's Head, at Witney, in the County of Oxford, if not before disposed of by private Contract, of which due Notice will be given in this Journal, the following ESTATES, in Two Lots:
    Lot 1. All that Dwelling-House, Brew-house, Out-Houses, and Garden, now in the Occupation of the said Hen. Bolton, pleasantly situated on the East Side of the Church-Green at Witney aforesaid, at the yearly Rent of £7 10s. ...'

Oxford Chronicle and Reading Gazette – Saturday 19 November 1842
'The Harriers Public House, in Witney. TO BE SOLD BY AUCTION, By Mr. LONG, On the premises in Westend-street, Witney, on Wednesday next the 23rd of Nov., at Two o'clock, – The well-known and long-established PUBLIC HOUSE, called The Harriers, in the occupation of the proprietor, Mr. Thomas Wells. The Premises comprise capital underground cellaring, brewhouse, kitchen, parlour, 3 bedrooms, back parlour, large club room, and other offices, an excellent well of water and lead pump, yard, and productive garden, the whole in good repair and condition. Particulars may be had and the premises viewed on application to Mr. Wells, on the premises, or the Auctioneer, Witney.'

Witney Gazette and West Oxfordshire Advertiser – Saturday 27 November 1886
'WITNEY, OXON. VALUABLE COPYHOLD PROPERTY. JOHN HABGOOD & SON have received instructions from Mr. W. Cook, who is retiring from business, to SELL by AUCTION, at "The Harriers," West End, Witney, on Friday, December 3rd, 1886, at 5 for 6 o'clock in the evening, – The fully licensed. PUBLIC HOUSE known as "The Harriers," situate in the West End, Witney, in which a good business has been carried on by the present owner upwards of 25 years; and about 2 Acres of Garden or Building LAND, (IN 5 LOTS.) With Barn, Stable, Outhouses, Loft, and Piggeries, situate at Costall, in the Hamlet of Hailey, and close to the Market town of Witney. Particulars and conditions of Sale may be obtained of N. G. Ravenor, Esq., solicitor Witney, and of the Auctioneers, Witney, Oxon, and Faringdon, Berks.'

Witney Gazette and West Oxfordshire Advertiser – Saturday 09 June 1900
'PETTY SESSIONS, Thursday. TRANSFERS. The license of the "Harriers" Inn, West End, Witney, was transferred from Mrs. Walker to Charles Piper.'

Witney Gazette and West Oxfordshire Advertiser – Saturday 13 October 1900
'HOLDOVER. Mr. Rigden applied for a holdover of the license of the "Harriers," West End, Witney, from Charles Piper to Mr. G. H. Hedges.'

Witney Gazette and West Oxfordshire Advertiser – Saturday 02 December 1905
'PETTY SESSIONS. ALTERATIONS. Alteration to the "Harriers" Inn, Witney, were submitted and approved.'

Witney Gazette and West Oxfordshire Advertiser – Saturday 20 February 1909
'INTERESTING WITNEY NEWS. Will it interest you? When you have read it you'll probably thank the Witney man who sends it.

Mr. R. G. White, of "The Harriers" Inn, West End, Witney, says: – "It is some time since I felt the first sign of kidney complaint - a severe pain across the back. It used to attack me severely at intervals, and made work very trying. There were also distressing urinary troubles; the kidney secretions were irregular and unnatural.

"I am pleased to say that I have found a medicine that has cured both these symptoms. That medicine is Doan's backache kidney pills. They very rapidly restored me to good health, and I can highly recommend them. (Signed) R. G. White."

Doan's Backache Kidney Pills are two shillings and sixpence per box (six boxes for thirteen shillings and ninepence). Of all chemists and stores, or post free, direct from Foster-McClellan Co., 8, Wells-street, Oxford-street, London, W. Doan's are the pills that cured Mr. White.'

Licensees:

1757–1764	Edward Joynes
1767–1774	John Shorter
1777–1787	Edward Joynes
1788–1843	Thomas Wells
	Age 82, wife Constance age 82 (1841 Census)
1840	Public House Garden &c. owned by Thomas Wells
1842	The Harriers was to be sold by auction in November
1843	Thomas Wells died end of year
1854–1867	William Cook snr
	Age 71, born in Coggs, Oxon. Coal Dealer. Wife Elizabeth age 69 (1861 Census)
1867	William Cook snr died October
1868–1886	William Cook jnr
	Age 35, born in Coggs, Witney. Weaver. Wife Eleanor age 45 (1871 Census)
	Age 44, born in Coggs, Oxon. Innkeeper. Wife Eleanor age 52 (1881 Census)
1886	The Harriers was to be sold by auction in November
1887	Job Fowler
1891	William Harding
	Age 60, born in Buckland, Devon. Wife Mary age 61 (1891 Census)
1895–1900	Mary Walker (Mrs.)
1901–1903	George Kilmaster Hedges
	Age 62, born in Wootton, Oxon. Wife Rhoda age 59 (1901 Census)

1925	Owned by Hunt Edmonds & Co
1906–1935	Robert George White
	Age 38, born in Deddington, Oxon. Wife Emily Jane age 37 (1911 Census)
1936–1941	James Edward Poole
	DOB 16 Jun 1883 Publican. Wife Maggie dob 14 Nov 1904 Unpaid Domestic Duties (1939 Register)
1942	James Poole died age 58
1942–1946	Maggie Poole
1947–1959	Geoffrey Richard Bollam
1960–1961	James William Winfield
1962–1966	William John Hagar
1967–1975	Eric A. Harbord
1976–1977	Eric W. Sharp
1978	Derek C. Tooth

House of Windsor (King of Prussia, Czar of Russia), 31 West End (1770–2010)

(Currently a private residence)
(1840 Tithe Awards Map ref 664)

From the newspapers:

Oxford University and City Herald – Saturday 10 January 1807
'PUBLIC HOUSE TO BE LET. TO BE LET, AND ENTERED ON IMMEDIATELY, THAT Old, Well-accustomed, and Neat PUBLIC HOUSE called the KING of PRUSSIA, situated in a Street called West End, in the Hamlet of Hailey in the Parish of Witney, in the County of Oxford, with a good garden, cellar, brewhouse, stable, and every other necessary out-building, and convenience; together with an enclosed ground, containing about two acres. For farther particulars, apply to Mr. Philip Coombs of Witney aforesaid.'

Oxford Journal – Saturday 13 June 1807
'Soon will be SOLD by AUCTION, if not previously disposed of by Private Contract,- That neat, commodious, and well-accustomed Public House, The KING of PRUSSIA, together with two Acres, more or less, of Arable Land, situate at Witney, in the County of Oxford. Further Particulars may be had of Mr. Westell, Solicitor, Witney.'

Oxford Chronicle and Reading Gazette – Saturday 08 March 1856
'Free Public House, TO BE LET, and possession had at Lady Day, an Old Established House, with a spirit and wine licence. Situate in West End Street, Witney, known by the sign of the KING OF PRUSSIA. Apply at No. 12 High Street, Oxford.'

Oxford Journal – Saturday 03 May 1856
'MARRIED. – April 22, at St. Mary's Church, Witney, by the Rev. R. Sankey, Mr. Mark Reeves Prat, upholsterer, to Mrs. Davis, widow of the late Mr. Davis, landlord of the King of Prussia, West End.'

Witney Gazette and West Oxfordshire Advertiser – Saturday 07 November 1903

'PROPERTY SALE. – On Wednesday last Mr. R. Gillett offered for Sale, in two lots, at the Fleece Hotel, a dwelling-house at West End, formerly known as the "King of Prussia" Inn and a copyhold building site, measuring 2 acres 35 poles on the Crawley Road, the yearly rental of the two lots being £14 a year. The dwelling house was bought by Mr. John Godfrey, the tenant, for £190, and the building site, after a spirited competition, was knocked down to Mr. F. J. D. Westell for Mr. W. H. Young for £207 10s. od.'

Faringdon Advertiser and Vale of the White Horse Gazette – Saturday 18 September 1915

'LICENSING. Mr R. Wakeford, architect to Messrs. H. and G. Simonds, brewers, of Reading, presented plans of proposed alterations at the "Czar of Russia," West End, Witney, which were allowed.'

Oxford Times – Friday 19 December 2003

'Pub regulars hope for Royal backing. The landlord of a Witney pub has been refused the go-ahead to convert it into a private house. The lowlands planning sub-committee of West Oxfordshire District Council voted nine to three on Monday to reject David Thomas' plans for the House of Windsor. Mr. Thomas told the planners that the pub was not viable and that there are ten other pubs within half a mile of the premises in West End, Witney. The House of Windsor, formerly the King of Prussia pub, in West End, has been a pub since 1774 and is listed in the Campaign for Real Ale's *Good Beer Guide*. Customer Paul Creighton, of the Save our Windsor Action Group, said: "We've written to Prince Charles and are awaiting a reply. We know he has supported campaigns to prevent closure of pubs in the past. The pub is a vital part of community life in West End and is the only one in the country called The House of Windsor." Planning officers recommended permission be given for the conversion, but the sub-committee decided not to accept the advice. Mr. Thomas said he was considering whether to appeal.'

Licensees:

1770–1786	John Rowles
1787–1792	Thomas Redgate
1793–1802	William Rowles
1804–1806	John Collins
1807	The King of Prussia was to be let in January
1807	The King of Prussia was for sale by auction in June
1808–1822	Thomas Andrews
1830	Charles Gardner
1840	Public House Garden &c. owned by Joseph Clarke
1842–1844	James Gardner
1847–1854	William Davis
	Age 42, born in Worcester. Wife Dianah age 38 (1851 Census)
1856	The King of Prussia was to be let in March
1864–1901	George Hudson
	Age 59, born in Hailey, Oxon. Butcher. Wife Mary age 59 (1881 Census)

	Age 69, born in Hailey, Oxon. Widower (1891 Census)
	Age 79, born in Hailey, Oxon. Widower (1901 Census)
1901	George Hudson died in the middle of the year age 79
1901–1902	Emma Hudson
1903	George Weller
1903	A dwelling house formerly known as the King of Prussia
1904–1914	Jane Weller (Mrs.)
	Age 64, born in Witney, Oxon. Widow (1911 Census)
1914	Jane Churchill Weller was buried on 28 November 1914 aged 67
1925	Owned by Simmonds & Co Reading
1918–1941	Alfred Bourton
1942	Bourton Alfred of 31 West End Witney Oxfordshire died 13 April 1942 at Radcliffe Infirmary Oxford Probate Oxford 4 July to Harriett Emily Bourton widow Frederick John Bourton grocers manager and Lindzey Robert Feaviour furniture buyer. Effects £358 9s. 4d.
1942–1945	Harriet Emily Bourton
1946–1959	Philip Baston
1960–1968	George William Manning
1969	Samuel R. Carr
1970–1972	Gwendoline M. Carr
1973–1975	Peter E. Stevens
1977–1980	Leslie J. Robinson
2003–2007	David Thomas
2007–2010	Terry McHugh Closed

Jolly Tucker (aka Tucker), 10 West End (1774–1908)

(Currently private residences)
(1840 Tithe Awards Map ref 699)

From the newspapers:

Gloucestershire Chronicle – Saturday 09 March 1839
'DEATHS. On the 20th ult., Mr. John Rawlins, of Wood Green, formerly of the Jolly Tucker, Witney'

Oxford Journal – Saturday 26 June 1841
'WITNEY, June 24. Died, this day, of a decline, in the 50th year of his age, Mr. Colegrave, of the Jolly Tucker; his loss will be sincerely felt by his numerous friends and relatives.'

Oxford Chronicle and Reading Gazette – Saturday 23 February 1861
'BIRTH. – Feb. 20, at Witney, the wife of Mr. William Gammage, of the Jolly Tucker Inn, of a daughter.'

Oxford Chronicle and Reading Gazette – Saturday 21 February 1863
'DIED.- Feb. 12, in West End, Witney, Sarah Elizabeth, the wife of Mr. William Gammage, of the Jolly Tucker Inn, aged 37.'

Oxford Chronicle and Reading Gazette – Saturday 21 March 1863
'Jolly Tucker Inn, Witney, Oxon. SEELY and BUCKINGHAM will SELL by AUCTION, on the Premises in the occupation of Mr. Gammage, on Wednesday

next, the 25th day of March, commencing at 11 o'clock, – The HOUSEHOLD FURNITURE, BREWING PLANT, Stock of Home-brewed BEER, Casks, and Effects, described in the catalogues now in circulation. Further particulars may be known on application to the Auctioneers, High Street, Witdey (sic.).'

Oxford Chronicle and Reading Gazette – Saturday 23 May 1863
'FREEHOLD PROPERTY, In WITNEY OXON. A Valuable MODERN RESIDENCE and GARDEN, Six DWELLING HOUSES and Appurtenances. Four COTTAGES, the "JOLLY TUCKER" PUBLIC HOUSE, also a spacious MALTHOUSE and Premises,

TO BE SOLD BY AUCTION Mr LONG, At the "King's Arms" Inn, Witney, on Wednesday, the 3rd of June, 1863, at 5 o'clock, in 8 lots (by order of the Executors of the late Miss Lane, deceased.) ...

Lot 7. – That well frequented and old established PUBLIC HOUSE and Premises, well known as the "JOLLY TUCKER," situate in West End, comprising Tap Room, Bar, Parlour, Kitchen, 3 Bedrooms and Attics, an excellent Cellar and Brew-house attached, Yard, and Back Entrance, with a good GARDEN.

Lot 8. – A spacious Nine-Quarter MALT-HOUSE in West End, comprising Barley and Malt Granaries, Grinding Room, Warehouse, and Premises attached, also a good substantial DWELLING HOUSE adjoining, and fronting West End Street, with right of entrance through the gateway, use of pump, &c.

Printed particulars, with the description of each lot and conditions of sale, may be had at the Office of Messrs. Bullen and Ravenor, solicitors, Witney, and of the Auctioneer, Witney.'

Oxford Chronicle and Reading Gazette – Saturday 17 February 1866
'Died. – On the 11th inst., at Ramsden, late of the Jolly Tucker Inn, Witney, Mr. W. Gammage, aged 42.'

Oxford Chronicle and Reading Gazette – Saturday 15 June 1867
'Clubs. – On Monday the Benefit Societies held their annual feasts at the Elm Tree, Jolly Tucker, Court Inn, and Butchers' Arms, Witney. – On Tuesday the Benefit Club held their annual dinner at the Griffin Inn, New Land, Coggs. The Witney Band were engaged playing through the principal streets, after their return from Coggs Church.'

Oxford Journal – Saturday 23 November 1872
'BAMPTON EAST DIVISION. – Witney, Nov. 21, ... Alfred Thornett, of Hailey, was charged with being drunk in the Jolly Tuckers, Witney, on the 18th instant, and refusing to quit; committed for fourteen days imprisonment.'

The Stage – Thursday 12 December 1901
'WANTED, through disappointment, Pianist, to open at once. One used to Portable Theatre preferred. – Lowest terms, Allen, Jolly Tuckers, West End, Witney, Oxfordshire.'

Oxford Times – Saturday 29 August 1903
'... George Broome, licensed victualler, of the "Jolly Tucker," West End, Witney, was summoned by Elisa Ann Broome, his wife, for assaulting her on the 11th inst.

Mr. Andrew Walsh appeared for the defendant, and in the absence of the wife, the Bench allowed the case to be withdrawn.'

Witney Gazette and West Oxfordshire Advertiser – Saturday 12 September 1903
'PETTY SESSIONS, Thursday. HOLDOVERS. Applications for the holdover of the license of the "Jolly Tucker," Witney, from George Broom to Edward George Conway; ...'

Oxford Times – Saturday 26 September 1903
'PETTY SESSIONS, Thursday. TRANSFER. – The licence of the ... that of the "Jolly Tucker," Witney, from George Broom to Edward Conway; ...'

Oxford Times – Saturday 02 June 1906
'LICENCES AT WITNEY. The Clerk of the Peace said the first cases were licences from the Bampton Petty Sessional Division, and he was in a position to prove that the notices had been given and advertised. The licences in question were "Jolly Tucker," West End, Witney, and the "Malt Shovel," Corn-street, Witney.

Mr. Ames, of the Oxford Circuit, instructed by Messrs. Ravenors, solicitors, Witney, appeared for the Witney Justices, and Mr. Andrew Walsh, solicitor, Oxford, appeared for tenant and the owners.

Mr. Ames said he proposed to take the two cases together.

Mr. Walsh pointed out that the evidence would be different.

Mr. Ames said then he would go on with the "Jolly Tucker."

The Chairman said from their report the Justices thought there was prima-facie case with regard to the "Jolly Tucker," and Mr. Ames would have to show why this particular public-house should be selected to be done away with.

Mr. Ames said the "Jolly Tucker" was at the corner of West-street and Bridge-street, and if a radius of 500 feet was taken it would be seen by the map that there were five licensed houses in the circle and one just outside, and of these Messrs. Clinch owned three. The history of how the "Jolly Tucker" came to be selected was this: The Justices came to the conclusion that there were too many public-houses in Witney, and they called upon the superintendent of police to make a report as to the accommodation and various characteristics of these different public-houses. They considered the report in committee and selected four houses for inspection. Two, the "Jolly Tucker" and the "Harriers," were visited, and they decided that in point of accommodation that at the "Jolly Tucker" was inferior to that at the "Harriers"; there was no accommodation for lodgers and no stabling, whereas at the "Harriers" a considerable sum had been recently spent in making the place better adapted as a public-house, and, in fact, was particularly well adapted for it. There was a back entrance to the "Jolly Tucker," which was kept locked by a particular arrangement with the landlord: it would be possible to evade that undertaking, but he did not suggest that it had been done. He was not suggesting that the house was structurally unfit for a public-house, but he had to draw a comparison between the two houses. There was another point, apart from the house, that of differentiation, which was a great factor. Messrs. Clinch owned 15 houses out of 29 in Witney; no one else owned more than four, and the rest were owned by separate owners, and what the Justices felt was this, that if they took a licence away from one of these separate owners they would be enormously increasing the monopoly of Messrs. Clinch, and would also interfere with the convenience of the public to a certain extent, because there would not be the opportunity of getting the beer they wanted. Another point was that the tenant worked at the Mills, and that was a matter of differentiation, for this reason - it was not a point connected with the fitness of the holder of the licence, because there had been no complaint of the conduct of the house, but it was an indication that the trade of the house could be a general one only of an evening, if the licensee could spend his day elsewhere.

Mr. Walter George Eaton, surveyor and sanitary inspector, Witney, deposed to having prepared a map showing the position of the licenced houses in the town, and within a circle of 500 feet there were five fully-licensed houses and one wine licence. The approximate number of houses in the circle was 145 and the number of inhabitants 561; the average was one public-house to every 28 men. The distance of the "Jolly Tucker" from the "Harriers" was 191 feet, from the "Elm Tree" 336 feet, from the "King of Prussia" 500 feet, from the Court Inn 171 feet, and from the "Black Head" 328 feet. He stated the accommodation of the house, and said there were no rooms for lodgers and no stabling. The "Harriers" had good accommodation for lodgers and some stabling, and with regard to the other houses in the circle he described the accommodation they possessed of this character. At the "Jolly Tucker" there was a back door into a passage.

In reply to Mr. Walsh, the witness said the "Jolly Tucker" was at the corner of two streets, where the road was narrow. He should call the place where a home could be put a shed rather than a stable. He should think the "Jolly Tucker" was more used by the public than the "Harriers." The landlord of the "Harriers" was a fish-hawker − he did not know that be was a barber as well. He could not say there were other houses in Witney which were less required than the "Jolly Tucker."

Supt. Hawtin said he had visited all the houses in the town by order of the Bench of Magistrates. He agreed with Mr. Eaton's description of the houses in the circle. There was a large shed at the "Jolly Tucker," which could not be called a stable. The back door at the "Jolly Tucker" he had every reason to suppose was always locked when the house was closed. The tenant was a foremen at Messrs. Smith's Mill, and his customers were working-men. The same kind of beer could he obtained at the "Black Head" as at the "Jolly Tucker." He had no complaint whatever as to the conduct of the house.

By Mr. Walsh: He did not complain of the back door, but the fact remained that it was there. The present tenant had been there three years, and he believed the previous tenant was there eight or nine years. From common observation he thought the house did a fair trade, and that it did more than some of the other houses, but he did not think he could go so far as to say that therefore it was more needed. There had been three tenants at the "Harriers" in the last six years, and for some time the spirit licence for that house was not taken out, but last year it was again taken out. In 1906 an application was made for a spirit licence for the New Inn, Minster Lovell, the proposal being that the spirit licence of the "Harriers" should be transferred if the application was granted. The objection to the "Jolly Tucker" was that were too many licensed houses in Witney. There were one or two houses doing less trade than the "Jolly Tucker." The landlord of the "Harriers" hawked fish for sale.

Mr. John Bryan, chairman of the District Council, and a Justice of the Bampton Division, said he had been round the town of Witney with Mr. Staples-Brown and Mr. Dawkins, and found there were 29 public-houses to a population of 3,700, or one to every 124. Of the "Jolly Tucker" and the "Harriers" he considered the latter was the better house. After a great deal of consideration two houses were selected to be done away with. He considered the position of the "Jolly Tucker" was inconvenient on account of the narrowness of the road. The landlady told him that there was not sufficient trade at the house, and that her husband had to go out to work.

By Mr. Walsh: The two houses selected were taken on account of Messrs. Clinch having other houses in the immediate district, and that people could get that particular beer there.

This was the case for the Justices.

The tenant, Mr. Conway, was called, and stated that he worked at Messrs. Smith's Mill. He paid £15 a year rent, and the house was tied for beer and spirits. His weekly trade was 3½ barrels of ale, 18 gallons of bitter, and 9 gallons of stout. He did not take "policeman's lodgers" (tramps) in. He had full accommodation for his trade, and had never heard of the inconvenience of the position the house.

Mr. John R. Wilkins, architect, Oxford, stated the dimensions of the bar and rooms for the public at the "Jolly Tucker," and said he considered the accommodation was as good or better than that of some of the houses in the locality. There was a good building, which he should think was erected for a stable, although there were no stalls or manger: the way to it was by the back door. About £70 had been laid out in sanitary improvements.

Mr. Charles Storey, manager to Messrs. Clinch and Co., said the "Jolly Tucker" did a good trade, better than the "Black Head," and better also than some other of the firm's houses.

Mr. Walsh said he had one or two matters which he thought the Bench ought to take into consideration. It seemed to him quite obvious that the renewal authority when they decided to pick out this licence did not and indeed could not, have in mind the decision in the Dartford Brewery case, that there must be direct evidence before them of differentiating one house from the other. It was quite plain from what Mr. Bryan said, and from the whole trend of his friend's case, that these two houses were picked out somewhat haphazard in what one might call a congested area from the of Messrs. Clinch and Co., and without reference to whether their houses were more required or not, than the other houses in this locality. Surely this matter had to be decided on a question of public need. That he understood was the way which magistrates had to look at these matters, and if his clients' 15 houses were more required for the wants of the neighbourhood than the other houses in

Witney, all he could say was that in common justice one or other of those houses ought to go without any reference whatever to the ownership of any particular house at all. His friend, having in his eye on the decision in the Dartford Brewery case, had dragged in in order to come within that decision different matters which were not before the renewal authority with regard to the accommodation, the back entrance, and so on, which he admitted were quite immaterial when dealing with the question of redundancy in the neighbourhood. He submitted that the whole question was one of trade, that whether a house was needed or not must be shown by the number of persons who used it, and as a direct consequence the amount of trade done there. It was admitted by the witnesses who appeared for the opposition, reluctantly, and therefore it was of infinitely more value to him, that this house did a good trade, and some of them said it did a better trade than a good many of the houses in Witney. In addition to that there was the evidence of Mr. Storey, the manager to Messrs. Clinch, who told them that this particular house did a better trade than that done by the "Black Head," which Superintendent Hawtin had said was a good house. What he submitted was this, that there were other houses in Witney which were less needed than these two, and that in the matter of trade, which showed if there was a necessity for the house or not, he had made out a good case for the renewal of the licence, and that there was not sufficient evidence of any real substantial difference between the houses in this area as to allowed them to say that this house ought go. It had been shown that the trade of this house was larger than in the majority of the houses in that particular district, and on that ground alone he admitted that the licence should be renewed.

Mr. Ames having briefly replied.

The Committee retired, and after a short absence, the Chairman said they were agreed in confirming the decision of the licensing justices.'

Banbury Advertiser – Thursday 03 January 1907
'OXFORDSHIRE QUARTER SESSIONS. ... The Chairman said the next business was the report of the Licensing Committee. The report was as follows: ... At the general annual licensing meetings in the present year, the question of the non-renewal of nine licences of public houses was referred to the Committee by the licensing justices, with reports, under section 1 of the Licensing Act 1904- five such licences being from the Borough of Banbury, two from the Bampton East Division, and two from the Henley Petty Sessional Divisional. After hearing the persons interested, as well as the licensing justices and their counsel, solicitors and witnesses, the Committee decided to refuse the renewal of six of the licences referred to them, and not refuse the renewal of the remaining three licences. With regard to the six cases where the licences were extinguished, the Committee gave consideration to the claims made for compensation, and after taking the advice of Mr. Arthur Vernon, of High Wycombe, as valuer upon the amounts submitted by the claimants, and also hearing the parties interested, and their counsel and solicitors, the Committee approved of the award of compensation at the sums ultimately agreed upon by the parties in the following four cases - the shares in which the amount was divisable between the owners and licensees being also

agreed upon: – Malt Shovel beerhouse, Witney, £761; Jolly Tucker alehouse. Witney, £1,250; ...'

Licensees:

1774–1776	James Cook
1777–1779	Anthony Geeves
1781–1818	William Rawlins
1819–1838	John Rawlins
1839	John Rawlins died in February
1839–1841	William Colegrane
1840	Public House Garden &c. owned by Edward Rawlins
1841	William Colgrave died in June aged 50
1842–1844	John Shepherd
1847–1854	Joseph Gardner
	Age 39, born in Witney, Oxon. Wife Catherine age 42 (1851 Census)
1861–1863	William Gammage
	Age 37, born in Hailey, Oxon. Wife Sarah age 35 (1861 Census)
1863	The Jolly Tucker was to be sold by auction in June
1864–1868	Howell Buckingham
1866	William Gammage died in February aged 42
1869–1887	James Fowler
	Age 37, born in Witney, Oxon. Master Carpenter (employing 2 men) & Licenced Victualler. Wife Esther age 36 (1871 Census)
1891–1895	Harry Herbert Hinton
	Age 24, born in Coggs, Oxon. Wife Mary age 22 (1891 Census)
1899–1903	George Broom
	Age 34, born in Witney, Oxon. Wife Eliza A age 30 (1901 Census)
1904–1908	Edward George Conway Closed

Nelson, 27 West End (1840–1901)

(Currently a private residence)
(1840 Tithe Awards Map ref 650)

From the newspapers:

Oxford Chronicle and Reading Gazette – Saturday 26 December 1846
'HOUSEBREAKING. – A most daring robbery was committed on Sunday evening last, between the hours of 6 and 8 o'clock, at the house of Mr. John Harris, West end, in Witney, baker. It seems, that in the absence of Mr. and Mrs. Harris, who were attending the Wesleyan chapel, the thieves entered the house by wrenching the lock off the street door; they then went into a sitting room, ransacked several small boxes, and not finding anything to them very valuable, proceeded up stairs, where they burst the locks of 3 drawers, and a trunk, standing in the bedroom, and abstracted two purses containing gold and silver amounting to £40 and upwards, two gold rings (one a keeper), a brooch, and several other articles of jewellery. After having strewed the contents of several drawers and boxes on the floor, they decamped with their booty, leaving no clue to lead to their discovery. From the impression left on the door, they must have used an iron bar or some other strong

instrument in effecting an entrance. Mr. Harris has offered a reward of £5 for the apprehension of the thieves. Added to the above there was an attempt made to get into Mr. Judd's house in Corn street, but the depredators were disturbed and took to their heels.'

Witney Gazette and West Oxfordshire Advertiser – Saturday 18 May 1901
'DEATH OF MR G. HUDSON. - We regret having to record the decease of a very old townsman, in the person of Mr. George Hudson, of the "Nelson" inn, Witney, who died on Wednesday in last week. The deceased, who was highly respected by all who know him, was the oldest licensed victualler in Witney, having had a license ever since the year 1853. For some 35 years also carried on the business of a butcher. The deceased, who is deeply mourned by his friends, was buried at Hailey, on Saturday.'

Witney Gazette and West Oxfordshire Advertiser – Saturday 25 May 1901
'The holdover of the license of the "Nelson" Inn, Witney, from George Hudson to Jane Weller was granted.'

Licensees:

1840	Public House Garden &c. owned by John Harris
1840–1846	John Harris
	Age 45, Baker. Wife Sarah age 45 (1841 Census)
1851–1853	John Hudson
	Age 65, born in Minster Lovell, Oxon. Landlord & Baker. Wife Mary age 65 (1851 Census)
1853–1901	George Hudson
	Age 39, born in Hailey, Oxon. Butcher & Publican. Wife Mary age 39 (1861 Census)
	Age 49, born in Hailey, Oxon. Butcher & Farmer, farming 27 acres of land, employing 1 man. Wife Mary age 49 (1871 Census)
	Age 59, born in Hailey, Oxon. Butcher. Wife Mary age 59 (1881 Census)
	Age 69, born in Hailey, Oxon. Inn Keeper & Butcher. Widower (1891 Census)
	Age 79, born in Hailey, Oxon. Publican. Widower (1901 Census)
1901	HUDSON George of West-end Witney Oxfordshire publican died 8 May 1901 (*aged 79*) Probate **Oxford** 26 June to John Henry Humphris restaurant-keeper Effects £529 1s 3d.
1901	Jane Weller

Three Tuns, West End

From the newspapers:

Oxford University and City Herald – Saturday 24 January 1807
'TO BE SOLD BY PRIVATE CONTRACT, THAT Long-established and Substantial PUBLIC HOUSE called the THREE TUNS, having a good and convenient cellar, brewhouse, stable, and garden, with other necessary and suitable offices, and out-buildings, situated in a street called West End, in the hamlet of Hailey, in the parish of Witney, in the county of Oxford, and near to

the Turnpike Road leading from Witney to Charlbury, Chipping Norton, &c. For further particulars apply to Mr. Turner, of Witney aforesaid.'

Oxford Journal – Saturday 04 April 1807

'TO be SOLD by AUCTION, by W. LONG, at the Lamb Inn, in Witney, Oxon, on Thursday next, April the 9th, 1807, at Three o'Clock in the Afternoon, - That long-established and substantial PUBLIC HOUSE, called the Three Tuns, with the TENEMENT adjoining, having a good and convenient Cellar, Brew House, Stable, and Gardens, with other necessary and suitable Offices and Outbuildings, situated in a Street called West End, in the Hamlet of Hailey, in the Parish of Witney, Oxon, and near to the Turnpike Road leading from Witney to Charlbury, Chipping Norton, &c.-For a View, and further Particulars, apply to W. Turner, Witney.'

Wheatsheaf, West End (1762–1858)

From the newspapers:

Oxford Journal – Saturday 10 June 1780

'SELLING off, at Witney, in the County of Oxford, The ENTIRE STOCK in TRADE, and WORKING UTENSILS of the late William Lewis, deceased, consisting of a large Quantity of Kiln Plate, Bar Iron, Smith's Iron, Bushel Iron, Bristol Steel, &c. one Pair of Forge Bellows, almost new, Kiln Plate Tools, together with a great Variety of other Tools. – They who are inclinable to purchase any of the above-mentioned Articles, are requested to apply to the Widow Lewis, at the Sign of the Wheat-Sheaf, in Witney aforesaid, who has likewise laid in a large Assortment of Scythes, Reaping-Hooks, and Sickles, to be sold, Wholesale and Retail, upon the most reasonable Terms.'

Oxford Chronicle and Reading Gazette – Saturday 10 July 1858

Refer to page 161 for full article for the sale of three Public Houses in Witney.

Licensees:

1762–1771	John Luckett
1774–1779	Benjamin Wiggins
1780	John Luckett
1781	Benjamin Wiggins
1782–1785	John Luckett
1858	The Wheatsheaf was for sale by auction

Around Witney

Windrush Inn, 60 Burford Rd (1954–present)

(Currently trading, owned by Heineken)

From the newspapers:

Oxford Times – Friday 08 November 1963
'BEATLES' QUIET WITNEY LUNCH The Beatles were in Witney on Friday – and Witney did not know. That is, only a handful of people knew, and they were customers in the Windrush Inn on the Burford Road, where the famous group stopped for lunch. When a black Austin Princess saloon halted on the forecourt outside the inn on the main A40 road, it was not given a second glance by passers-by. A member of the entourage entered the premises and asked if lunch could be served to a small party. "The man said it was for the Beatles," said Mr. Ted Thompson, the landlord of the inn. "They were feeling tired and could their presence be kept quiet." And that was why the Beatles, on their way to Cheltenham for an appearance on Friday night, were able to break their journey for an hour in peace. There they were, none of the maddening crowds such as they has experienced at London Airport the previous day on their return from their successful visit to Sweden. Mind you, this is not to say that the atmosphere in the Windrush Inn was not, well, a little electric to say the least. Mrs. Margaret Hill, who was doing the waiting in the dining room with Mrs. Pauline Grant, was bubbling over with excitement. "I didn't know whether I was coming or going," she said later. And Mrs. Marjorie Marchant, who served the drinks, was quite as excited. The distinguished quartet signed a menu for Mr. Thompson and obliged several others with their autographs. Their privacy was respected – as much as possible, and as they left the inn news of their presence had still not generally leaked out.'

Licensees:

1953	Planning permission was granted for a public house
1954–1972	Edwin Reid Thompson
1973–1980	Cecil R. Ward
1995–2003	Yvonne Laight
2003–present	Jeremy Laight

Rowing Machine (Flying Machine), 25 Fettiplace Rd (1962–present)

(Currently trading, owned by Greene King Retailing)

Licensees:

1960	Planning permission was granted for a public house
1961	Pub is built by West Country Breweries of Cheltenham
1962	Pub opens
1962–1964	Abraham Payne
1965	Leslie J. Townsend

1967–1968	James Elias
1969	Derek T. Haywood
1970–1975	Thomas M. Morgan
1976–1977	Clive E. Hagger
1978	Michael H. Shearing
1979	John C. Pearce
1980	Ethel M. Addison
2005	Pub owned by Greene King Retailing
2005–2007	Nigel Russell
2007	Christopher Snell
2008	Sheila Haines
2009–2010	Paul Wakefield
2011	Caroline Perry
2011–2014	Sarah Milligan
2014–2017	Shelley Barlow
2017–present	Thomas Parker

Robin Hood, 81 Hailey Rd (1775–2005)

(Currently a private residence)

From the newspapers:

Oxford Journal – Saturday 14 December 1878
'HAILEY FIELD, NEAR WITNEY. Excellent BREWING PLANT, with Copper, Pump, &o., complete, Beer Casks, Iron-axle Wagon, capital Spring Trap, two Milk Leads and Stands, various Implements, and a few lots of FURNITURE and Effects, TO BE SOLD BY AUCTION, By WILLIAM F. LONG, On the premises, at the Robin Hood, Hailey Field, near Witney, on Monday, December 23, at Twelve o'clock. The brewing plant, which is in excellent condition, is sold only on account of the proprietor having discontinued brewing. Catalogues may be had at the place of sale, and of the auctioneer, West-end, Witney.'

Oxford Mail – Friday 16 February 2001
'Landlord hits target. Pub Licensee Kevin Bunyan is the toast of the town after scooping a double award for his beer keeping. Kevin, who is licensee of the Robin Hood, in Hailey Road, Witney, was given his second Cask Marque Award by brewers Greene King after their latest cellar inspection. He also scored 93 per cent in a mystery guest assessment, even though he was on holiday and the pub was being run by his family at the time of the visit. He said: "Cask Marque, cellar awards and high mystery guest assessments are a good reflection on the bar staff and my wife Elaine. It's a team effort running a local estate pub offering 11 different sporting events, bar meals and real ale. The cellar is my domain and as far as I'm concerned, if you keep it clean it's dead easy." It is his second Cask Marque at the Robin Hood – he received the award while a Morlands tenant.'

Licensees:

1775–1781	John Harbud
1899–1913	James Buckingham

1914–1949	Ernest Clements
	DOB 15 May 1868 Licensee. Wife Esther dob 2 Jul 1867 Unpaid
	Domestic Duties (1939 Register)
1950–1954	John Anthony O'Connor
1955–1966	William Wyatt
1967–1972	Godfrey Evans
1973–1976	James H. P. Saunders
1977	Brian McGhin
1978 - 1979	Leslie R. F. Goddard
1980	Roger V. Pitkethly
2001	Pub owned by Greene King
2001–2006	Kevin Bunyan
2007	Mark Holmes
	Lynne Kane
	Elizabeth Killeen
	Anna Key
2008	Sarah Woodcock
2009–2011	Kevin Bunyan
2012	Gary Nicholls
2013	Olwyn Newby
2013	Pub closed 5th August

Carpenter's Arms (Plaister's Arms), 132 Newland (1761–present)

(Currently trading, Free House)

From the newspapers:

Berkshire Chronicle – Saturday 12 June 1830

'LOCALITIES AND GENERALITIES. An inquest was held at the Carpenter Arms, Newland, on the body of William Robinson, of Shilton, Berks, apparently about 60 years of age, who was killed in the parish of Coggs, near Witney, by a van passing over his body, in the night of the 28th ult. Several of the ribs of the left side were dreadfully fractured, and his back much bruised; the left arm was also literally crushed from the elbow to the shoulder. The van was the property of Mr. Haines, and was proceeding from Oxford to Cheltenham; the deceased was driving for James Maisey, who gave up the whip to Robinson at Ensham, and got inside; nor was he aware of the accident having happened until his horses were stopped in the town of Witney, by a man who found the deceased on the road, and ran after the van. There were two or three other persons with Maisey in the van, and it appeared he was perfectly sober. It is proper to state, as some excuse for Maisey having given up the whip to the deceased, that Robinson was in the constant habit of driving for him, and travelled by the van from Burford to Oxford every week. His death must have been instantaneous, as the man who found him had walked from Ensham behind and within sight of the van. The Jury returned a verdict of Accidental death, and imposed a deodand of 2s. on the wheel causing the death.'

Oxford Chronicle and Reading Gazette – Saturday 15 May 1847
'MONEY STEALING. – On Saturday last, Clift and Richard Ashfield the younger, were apprehended and brought before Walter Strickland, Esq. on a charge of stealing money from the house of Mr. Castle, the Carpenter's Arms, Witney. Clift found bail for his appearance at the sessions, and Ashfield was acquitted, there being no evidence to support a committal.'

Oxford Chronicle and Reading Gazette – Saturday 17 July 1847
'Oxfordshire Summer Assizes. John Clift, 25, was charged with stealing six sovereigns, a silver watch, two gold studs, and other property, at Coggs, the property of Watkin Castle. Mr. Pigott for prosecution, Mr. Keating defended prisoner. Maria Castle deposed that she is the wife of Watkin Castle, who keeps the Carpenters' Arms, at Coggs, near Witney. On Saturday evening, 8th May, heard some one up stairs, and had a glimpse of a man on the landing. She fetched her father. He went up stairs, and she followed him. Saw some one near the drawer in which their money was. Her father said he was gone out of window. They found the drawer had been forced open. There were two small boxes in the drawer, in which were 2 £5 notes and 5 sovereigns, and 2 gold studs, which belonged to the club. The drawer was locked. There was another small box in the drawer, in one were 6 sovereigns and about £2 in silver. The money was gone. The box was left in the drawer. She saw it safe an hour and a half before. She had left a watch on the shelf near the window, that was gone. Prisoner used to lodge in the house. Had seen him in the house the day the money was lost. The room in which the prisoner had slept adjoined the one from which the money had been taken...

The learned Judge said, he thought the case a very weak one. The Jury returned a verdict of not guilty, and prisoner was immediately discharged.'

Oxford Chronicle and Reading Gazette – Saturday 18 July 1863
'SUDDEN DEATH. On the 13th instant, an inquest was held, before F. Westell, Esq., coroner, at the Carpenters' Arms Inn, Newland, Coggs, on the body of a young man unknown. The deceased had stayed at a lodging house on Saturday night, in Corn street, and kept raving the greater part of the night about some one going to kill him by smothering him. He got up at 5 o'clock on Sunday morning and went off. He complained of a sore throat. At 11 o'clock on Sunday he was seen by George Harris, of Coggs, when he was raving and talking a lot of nonsense... Death was caused by inflammation of the membrane of the brain, brought on by excitement and extreme heat of the weather. Verdict accordingly. Deceased's stockings were marked "H. M. S. 12."'

Oxford Times – Saturday 12 April 1879
'FOUND DEAD. – An inquest was held on Monday last, before Mr. Coroner Westell, at the Carpenter's Arms, Newland, Coggs, on the body of Zelpha Ball, wife of Charles Ball, of Coggs, labourer, aged 72 years. It appeared that the deceased had been very well with the exception of a cough. On the night preceding her death she ate her supper as usual, and then went to bed. Her husband stated that

he did not hear anything of his wife in the night, but about five o'clock on the morning of the inquest, he awoke and found he could not hear her breathe, and then discovered that she was dead. Medical evidence tended to show that death resulted from disease of the heart. Verdict accordingly.'

Witney Gazette and West Oxfordshire Advertiser – Saturday 04 October 1884
'FATAL ACCIDENT. An accident, which unhappily proved fatal occurred to a man named Isaac Calcutt. The deceased was well known in the neighbourhood as one of the draymen employed at the Eagle Brewery. He was a respectable young man, and was to have taken possession of the "Carpenter's Arms" Inn, on the following day. The particulars of his death will be found below...' *(see the Griffin below.)*

Witney Gazette and West Oxfordshire Advertiser – Saturday 23 May 1891
'NEWLAND CLUB. The members of the above club had their annual dinner on Whit-Tuesday. After attending Divine Service at Coggs Church in the morning, the members headed by the Ramsden Brass Band, marched in procession through the town to the "Carpenter's Arms," where a capital spread was provided by Host Cripps.'

Oxford Journal – Saturday 19 September 1891
'INQUEST.-F. Westell, Esq., held an inquest at the Carpenter's Arms, Newland, on Tuesday, on the body of Harriett Rowles, who died early on Monday morning.-Edward Rowles deposed that the deceased was his wife, and that her breathing had been bad for some years. She vomited some clear water at 12 o'clock on Sunday night, and seemed to be better afterwards, but she gradually got worse, and died soon after 12 o'clock. - Edward Hyde, surgeon, stated that deceased had suffered from heart disease for some years, and be believed that was the cause of death.-A verdict to that effect was accordingly returned.'

Witney Gazette and West Oxfordshire Advertiser – Saturday 01 April 1893
'THE ALLOTMENT QUESTION. A meeting of the working men of Coggs, was held at the Carpenters Arms Inn, on Friday, for the purpose of considering the providing of allotments for those requiring them. About 20 men were present... The question as to what would be a fair rent was then discussed, when the general opinion seemed to be that they should be able to get their allotments at 30s. per acre. A vote of thanks to Mr. Dingle concluded the proceedings.'

Witney Gazette and West Oxfordshire Advertiser – Saturday 14 July 1894
'LOCAL GOVERNMENT. – On Wednesday evening many working men of Coggs assembled at the "Carpenters Arms" Inn for the purpose of hearing the Parish Councils Act explained. Mr. Blake, C.C, presided. Mr. S. J. Rose and Mr. I. Dingle addressed the meeting, the latter stating that the receipt of charity did not preclude a man from sitting on the Pariah Council.'

Witney Gazette and West Oxfordshire Advertiser – Saturday 08 June 1895
'CLUB FEAST. – On Tuesday last the members of the Carpenters Arms Friendly Society held their annual festivity at Newland, when Mr. Samuel Smith was

re-elected secretary, and Messrs T. Beeson and E. Haley as stewards. In the morning service was held at Coggs Church, conducted by the Rev. E. J. U. Payne. A collection was made in aid of the Witney Hospital Fund. After service the members, accompanied by the Ramsden Band, proceeded to their head quarters where a capital spread was served by Host Cripps. The Balance Sheet front May 18th., 1894 to June 4th., 1895 was read.'

Witney Gazette and West Oxfordshire Advertiser – Saturday 19 June 1897
'THE SUDDEN DEATH AT NEWLAND. INQUEST. On Friday evening last F. Westell, Esq., (coroner) held an inquest at the "Carpenters Arms," Newland touching on the death of William Rowles, an old man who died suddenly in his garden that morning. The following evidence was adduced: Hannah Mansell deposed: I lived with the deceased as his house-keeper at Coggs. He was 89 years of age. I left the deceased in the house at 9 o'clock this morning to go to my work. Deceased had his breakfast as usual...

Mr. W. D. Hyde deposed : I have occasionally seen deceased professionally. He suffered from giddiness. I have examined the body, and find nothing remarkable on it. I believe be died from disease of the heart. A verdict of death from heart disease was returned.'

Witney Gazette and West Oxfordshire Advertiser – Saturday 03 August 1901
'PETTY SESSIONS, Thursday. CHARGE AGAINST AN INNKEEPER. John Cripps, of Coggs, licensed victualler, was summoned by the police for permitting drunkenness on his licensed premises, the "Carpenter's Arms" Inn, Coggs, on the 30th June... John Cripps, landlord of the "Carpenter's Arms," deposed: I have been the landlord of the house for 13 years... The Bench imposed a fine of £3 including costs, the Chairman saying the Magistrates considered it a very bad case, but they had taken into consideration the fact that it was his first offence.'

Witney Gazette and West Oxfordshire Advertiser – Saturday 28 September 1901
'CARPENTERS ARMS INN Newland. Coggs. To be Sold by Auction by RICHARD GILLETT On Tuesday, October 1st , 1901 at 12 for 1 o'clock, on the premises, by order of Mr. Cripps, who is leaving, upwards of 150 Lots of HOUSEHOLD FURNITURE and EFFECTS, comprising Windsor and other Chairs, Iron Bedsteads, Chests of Drawers, Glasses, Tables, Clocks, Washstands, Cooking and Washing Utensils, &c., &c.'

Oxford Times – Friday 24 October 1975
'Publican Retires. Mr. Cliff Bayliss, the retiring landlord of the Carpenter Arms, Newland, Witney, was recently presented with a copper etching by his customers. Mr. Bayliss, who is 61 and a widower, has been the licensee of the public house for 27 years. The gift will also mark the end of an era for the Carpenter's Arms, for Courage the brewers are planning to close it, although the public house has been on the market since August, freehold and with full on-licence.'

Licensees:

1761–1776	Michael Jackson
1777–1796	Thomas Phipps
1797–1804	James Shayler
1819–1822	Thomas Turner
1830	John Cantwell
1839–1844	Swanley Harrod Polden
1847–1852	Watkin Castle
1853–1854	William Pool
1863–1868	John Cowley
1869–1883	Thomas Hinton
1887	Joseph Green
1888–1902	John Cripps
	Age 44, born in Alvescot, Oxon. Wife Mary age 51 (1891 Census)
1903–1906	Henry John Moss
1908–1919	Daniel William Weller
	Age 31, born in Witney, Oxon. Wife Esther Ryman age 33 (1911 Census)
1925	Owned by Clinch & Co
1920–1939	James William Staines jnr
	DOB 16 Feb 1879 Publican. Wife Eliza dob 30 Jun 1885 Unpaid Domestic Duties (1939 Register)
1940	Staines James Williams of The Carpenter Arms Newland Witney Oxfordshire died 1 April 1940 at the Radcliffe Infirmary Oxford Probate Oxford 15 July to Eliza Hannah Staines widow. Effects £288 4s. 2d.
1940–1947	Eliza Hanna Staines
1948–1975	Aubrey Clifford Bayliss
1975	Cliff Bayliss retired
1976–1978	Brian Evans
1979	Alexander Reader
1980	Graham L. Woolcott
2005	Pub owned by New Wood Inns Ltd
2005	Leslie Farris
2006	Pub bought by Black Rock Properties
2006–2008	Keith Millard
2011	Pub bought by Steven Williams & William Kelly
2009–2013	Robert Fletcher
2014	Martin Long
2015	Pub bought by Mark & Linda Forkner
2015–present	Mark Forkner

Griffin, 166 Newland (1780–present)

(Currently trading, owned by Wadworth Brewery)

From the newspapers:

Oxford Journal – Saturday 18 April 1807

'POOR TO BE LET. NOTICE is hereby given, That all Persons intending to contract for the Support and Maintenance of the POOR of the Parish of Coggs, from May 2, 1807, to the 2d of May following, are requested to attend a Meeting to be held at Mr. James Badcock's, at the Griffin Inn, at Coggs, on Tuesday next, April 21, for that Purpose.'

Oxford Chronicle and Reading Gazette – Saturday 05 January 1856
'MARRIED. On Thursday, 27th Dec., Mr. Thomas Stone, son of Mr. Stone, Griffin Inn, Newland, Witney, to Miss Matilda Brown, of the same place.'

Oxford Chronicle and Reading Gazette – Saturday 15 June 1867
'Clubs. – On Monday the Benefit Societies held their annual feasts at the Elm Tree, Jolly Tucker, Court Inn, and Butchers' Arms, Witney. – On Tuesday the Benefit Club held their annual dinner at the Griffin Inn, New Land, Coggs. The Witney Band were engaged playing through the principal streets, after their return from Coggs Church.'

Witney Gazette and West Oxfordshire Advertiser – Saturday 04 October 1884
'FATAL ACCIDENT... An inquest was held at the "Griffin" Inn, on Monday last, before F. Westell. Esq., coroner, on the body of Isaac Calcutt, when the following evidence was given:

Arthur Haynes deposed : I live at Coggs. I knew deceased; he is Isaac Calcutt, and is 41 years of age; I lived with him. On Saturday last deceased and I were gathering apples in the garden, at about 10 minutes past 6 o'clock in the evening. Deceased was standing on a ladder gathering apples from a tree, and I was beneath the tree. I saw that he was within 3 rounds of the top of the ladder, and he was reaching over the top of it, and in about a minute after I looed up and saw deceased falling from the ladder. No one else was near. I ran to fetch his wife, and she came back with me. He (deceased) said "Oh, my poor head," and was quite sensible. I went for a doctor.

Isaac Cantwell deposed : I live at Coggs. I went to see deceased last Saturday night. Mr Hyde came and attended the deceased until he died. He was sensible until about 4 o'clock yesterday morning, and he died at 7 o'clock. He complained of pain across the shoulders and the back of his head. He told me he was reaching after the apples, and that he took hold of a branch of the tree, which gave way, and that caused him to fall. Verdict – Died from injuries received from accidentally falling from a tree.'

Witney Gazette and West Oxfordshire Advertiser - Saturday 09 January 1886
'OBTRUCTING A FOOTPATH, Edward Lay, of Northleigh was charged with obstructing a footpath at Newland, Coggs, by leaving a horse and trap thereon, on the 20th ult. P.C. Porter deposed: On Sunday afternoon I saw defendant's horse and cart standing outside the "Griffin" Inn in such a manner as to obstruct the foot path. I watched it for 20 minutes and several persons had to turn out of the path. Defendant's wife said they had taken their daughter to the Doctor, and went to the "Griffin" Inn to visit her cousin. Fined, 2s. 6d., and costs, 13s.'

Witney Gazette and West Oxfordshire Advertiser - Saturday 03 September 1887
'PETTY SESSIONS, Thursday. This was the general annual licensing day, and superintendent Keel stated that he had no objection to the renewal of any license. There had not been a conviction during the year. The whole of the licenses were consequently renewed, that of the "Griffin" Inn, Newland, was transferred from John Basson, deceased, to Martha Basson.'

Gloucestershire Echo – Friday 19 March 1948
'WTD., a clean, respectable, honest middle aged woman with no ties; or a young girl; good wages, live in. One who would like to travel. – Apply Mrs. A. Harris, opposite Griffin Inn, Newland, Witney, Oxon.'

Licensees:

1780–1796	John Allsop
1797–1800	George Cooper
1801	Thomas Turner
1802	Thomas Hudson
1804–1807	James Badcock
1812	Job Harwood
1814–1818	Richard Tuffley
1839	John Busby
1842–1844	William Davis
1851–1854	Thomas Stone
	Age 40, born in Standlake, Oxon. Tailor. Wife Ann age 44 (1851 Census)
1863–1887	John Basson
1887	17 September. The Will of John Basson late of Newland Coggs in the County of Oxford Publican who died 14 June 1887 at Newland was proved at Oxford by Martha Basson Widow the Relict and William Cantwell Builder both of Newland the Executers. Personal Estate £307 0s 2d. Age 65
1887–1915	Martha Basson (Mrs.)
	Age 55, born in Coggs, Oxon. Widow (1891 Census)
1915	Basson Martha of Newland Coggs Oxfordshire widow died 17 July 1915 Probate Oxford 20 December to Alice Agnes Basson (wife of Arthur Judd Basson). Effects £575.
1915–1921	Arthur Judd Basson
1922–1925	James William Staines
	Owned by Garne & Sons Burford
1926–1933	Henry William Painter
1934	Painter Henry William of the Griffin Inn Newland Witney Oxfordshire died 8 July 1934 Probate Oxford 12 October to Sarah Jane Painter widow. Effects £897 11s.
1934	Sarah Jane Painter
1935–1948	James Thomas Smith
	DOB 21 Sep 1898 Licensee & Leather Glove Cutter. Wife Ada dob 12 Aug 1900 Unpaid Domestic Duties (1939 Register)
1949–1975	William Henry Lawson
1976–1980	Ernest R. Marshman

2005–2006	Robin Dyer
2007	Colin Lawler
	Roderick Jepson
	Zoe Pocock
2008–2016	Geoff & Jackie Patterson
2016–present	John Faherty

Three Pigeons (aka Pigeons), 31 Wood Green
(1760–present)

(Currently trading, owned by Enterprise Inns)

From the newspapers:

Oxford Journal – Saturday 05 July 1806

'TO be SOLD by AUCTION, by Messrs. PALFRY and WILKINSON, on the Premises at Wood Green, near Witney, Oxon, on Wednesday the 16th Day of July, 1806, at Five o'clock in the Afternoon, under Conditions of Sale then to be produced, in Three Lots, -All that old-established PUBLIC HOUSE, with a large Garden thereto belonging, known by the Sign of the Three Pigeons, situate on Wood Green aforesaid, in the Occupation of THOMAS ANDREWS; and Two other COTTAGES or TENEMENTS, and Gardens adjoining, in the several Occupations of J. PIESLY and ANN BROOKS, Tenants at Will, at low Rents. The Buildings have lately been completely repaired. And for further Particulars apply to Mr. Westell, Solicitor, or the Auctioneers, Witney.'

Oxford University and City Herald – Saturday 03 April 1841

'Tithe Commission. – Notice. The Tithe Commissioners for England and Wales hereby give notice, that a Copy of the Draft of Apportionment of the Rent-charge agreed to be paid in lieu of Tithes, in the Hamlet of Hailey, in the Parish of Witney, in the County of Oxford, has been deposited at the house of John Bowerman, called the Three Pigeons, in the said Hamlet, for the inspection of all Persons interested in the Lands and Tithes of the said Hamlet. ...'

Oxford Chronicle and Reading Gazette – Saturday 27 November 1841

'DEATHS. On Monday last at Hailey, Mr. Thomas Sheppard, many years landlord of the Three Pigeons, Woodgreen, aged 66.'

Banbury Guardian – Thursday 20 July 1848

'... Ann Gardner, Three Pigeons, Wood Green, Hailey, proved buying three mops of the prisoner, who said he bought his thrums of Master John Early, of Newland, that is the prosecutor, at sevenpence a pound. ...'

Oxford Journal – Saturday 12 July 1862

'DIED. – July 9, Mr. Lloyd, of the Three Pigeons Inn, Wood Green, Witney.'

Oxford Times – Saturday 17 July 1880

'Inquest. – An inquest was held on Woodgreen, at the "Three Pigeons," on Friday last, before F. Westell. Esq., coroner, on the body of the infant son of Eliza Beechey, of Witney, single woman, aged six weeks. It appeared that deceased had always had good health and seemed quite well when he was put to bed on the night preceding his death. He slept with his mother and grandmother and another child of Eliza Beechey's. His mother heard nothing of deceased from eleven o'clock until about six o'clock the next morning, when her mother awoke her and said "That child looks almost dead." She picked him up and saw that there was a great difference in his appearance. They called a neighbour who came and stayed about three minutes. Deceased died about ten minutes after his mother awoke. A Batt, Esq., M.D., of Witney, said that there was nothing remarkable on the body, which was well nourished. He could not tell the cause of death, but had no reason to believe but that it was natural one. Verdict, "Visitation of God."'

Faringdon Advertiser and Vale of the White Horse Gazette – Saturday 05 September 1903
'Two Sad Occurrences. – Quite a gloom has been cast over the town by the death, within a day of each other, of two of the most respected licensed victuallers in the town. Late on Thursday se'nnight, Mr W. H. Pratley, proprietor of the "Three Pigeons," Wood Green, was seized with violent vomiting, and, despite medical attention, died about 15 hours afterwards from gastric ulcer, perforation, and peritonitis. Mr Pratley, who was 37 years of age, had been house-painting, and it is thought this was not unconnected with his illness. He leaves a widow, but no children. ...'

Witney Gazette and West Oxfordshire Advertiser – Saturday 05 September 1903
'DEATHS. PRATLEY. – August 28th, at "Three Pigeons" Inn, Woodgreen, Witney. William Pratley aged 37 years."

Witney Gazette and West Oxfordshire Advertiser – Saturday 12 September 1903
'PETTY SESSIONS, Thursday. HOLDOVERS. Applications for the holdover of the license of the ... "Three Pigeons," Witney, from William Pratley , deceased, to Harriet Pratley; ...'

Oxford Times – Saturday 26 September 1903
'PETTY SESSIONS, Thursday. TRANSFER. – The licence of the "Elm Tree," West End, Witney, was transferred from T. Smith to F. Moore; that of the "Jolly Tucker," Witney, from George Broon to Edward Conway; Bull Inn, Witney, from the late Charles Howell to his widow, Ann Howell; "Three Pigeons," Witney, from the late W. H. Pratley to his widow; of the "Black Head," Witney, from Stephen Harwood to Elijah Miles; ...'

Coventry Evening Telegraph – Saturday 10 October 1970
'LICENSEE DIES IN CAR CRASH. A HEAD-ON collision between two cars resulted in the death of a Midland licensee and blocked the Banbury to Chipping Norton Road for over an hour last night. Mr. Robert Alexander Burnett, 39-year-old licensee of the Three Pigeons, Wood Green, Witney, who died, was driving towards Chipping Norton when his Morris 1000 was in collision with a Ford Cortina driven by Airman First Class Gregory Joseph Seyk, aged 22, of the United States Air Force Base at Upper Heyford, near Banbury. ...'

Licensees:

1760–1774	Joseph Collier
1781–1788	Robert Godfrey
1789–1799	William Burdon
1800–1802	Thomas Wheeler
1804–1807	Thomas Andrews
1806	Three Pigeons was to be sold by auction in July
1808	William Wright
1809	William Wright was buried on 30 January age 56
1809–1811	Mary Wright
1812–1820	Thomas Sheppard
1821–1830	James Curtis
1841–1844	John Bowerman
1847–1848	Ann Gardner (Mrs.)
1851–1852	George Young
	Age 38, born in Charlbury, Oxon. Wife Sarah age 38 (1851 Census)
1853–1854	John George
1861	James Lloyd
	Age 32, born in Witney, Oxon. Woolen Weaver. Wife Sarah age 31 (1861 Census)
1862	James Lloyd died in July
1863	Mrs. J. Lloyd
1869–1876	James Bull
1891–1895	Lewis Frederick George
	Age 35, born in Witney, Oxon. Carpenter & Joiner. Wife Martha age 34. (1891 Census)
1899–1903	William Haynes Pratley
	Age 34, born in Witney, Oxon. Carpenter & Joiner. Wife Harriet age 29. (1901 Census)
1903	William Pratley died in August aged 37
1904–1909	Harriett Pratley (Mrs.)
1910–1926	John Holland
	Age 46, born in Witney, Oxon. Painter. Wife Harriett age 39. (1911 Census)
1925	Owned by Clinch & Co
1927–1935	Charles William Holland
1936	Charles Holland died age 52
1936	Elsie Kate Holland
1937–1945	Francis James Rowles
	DOB 6 Jun 1900 Road Foreman Public Works. Wife Elsie dob 12 Oct 1887 Unpaid Domestic Duties (1939 Register)
1946–1958	Ernest Franklin
1959–1961	Marjorie Norah Franklin
1962–1965	Brian Morris Day
1968–1970	Robert Alexander Burnet
1971–1972	Josephine M. Burnet
1973–1980	John K. Goodman
1981–1992	Wally & Rose ?
1993–present	Joy Gosling

Appendix 1

Other Inns, Taverns and Beerhouses mentioned but no indication of their location

The following un-located licensed premises may have been small, short-lived, beerhouses where, in order to secure a licence to sell beer, the applicant had to give a name for the premises. These beerhouses would only have sold beer and cider, and probably from their front parlour.

No indication of their whereabouts has been found other than that they were in Witney.

2 Brewers

Licensees:

1772–1792	Mary Lucket
1793–1796	Job Fidler
1797–1802	Mary Fidler
1804–1806	Thomas King

Adam & Eve

Licensees:

1767–1774	John Ashfield

Admiral Vernon (Squirrel?)

Licensees:

1762–1785	Joseph Wiggins (1781–1782 at the Squirrel)
1785	Joseph Wiggins died 3 October 1785 age 62
1786–1787	Ann Wiggins
1788–1793	Philip Kent

Ax, Coggs

Licensees:

1774–1778	Thomas Turner
1778	Buried on 14 September 1778
1779	Sarah Turner
1780–1785	Thomas Birdseye

Bear

Licensees:

1753–1778	William Green
1779	Buried on 18 April 1779
1779	Mary Green
1795	Ben Trundle

Blue Ball

Licensees:
1765–1778   James Bunting
1779–1783   William Norton

Bull

Licensees:
1777–1790   Joseph Draper

Carpenter's Arms, Corn St (north side)

Licensees:
1781–1785   Robert Simms

Cart & Horses

Licensees:
1764–1784   David Thorley (1777–79 at the Cart & Horses)
1784   Buried on 22 October 1784
1785–1786   Mary Thorley

Crown (Three Crowns)

From the newspapers:
Oxford Journal – Saturday 25 December 1756
'...And such Person or Persons, who have a Mind to enlist themselves as aforesaid, are desired to enquire for Serjeant Stafford, at the Three Crowns in Witney, Oxfordshire...'

Licensees:
1782–1785   Benjamin Wiggins
1785   Died 25 December 1785 age 60
1786–1788   Elizabeth Wiggins
1789–1793   William Bancham
1794–1800   William Burham

Digging Dick

Licensees:
1753–1783   William Townsend

Fox Inn

From the newspapers:
Oxford Journal – Saturday 07 July 1860
'CLUB FEAST. – At this annual feast, held on Tuesday last, our town was enlivened by the Witney and Burford bands, orchestras being erected for them in front of the Blue Boar and Fox Inns. ...'

Licensees:
1782   Edward Hawks
1783–1801   Edward Seeley
1802   William Fletcher

1804	Edward Harris
1807	Thomas Hanks
1812–1814	John Wiggins
1861–1869	Thomas Kimble
	Age 41, Grocer. Wife Mary age 46 (1861 Census)

Golden Ball (1)

Licensees:

1775–1802	William Wright
1804	Daniel Seeley
1805–1806	Richard Grant
1807–1808	William Grant

Golden Ball (2)

Licensees:

1768–1787	Henry Empson (1774–1779 at the Balls)
1788	Anthony Fisher
1789	Thomas Fisher
1799	Thomas Wells

Greyhound

Licensees:

1765–1774	Charles Green
1775–1776	William Green
1777–1779	Charles Green

Hen & Chickens

Licensees:

1775–1799	John Clark
1800–1802	John Jackson
1804–1830	William Brice

Mother Red Cap

Licensees:

1764–1783	Sarah Mills
1784	Buried on 5 September 1784
1784–1891	Ann Sheppard

White Horse

Licensees:

1764–1772	William Hartley
1772	Buried on 22 July 1772
1772–1778	Ann Hartley
1779–1797	Moses Potter
1798–1799	William Collier
1800–1804	Samuel Walker
1807	John Green

Appendix 2

The Blanket Hall/White Hart Brewery

A first hand account of the Blanket Hall Brewery taken from the autobiography of William Smith, November 1872.

'In 1846 I undertook the mop making department of J. Early & Co., the returns for which added materially to my interest and my fifty pounds soon swelled to a hundred.

At this juncture my employer (Mr. E. Early) proposed a partnership between myself and his son Joseph, and a preliminary meeting was arranged for the purpose, when Mr. E. Early proposed that we should start a small family brewery at my residence "The Blanket Hall" and call the Brewery by that name. (A singular business to propose to one who had been a Teetotal upward of five years!). The question of capital and profits were then discussed, and as my intended partner had no capital I kept my own in the back ground, and we started a small business upon the credit system, with the understanding that our position should be supported by my employer.

There was already on the premises the original brewing plant of the Blanket Makers Company with several casks in the Cellar including the cask "Queen Anne" which was supposed to be the relick of the original as presented by the Queen of that name, who granted a special Charter to the Witney Blanket Makers, which gave them many privileges in the manufacture of their Blankets.

With this small plant (12 Bushels *[96 gallons, 2.5 barrels, Ed.]*) we commenced our brewing business, and added vats and casks as fast as required for use, upon credit. In the course of a little time, money was required for the Cooper, and on submitting the bill to our volunteer backer, was surprised to learn that I must stand upon my own resources, and for some unexplained reason his son had withdrawn from the speculation.

Nothing daunted, I proceeded upon my hundred pounds reserve. My business increased from week to week and proved very lucrative. In the course of time I wanted to enlarge my borders and proposed the building of a new brewhouse to take a three quarter plant, and use the old brewhouse as Cellarage, with an increase of rent of 7½ per cent on the outlay. This arrangement was entered into and carried out. My business still increased, and soon became of considerable importance and became a temptation to my original but now defunct partner, who had never spent a penny nor an hour's interest in the concern from first to last.

Being a yearly tenant only, I was served with a notice to leave, but I ultimately found that the object of the notice was to restore the original partnership, or relinquish the business that I had cultivated (with great trouble and care), in favour of the same individual at valuation. I resented this inroad upon my privileges of course, and showed by facts and figures that my business was now worth many hundreds of pounds, and was increasing in value every year. However, all my remonstrance was in vain till at last a gentleman came forward and offered to arbitrate. This person, Mr. M. Long, was supposed to be a friend to both parties, but in the course of negotiation I found the balance to be in favour of my adversary. At length I determined to adhere to the notice, and prepared for a removal altho' my new plant, with pumps, fixtures, pipes, vats and casks, would involve great difficulty and expense. Without further ceremony I went to Mr. Hollis of Cogges and took my present residence *(The White Hart, Bridge Street, Ed.)* to shift at my convenience, which was commenced forthwith. In the construction of the brewhouse I was now leaving, I had provided for such an emergency, and the doorway entrance was of sufficient dimensions to allow the largest vessel to pass through. It was now only a question of time, trouble and expense. I at once commenced sinking a well at my new residence, and with the material from the well built a copper stack and had the whole in working order in a month, and closed the Blanket Hall door and put the key in my pocket.

I was now placed in a very critical position. A Member of the Wesleyan Society, brought into a public house with a family of seven children, and upwards of three thousand galls of ale shifted from one position to another, and in danger of being spoiled and quite unfit for general family use.

My only course open was a retail license. Most of my old friends and acquaintances deserted me, and I had to work out my own problem, and this I did with fear and trembling. My first resolve was to keep holy the Sabbath day, I therefore closed my sale of everything from Saturday to Monday, but as my ale was recommended by the medical faculty for convalescents, we were frequently called upon to let the tap run on the Lord's day, but it was invariably presented in honour of Him who had set the day apart for rest.

I soon disposed of my old stock and replaced it with a new supply. Prosperity attended every step, and I was thereby enabled to commence a malting business for my purpose exceedingly well.

My hop Merchant was Mr. J. Pike of Oxford who always took an interest in my welfare, and by his advice I made many good little speculations. I remember on one occasion when hops were low in price and good in quality, by his advise I bought to the extent of my means, and after using from the bulk for 6 months, my hops that remained were more in value than when I first made the purchase. Nevertheless my heart was among the wool, and my ideas among the Mops, and altho' my business had reached considerable dimensions I was constantly looking for a change.'

(Reproduced from 'My Heart was among the Wool, The Autobiography of William Smith 1872' by kind permission of David J. Smith)

From the newspapers:

Oxford Chronicle and Reading Gazette – Saturday 01 July 1854

'White Hart Brewery, Witney, Oxon. MR. SMITH, who is relinquishing the Brewery Business, and is requiring his premises for manufacturing purposes, has instructed MR WILKINSON To SELL by AUCTION, on the premises, on Wednesday, the 12th July, the whole of his valuable STOCK-IN TRADE, comprising a most complete three-quarter BREWING PLANT, with refrigeration apparatus, in excellent working condition, Six BEER VATS, varying from 350 to 1100 gallons; 20 Casks, from 100 to 280 gallons; and 120 smaller Casks, from 4½ gallons upwards; about 3000 GALLONS of sound old BEER, 5 pockets of HOPS, very excellent malt mill, light brewer's dray, two-wheel truck, two spring carts, dog cart (nearly new), set of plated harness, Nag Mare in foal, by "Flying Buck," the fixtures and movables of Tap Room, comprising 4-pull beer engine, with 200 feet of piping, settles, tables, measures, cups, &c., &c. ; also 100 small maiden ASH TREES, and lot of oak posts and planks...'

Cheltenham Examiner – Wednesday 16 October 1867
'A REGULAR SUPPLY of Good Solid YEAST can be had at low prices at Shillingford Brothers, Blanket Hall Brewery, Witney. – Welsh's Van every Wednesday.'

Oxford Chronicle and Reading Gazette – Saturday 04 September 1869
'TO LET, at Michaelmas, the RED HORSE," - and LAND, at Ramsden.- Apply at the Blanket Hall Brewery, Witney.'

Oxford Journal – Saturday 19 December 1874
'TO LET, at Christmas Day next, - A good BEER HOUSE, with Butcher's shop attached; position good in a market town. Rent £16. – Apply to Shillingford Brothers, Blanket Hall Brewery, Witney.'

Oxford Times – Saturday 27 January 1877
'WANTED, - A NIGHT MAN, used to brewery work. Good wages. – Apply at the Blanket Hall Brewery, Witney.'

Oxford Times – Saturday 11 May 1878
'TO BE LET, with immediate possession, - The "Maltshovel" PUBLIC HOUSE, Corn-street, Witney. – Apply at the Blanket Hall Brewery, Witney.'

Oxford Times – Saturday 10 August 1878
'HENRY DRUCE, For Twenty Five Years at the Blanket Hall Brewery, Will commence business on August 1st, at Minster Mill as miller and maltster...'

Oxford Journal – Saturday 31 August 1878
'TO be LET, with possession at Michaelmas next, - The "White Hart Inn," Eynsham, Oxon. Now in full trade. – For particulars apply to Shillingford Brothers and Co., Blanket Hall Brewery, Witney, Oxon.'

Oxford Times – Saturday 15 February 1879
'TO BREWERS DRAYMEN. - WANTED. - A middle-aged Man, accustomed to the work, and whose character will bear investigation as to honesty and sobriety. – Apply, Shillingford Brothers and Co., Blanket Hall Brewery, Witney.'

Oxford Journal – Saturday 26 July 1879
'FULL-LICENSED PUBLIC HOUSE. TO be LET, from the 29th day of September next. – The ANGEL INN, Witney, Oxon, situated near the Market

Place, and in a good position for business... For particulars apply to Shillingford Brothers and Co., Blanket Hall Brewery, Witney, Oxon.'

Oxford Journal – Saturday 07 February 1880
'WANTED. – A Middle-aged WORKING HOUSEKEEPER for two single gentlemen; must be a good cook and of undoubted respectability. – Address J.C., Blanket Hall Brewery, Witney.'

Oxford Journal – Saturday 24 July 1880
'TO LET, with possession on the 29th day of September next, - That Old-established and Fully-licensed INN, with good Yard, Garden, & Out-buildings, known by the name of the King's Arms, and situate in High-street, Witney, Oxon. - For particulars apply at the Blanket Hall Brewery, Witney.'

Oxford Journal – Saturday 25 December 1880
'TWO BREWING PLANTS FOR SALE; coppers in good condition, and every requisite complete. Suitable for large family or small brewery. – May be seen on application to the Blanket Hall Brewery, Witney.'

Reading Mercury – Saturday 09 July 1881
'FIRST-CLASS Family and Commercial Hotel. – TO LET, with immediate possession (if desired), the "Fleece Hotel," commanding one of the best positions for business, in the manufacturing town of Witney, Oxon, and where a good and increasing trade has been carried on for some years. – For particulars, apply the present tenant (Mr. F. Townsend), or to Messrs. Shillingford Bros., and Co., The Blanket Hall Brewery, Witney.'

Oxford Journal – Saturday 25 November 1882
'Cross Keys Inn, Witney, Oxon. TO LET, - the above Old-established and Fully-licensed INN, consisting of large and convenient Premises, situated in the centre of the town and near the Market. It has been in the hands of the present tenant upwards of 11 years, to whom apply for further particulars, or to Shillingford Bros., and Co., Blanket Hall Brewery, Witney.'

Gloucester Journal – Saturday 03 November 1883
'BLANKET HALL BREWERY, WITNEY, OXON, Messrs. Shillingford Bros. & Co. beg respectfully to inform their numerous Friends and Customers that on and after November 1st, 1883, the above Old-established Business will be carried on under the Style or Firm of Shillingford and Bateman, to whom in future all business communications should be addressed.'

Witney Gazette and West Oxfordshire Advertiser – Saturday 11 July 1885
'BLANKET HALL BREWERY, Witney. NOTICE. THIS Brewery will be CLOSED on Tuesday July 14th, for the purpose of affording the employees an opportunity of joining the Trip to Portsmouth.'

Wilts and Gloucestershire Standard – Saturday 20 February 1886
'BLANKET HALL BREWERY, WITNEY, NOTICE. THE PARTNERSHIP lately existing between JAMES EDWARD SHILLINGFORD and ARTHUR

BATEMAN has this day been DISSOLVED by mutual consent, and the business in future will be carried on by ARTHUR BATEMAN exclusively, who respectfully solicits a continuance of that patronage and support so liberally bestowed on the late firm. January 30th, 1886.'

Witney Gazette and West Oxfordshire Advertiser – Saturday 26 March 1887
'THE "ROYAL OAK" INN, at COOMBE. TO LET, from the 24th day of June next. Preference will be given to a married couple without encumbrance, and possessing a knowledge of the trade. – Apply for particulars to the Blanket Hall Brewery, Witney.'

Witney Gazette and West Oxfordshire Advertiser – Saturday 13 October 1888
'"Cross Keys" Inn, Witney, TO LET, from 1st December next, For particulars apply to the Manager, Blanket Hall Brewery, Witney.'

Witney Gazette and West Oxfordshire Advertiser – Saturday 08 June 1889
'DEATHS. BATEMAN – On Thursday, June 6th, at Oriel House, Church Green, Witney, after a short and severe illness, Arthur Bateman, aged 54 years.'

Witney Gazette and West Oxfordshire Advertiser – Saturday 26 October 1889
'We understand that the executors of the late Mr. A. Bateman have sold the Blanket Hall Brewery, Witney, together with all the public-houses belonging thereto, to Messrs. W. Clinch & Co., of Witney.'

Witney Gazette and West Oxfordshire Advertiser – Saturday 21 December 1889
'BLANKET HALL BREWERY, WITNEY. NOTICE. THE above Brewery will be CLOSED on and after January 1st. 1890, for the Sale of Beer. OFFICE ONLY will be open after that date for the receipt and payment of Accounts connected with the Estate of the late Arthur Bateman. Witney, Dec 20th, 1889.'

'Blanket Hall Brewery. ARTHUR BATEMAN DECEASED. ALL PERSONS having CLAIMS against the estate of Arthur Bateman, late of Witney, Oxfordshire, Brewer and Maltster, deceased who died on the 6th day of June 1889, are requested to immediately send full, particularsthereof (*sic*) to Mr. A. C. Bateman, Oriel House, Witney, or to the undersigned.

And ALL PERSONS owing money to the deceased, are requested to pay the same forthwith to Mr. A. C. Bateman's credit, at the OFFICE of the Blanket Hall Brewery aforesaid.

Dated this 12th day of December 1889. SEWELL & SONS, Solicitors, Cirencester.'

Witney Gazette and West Oxfordshire Advertiser – Saturday 22 November 1890
'SALE BY AUCTION The Valuable and Modern BREWERY PLANT of the BLANKET HALL BREWERY Witney, Oxon, comprising... An excellent 22

barrel dome copper With pan to take 10 barrels, with Sluice Valve, &c. An English Oak Sqr. Mash Tun With steam copper ploughs, Caves false bottom, rakes and gearing and mashing machine...Will be sold in lots by auction by Messrs H. S. Couchman & Roberts Brewer's Auctioneers, & Valuers On Tuesday, November 25th, 1890, at 1 o'clock sharp...'

Oxford Times – Saturday 07 April 1900
'TO LET. – BLANKET HALL BREWERY PREMISES at Witney. Suitable for Warehouse, Stores, etc. – Apply Clinch and Co., Witney, Oxon.'

Appendix 3

Tithe Awards 1840

The Tithe Awards only state a reference number, the name of the person in the dwelling and the type of property as a Public House. The name of the Public House may be deduced from the position of the reference number on the Tithe Map and names from the 1841 Census and an 1839 Trade Directory.

Map Ref.	*Occupant*	*Pub Sign and Address*
47	John Ellis	Bull Inn, 46 Market Sq
48	Charles Fisher	George Inn, 44 Market Sq
50	John Mourby	Angel, 42 Market Sq
53	Henry William Clarke	Red Lion, 1 Corn St
62	John Stevens	Malt Shovel, 17 Corn St
75	Richard Willett	Holly Bush, 35 Corn St
86	George Dailey	Chequers, 47 Corn St
97	James Tilman	Bell Inn, 57, Corn St
156	Thomas Pumfrey	New Inn, 111 Corn St
249	void	Rocket Tavern, 152 Corn St
326	Robert Spittle	Butcher's Arms, 104 Corn St
328	Richard Redgate	Nag's Head, 100 Corn St
343	John Andrews	Three Horse Shoes, 78 Corn St
391	Giles Clarke	Coach & Horses, 32 Corn St
397	Richard Gilbert	Lamb Inn, 36 Market Sq
400	James Gillett	Marlborough Arms, 28 Market Sq
458	Emmanuel Lambourn	Royal Oak, 17 High St
479	Joseph Clarke	Britannia, rear of 57 High St
542	Thomas Sylvester	New Inn, 101 High St
625	Joseph Clarke	Roebuck, 15 Bridge St
642	Thomas Wells	Harriers, 15 West End
647	Job Baugham	Elm Tree, 21 West End
650	John Harris	Nelson Inn, 27 West End
664	John Dyke	House of Windsor, 31 West End
699	William Colegrave	Jolly Tucker, 10 West End
750	Joseph Masters	Staple Hall Inn, 30-32 Bridge St
754	Thomas Beckinsale	Black's Head, 26 Bridge St
766	Joseph Masters	White Hart Inn, 10 Bridge St
778	Joan Payne	King's Arms Inn, 106 High St
782	Thomas Collier	Plough, 98 High St
798	Thomas Lindsey	Jolly Waggoner, High St

800	Hannah East	King's Head, 74 High St
917	John Steptoe	Cross Keys, 1 Market Sq
944	William Grace	Crown Hotel, 27 Market Sq
983	William Bond	Marlborough Head, 11 Church Gn

Other Property and Owners

Map Ref	Owner	Property Description and Address
44	John Williams Clinch	House Brewery Garden, Market Sq
45	John Williams Clinch	Brewery Close, The Crofts
46	John Williams Clinch	Malt House Hovel & Close, Eagle Maltings
96	Thomas Dix	House Malt House &c., Corn St
402	Charles Keake	Malt House & Yard, Marlborough Lane (Behind the Marlborough Arms)
630	Hugh Eldrid	House Outbuildings & Garden
633	George Cooper	House Malt House Garden &c., Bridge St (Site of Court Inn)
640	Edward Rawlins	Malt House & Yard, West End (Behind 11 West End)
681	James Long	House Malt House Garden &c., West End (Now Spinners Court)
772	Joseph Francis	Malt House & Yard, Bridge St (On the banks of the Windrush)
865	John Williams Clinch	Malt House & Yard, High St
927	William Shuffrey	House Malthouse & Garden, Market Sq
934	John Williams Clinch	Malt House &c., Market Sq (Behind the Crown Hotel)
965	Mary Ann Waine	Malt House & Yard, Church Green
966	James Clinch	Malt House & Yard, Church Green

Witney 1840 Tithe Award Map

Overall Tithe Award Map. See following pages for enlarged
detail maps of different areas of town

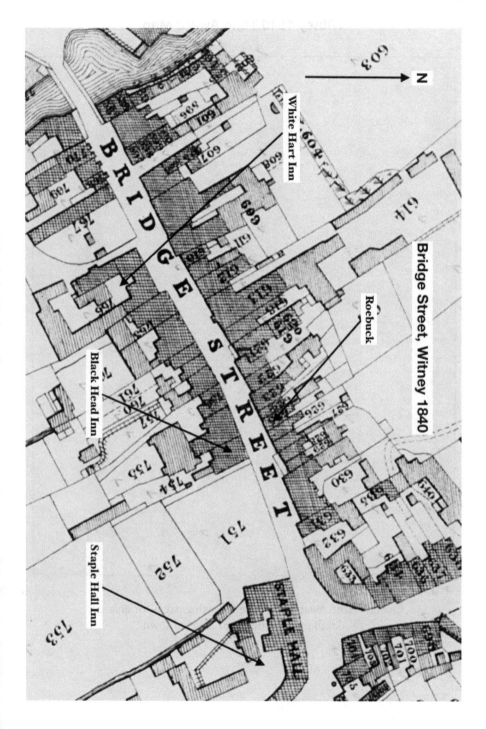

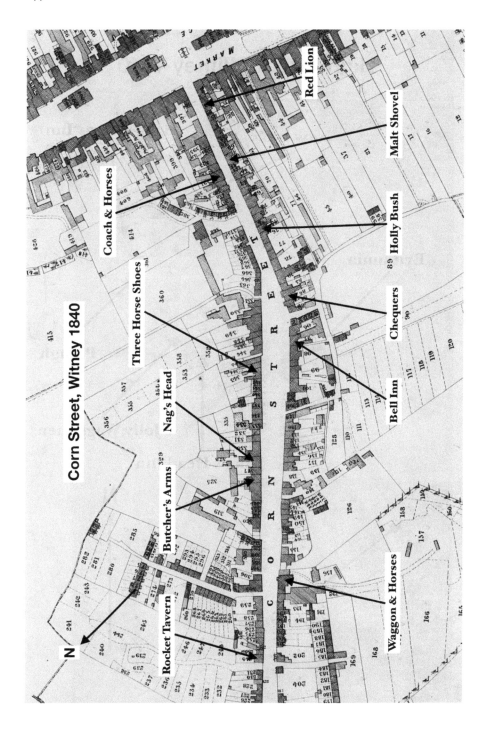

Corn Street, Witney 1840

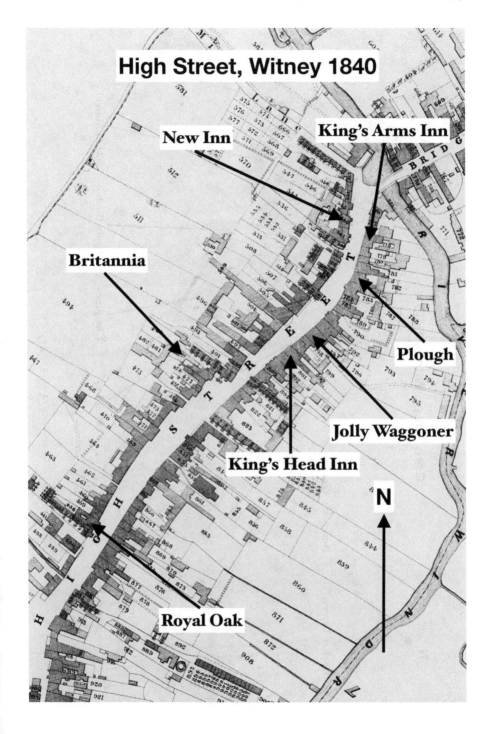

High Street, Witney 1840

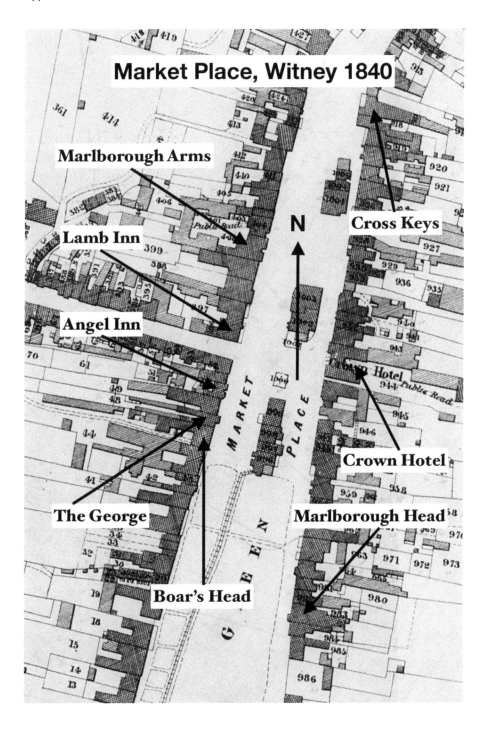

Market Place, Witney 1840

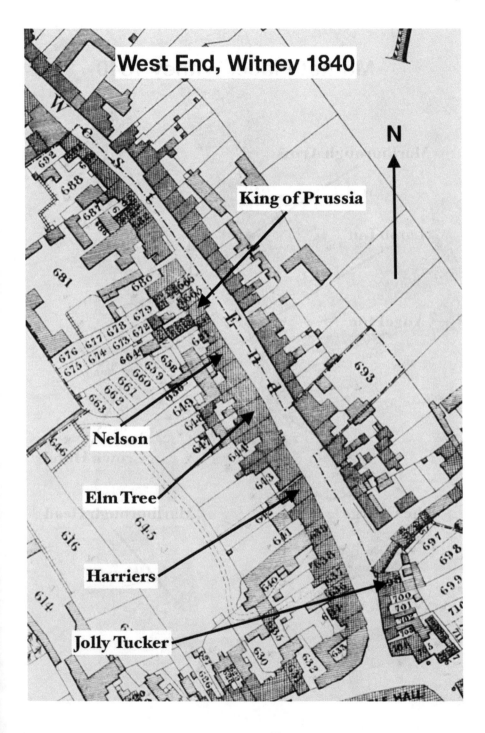

West End, Witney 1840

Appendix 4

Full newspaper article on the sale of three Public Houses

Oxford Chronicle and Reading Gazette – Saturday 10 July 1858

'To Brewers, Maltsters, Liquor Merchants, &c.

Freehold Public Houses, Malthouse, Close of Land, Residences, &c.,

In WITNEY, Oxon,

TO BE SOLD BY AUCTION

By Mr. LONG,

At the King's Arms Inn, in Witney, on Wednesday next, the 14th July, at 4 o'clock, under conditions of Sale to be then produced, in the following lots, and by order of the Trustees for Sale, named in the Will of the late Mr. George Cooper: - THREE FREEHOLD PUBLIC HOUSES, TWO DWELLING HOUSES, and MALTHOUSE, Close of LAND, BLACKSMITH'S SHOP and PREMISES, respectably situate in West End, Bridge Street, and the Market Place, Witney, and all tenanted except the Dwelling House.

Lot 1 – A FREEHOLD DWELLING HOUSE, in West End Witney, late in the occupation of Mrs. Walker, deceased, comprising sitting room, parlour, two bedrooms, and attics, underground cellar, washhouse, court yard and premises, garden, &c.; also adjoining, a 7-quarter malthouse, with suitable floors and kiln, barley and two malt granaries adjoining, a DWELLING HOUSE, in Bridge Street, with gateway entrance, sitting room, parlour, three bedrooms, and two attics, back kitchen, cellar, and offices, and warehouse over, a 4-stall stable, with two lofts over, smith's shop, shed, garden, yard, and premises, now in the occupation of Mr. Thomas Birdseye, Smith and Farrier. The whole commanding a frontage to the street of nearly 200 feet in extent. The rental and apportioned rent of the late Mrs. Walker's House is £39.

Land Tax, 10s. 2d. Quit Rent. 1s. 10½d.

Lot 2. – A substantially built FREEHOLD PUBLIC HOUSE, known as the Wheatsheaf, in West End, Witney, with gateway entrance, and 32 feet frontage to the street, comprising two front rooms, three bedrooms, and attics, bar, cellar, and offices, excellent bakehouse, with spacious oven, flour room, warehouse, stable, cart shed, granary, two pigstyes, yard, &c., now in the occupation of James Brown, at a rental of £15 per annum.

Land Tax, 7s. 6d. Apportioned Quit Rent, 1s.

Lot 3. – A valuable Close of FREEHOLD LAND, by admeasurement, 1 Acre and 17 Poles, with a summer house and timber thereon, situate at the back of the last lot, with entrance for carts and carriages from West End Street, now in the occupation of Mr. Harris, at £4 per annum.

Land Tax, 1s. Apportioned Quit Rent, 10d.

Lot 4. – The FREEHOLD well-known BLACK HEAD PUBLIC HOUSE, situate in Bridge Street, Witney, and adjoining the new County Courts, comprising a passage entrance, front taproom, three bedrooms, two attics, brewhouse, cellars, back kitchen, coalhouse, stable and loft over, pigstye, yard, garden, &c., and is now in the occupation of Mr Thomas Beckinsale, at the yearly rent of £20.

Land Tax, 4s. 3d.

Lot 5 – The ANGEL PUBLIC HOUSE, FREEHOLD, in the Pig Market, Witney, comprising a passage entrance, taproom, parlour, bar, club room, three bed rooms, and attics, back kitchen, brewhouse, cellar, stabling, pigstye, yard and premises, in the occupation of Mr. James Smith, at £20 per annum.

Land Tax. 8s. 6d. Quit Rent, 6d.

The attention of Brewers and Maltsters is particularly called to the sale of the property comprised in the last two lots, there being in each house a large consumption of beer.

The respective Tenants will show the property, and particulars may be had of Mr. Frederick Westell, Solicitor; Messrs. H. C. Townsend and Edward Early, of Witney, the Trustees; of the Auctioneer; and at the Place of Sale.'

Appendix 5

Witney's Pubs in the early 21st Century

From the newspapers:

Oxford Mail – Friday 31 August 2012

WITNEY has the same number of pubs it did 30 years ago, *(refer to Appendix 8, ed.)* which makes it "unique" in bucking the pub closure trend, say campaigners. The Oxford branch of Campaign for Real Ale (CAMRA) said no other UK market town had achieved this feat.

Only one Witney pub, The House of Windsor, has closed in the last three decades – it was in West End and shut in 2011. However, the town has gained a JD Wetherspoon pub.

The figures are in stark contrast to the picture across Oxfordshire, where 50 pubs have closed in five years.

Witney landlords believe the achievement is down to the town's pub culture and its expansion, and think the trend may continue.

Tony Goulding, CAMRA Oxford pubs officer, said: "Witney is unique for the size of town that it has always had 24 pubs for the last 30 years.

"For a town of its size, for them to be almost intact is unprecedented in the country. It is absolutely amazing."

But he did not know why the town's trade had been so successful, when nationally 4,500 have shut in the last four years.

The Royal Oak landlord Lesley Semaine said: "It's because Witney is such a thriving town. The councils have worked hard to keep the town clean, safe and prosperous and it is an attractive place for people to come to.

"People are also good at supporting their local pubs, shops and restaurants. It is a really good community."

She added: "I've been here 28 years and we've all had bad times – the smoking ban and recession – but we seem to get past it. The future looks good."

A handful of pubs have closed for short periods in Witney in the last three decades, including The Eagle Tavern and The Butchers Arms, but have all reopened.

The town has a long history with alcohol and a brewery has been based in the town for decades. The Wychwood Brewery currently operates from Witney.

In recent years the trade has matured, with bars such as Izi, Norton's and Fat Lil's opening and pubs diversifying into food and entertainment. Fat Lil's owner Paul Spink said: "There are a lot of factors as to why pubs have not closed, but one might be there's an embedded culture in Witney.

"People do not tend to move away and pubs are still part of the social fabric of Witney."

Witney historian Stanley Jenkins said: "Market towns have a lot of pubs because it is where farmers met to do business. The town has expanded so customers have come in."

He added that few establishments had been built in new estates, boosting town trade.

Appendix 6

Old Pub Games

Backgammon: is one of the oldest known board games. Its history can be traced back nearly 5,000 years to archaeological discoveries in the Middle East. It is a two-player game where each player has fifteen pieces (checkers), which move between twenty-four triangles (points) according to the roll of two dice. The objective of the game is to be first to bear off, i.e. move all fifteen checkers off the board. Backgammon is a member of the table's family, one of the oldest classes of board games.

Gleek: is an English card game for three persons. It is played with a 44-card pack and was popular from the 16th century through the 18th century.

Lodam: Losing Lodam. This British game was played in the 16th and 17th centuries, and is now obsolete. The aim, as in modern reverse games such as Hearts, was to avoid taking scoring cards in tricks. In this case the scoring cards were all aces (11), kings (3), queens (2), jacks (1) and tens (10).

Maw: Spoil-Five (also Spoilt Five and Five and Ten) is the traditional book version of the Irish national card game called Twenty-Five, which underlies the Canadian game of Forty-Five. Charles Cotton describes it in 1674 as "Five Fingers", a nickname applied to the Five of Trumps extracted from the fact that the Irish word cúig means both 'five' and 'trick'. It is supposed to be of great antiquity, and widely believed to have originated in Ireland. It may be identified with the game of Maw, of which James I of England was very fond.

Noddy: (also Noddie or Nodde) is a 16th century English card game ancestor of Cribbage. It is the oldest identifiable card game with this gaming structure and a relative to the more complicated 18th century game Costly Colours.

Shovelboard: Shuffleboard, more precisely deck shuffleboard, and also known as floor shuffleboard, is a game in which players use cues to push weighted discs, sending them gliding down a narrow court, with the purpose of having them come to rest within a marked scoring area. As a more generic term, it refers to the family of shuffleboard-variant games as a whole.

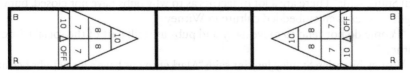

Top view of shuffleboard

Appendix 7

Glossary

Opening and closing dates are subject to verification as some of them are the first or last mention to be found.

Information for the Licensees from 1964 to 2004 was taken from the Electoral Registers, so may not be the actual licence holder.

'Messuage': A dwelling house with outbuildings and land assigned to its use. Late Middle English: from Anglo-Norman French, based on Latin *manere* 'dwell'.

'Hovel': An open shed or outhouse, used for sheltering cattle or storing grain or tools.

'Quitrent': A fixed rent payable to a feudal superior in commutation of services.

Beer Retailer: A person licensed to sell beer and cider.

Victualler: (also licensed victualler) A person licensed to sell beer, cider, wine and spirits.

Originally beer houses and alehouses only sold ale or beer whilst taverns sold additional beverages such as wine and spirits.

In 1830 the Beerhouse Act, passed to encourage the sale of beer, brought into being beer retailers who kept beer shops, or beer houses; they could only sell beer and cider (as against public houses which could also sell wine and spirits). Licence for these could be obtained on demand from the local excise office; beer retailers did not have to acquire a licence at the annual Brewster Sessions.

Public houses, or 'alehouses', have been subject to licensing for many centuries, and the first national licensing system was introduced by the Alehouse Act of 1552. Under this act, persons wishing to sell ale had to be licenced by a Justice of the Peace at the Quarter Sessions. This meant entering into a bond, or 'recognizance,' in which the victualler pledged to abide by the Act and maintain good behaviour in his alehouse.

This system continued throughout the 16th – 18th centuries, with minor alterations. Under the 1753 Licensing Act, victuallers could be licenced only if they had a certificate confirming their good character, and this had to be signed by a parish notable, but no further amendments to the system were made until the Acts of 1828 and 1830. These alterations meant that the licensing system moved from the jurisdiction of the Quarter Sessions to the Petty Sessions, but no provision was made for the Clerk of the Peace to keep licensing records. The records of licenced victuallers are less comprehensive, therefore, after 1828.

In the early 21st century it was becoming ever more difficult for a landlord to earn a reasonable living from selling just beer, wine and spirits and a few bar snacks. Those that did run such a pub have built their business and reputation by offering a larger than usual range of real ales and real ciders which are kept in top condition and regularly changed. These wet sales only pubs were in the minority and tended to be Free Houses, those that were not tied to a big pub chain company or brewery. The majority of pubs needed to diversify in order to increase their income and many did so by offering food. This presented a dilemma; were they a pub serving food or were they a restaurant serving beer? Nevertheless, this diversification in order to stay in business was not a modern trend.

What's in a name? Alehouse, Tavern, Inn or Pub: The existence of what we now call a 'Pub' goes back many hundreds of years. It seems our desire to meet and socialise over a tipple or two is timeless, stretching back across countless generations. Over the years, however, the public house has had many iterations – from alehouse to taverns and inns. Do you know the difference between them?

Alehouse: Alehouses have existed in the British Isles since before the Norman Conquest. However, it wasn't until the 14th century, when the hop arrived in Belgium that alehouses began to be established. The Black Death also meant that there was a labour shortage, which, in turn, drove up wages and meant that people had more disposable income. By 1577, there were around 24,000 alehouses in existence in the United Kingdom. However, like the name suggests, alehouses were simply houses in which ale or beer was sold and quite dissimilar to our pubs of today.

Tavern: A tavern was different to an alehouse in that it tended to be larger in size and concentrated more on serving wine as opposed to beer. They also tended to attract a better standard of customer. During the seventeenth century, a tavern was regarded as the meeting place for a gentleman, latterly being usurped by the introduction of coffee houses by 1800.

Inn: This was typically a house to accommodate travellers. There were generally two types of Inn – those that faced the road and those that were built around an inner courtyard. By the end of the seventeenth century, thanks to the growing coaching network and new turnpike roads, inns were increasing in number.

Public House: The term public house can be applied as the collective noun for taverns, inns and alehouses, with the first recording of the term appearing in 1669. Despite the fact that many public houses had a bar and a cellar – features that we now recognise in our modern day public houses – these establishments at this time remained quite primitive. By 1880 there was more regulation around licensing and standards. The difficulty in obtaining licenses meant that brewers began to acquire pubs, leading to a 'golden age' of pub building with many fine buildings appearing in our towns and cities.

(Focus Magazine)

As some of the information in this history of Public Houses has been obtained from sources that due to the passage of time cannot be verified, there may be discrepancies or errors. Your assistance in the correction of any such errors, or with the completion of any missing information, would be most gratefully received.

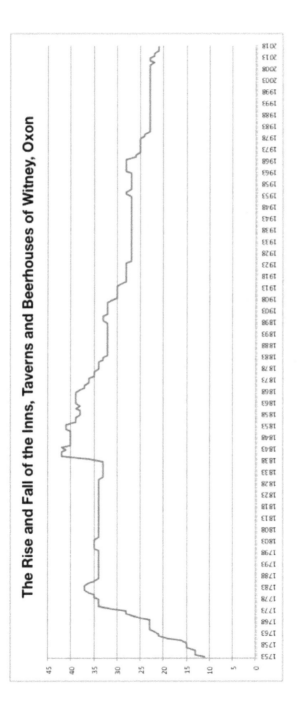

Appendix 8

Appendix 9

Sources of Information

Victuallers Recognizances 1753–1822

Tithe Awards 1840

Various Trade Directories 1823–1939

Census Returns 1841–1911

Register of Licences, Bampton East 1925–1963

1939 Register

Electoral Registers 1964–2004

ERS (Licensing) Publica Group 2005–2018

St Mary's Church, Witney Burial Records

England & Wales, Civil Registration Death Index, 1837–2007

Newspapers:-
    Banbury Advertiser
    Banbury Guardian
    Faringdon Advertiser and Vale of White Horse Gazette
    Oxford Chronicle & Reading Gazette
    Oxford Journal
    Oxford Times
    Witney Gazette & West Oxfordshire Advertiser
    and various others

A History of the County of Oxford: Volume 14

Universal British Directory 1793–1798 Vol. 4 N-Y

Further Reading

Brown, Mike, *Oxon Brews, The Story of Commercial Brewing in Oxfordshire* (Brewery
    History Society 2004)

Giles, J. A., *History of Witney* (first published in 1852, pages 58 & 59)

Honey, Derek, *Changing Faces of Witney Book One* (Robert Boyd Publications,
    1998)

Honey, Derek, *Changing Faces of Witney Book Two* (Robert Boyd Publications,
    2000)

Honey, Derek, *Witney Inns, Pubs and Breweries* (Robert Boyd Publications, 2007)

Steane, Kate (ed. Jenkins, Stanley C.), *Historic Inns & Alehouses in Historic Witney*
    (Lightmore Press, 2011)

Monk, W. J., *History of Witney* (first published in 1894, pages 34–36)

Alphabetical Index of Pubs

Pub Sign	Address	Status	Page
2 Brewers	Unknown	Closed	144
Adam & Eve	Unknown	Closed	144
Admiral Vernon	Unknown	Closed	144
Anchor	Bridge St	Closed	5
Angel	42 Market Sq	Open	90
Ax Coggs		Closed	144
Ball	98 High St	See Plough	82
Bear	Unknown	Closed	144
Bell Inn	57 Corn St	Closed	40
Black Head	26 Bridge St	Closed	5
Black Horse	70 West End	Closed	115
Black Swan	Corn St	Closed	43
Blackmore's Head	74 High St	See King's Head	78
Blue Ball	Unknown	Closed	145
Blue Boar	28 Market Sq	Open	93
Boar's Head	46 Market Sq	See Bull Inn	100
Britannia	57 High St	Closed	72
Bull	Unknown	Closed	145
Bull Inn	46 Market Sq	Closed	100
Butchers Arms	104 Corn St	Closed	44
Carpenter's Arms	Corn St (north side)	Closed	145
Carpenter's Arms	132 Newland	Open	134
Cart & Horses	Unknown	Closed	145
Chequers	47 Corn St	Open	47
Coach & Horses	32 Corn St	See Eagle Tavern	50
Company of Weavers	31 Market Sq	Open	102
Court Inn	39–43 Bridge St	See Old Court Hotel	9
Cross Keys	1 Market Sq	See Ye Olde Cross Keys	111
Crown	Unknown	Closed	145
Crown Hotel	27 Market Sq	Closed	102
Czar of Russia	31 West End	See House of Windsor	121
Digging Dick	Unknown	Closed	145
Duke's Head	15 West End	See Harriers	119
Eagle Tavern	22 Corn St	Open	50
Eagle Vaults	18-22 Market Sq	Open	105
Elm Tree	21 West End	Open	115
Fleece Hotel	11 Church Green	Open	31
Flying Machine	25 Fettiplace Rd	See Rowing Machine	132
Fox Inn	Unknown	Closed	145
George Inn	47 Market Sq	Closed	105
Golden Ball (1)	Unknown	Closed	146
Golden Ball (2)	Unknown	Closed	146
Greyhound	42 Market Sq	See Angel	90
Greyhound	Unknown	Closed	146
Griffin	166 Newland	Open	138
Harriers	15 West End	Closed	119
Hen & Chickens	Unknown	Closed	146
Holly Bush	35 Corn St	Open	55
Horse Shoes	78 Corn St	See Three Horse Shoes	69

Pub Sign	Address	Status	Page
House of Windsor	31 West End	Closed	121
Jolly Tucker	10 West End	Closed	123
Jolly Waggoner	78 High St	Closed	73
King of Prussia	31 West End	See House of Windsor	121
King's Arms Inn	106 High St	Closed	73
King's Head	74 High St	Closed	78
Lamb Inn	34 Market Sq	Closed	107
Malt Shovel	17 Corn St	Closed	58
Marlborough Arms	28 Market Sq	See Blue Boar	93
Marlborough Head	11 Church Green	See Fleece	31
Mother Red Cap	Unknown	Closed	146
Nag's Head	100 Corn St	Closed	61
Nelson	27 West End	Closed	129
New Inn	111 Corn St	Open	63
New Inn	101 High St	Closed	81
Old Court Hotel	39-43 Bridge St	Open	9
Old White Hart	13-15 Market Sq	Closed	108
Pigeons	31 Wood Green	See Three Pigeons	141
Plaister's Arms	132 Newland	See Carpenter's	134
Plough	98 High St	Open	82
Plough & Shuttle	98 High St	See Plough	82
Prince Albert	Bridge St	Closed	14
Prince of Wales	63 High St	Closed	85
Queen's Head	10 High St	Closed	86
Red Lion	1 Corn St	See Rocket	65
Robin Hood	81 Hailey Rd	Closed	133
Rocket	1 Corn St	Open	65
Rocket Tavern	152 Corn St	See Star Inn	68
Roebuck	15 Bridge St	Closed	15
Rowing Machine	25 Fettiplace Rd	Open	132
Royal Oak	17 High St	Open	86
Salutation	1 Market Sq	See Ye Olde Cross Keys	111
Squirrel	Unknown	See Admiral Vernon	144
Staple Hall Inn	30-32 Bridge St	Closed	15
Star Inn	152 Corn St	Closed	68
Sun	49 Market Sq	Closed	111
Sundial	49 Market Sq	See Sun	111
Swan	Corn St	See Black Swan	43
Three Crowns	Unknown	See Crown	145
Three Horse Shoes	78 Corn St	Open	69
Three Pigeons	31 Wood Green	Open	141
Three Tuns	West End	Closed	130
Tucker	10 West End	See Jolly Tucker	123
Waggon & Horses	111 Corn St	See New Inn	63
Wheatsheaf	West End	Closed	131
White Hart Inn	10 Bridge St	Closed	24
White Horse	Unknown	Closed	146
White Lion	37 Bridge St	Closed	29
Windrush Inn	60 Burford Rd	Open	132
Ye Olde Cross Keys	1 Market Sq	Open	111